Michael Chesher and Rukesh Kaura

Electronic Commerce and Business Communications

Springer

Michael Chesher
Kingston Business School
Kingston University
Kingston upon Thames
Surrey KT2 7LB

Rukesh Kaura
Chase Investment Bank Ltd
125 London Wall
London EC 2Y 5AJ

ISBN 3-540-19930-6 Springer-Verlag Berlin Heidelberg New York

British Library Cataloguing in Publication Data
Chesher, Michael
   Electronic commerce and business communications. - (Practitioner series)
   1. Business – Data processing
   I. Title II. Kaura, Rukesh, 1971–
   658'.05
   ISBN 3540199306

Library of Congress Cataloging-in-Publication Data
Chesher, Michael, 1942–
   Electronic commerce and business communications / Michael Chesher
and Rukesh Kaura.
      p. cm. -- (Practitioner series)
   Includes bibliographical references and index.
   ISBN 3-540-19930-6 (pbk. : alk. paper)
   1. Electronic commerce. 2. Business communication--Computer
networks. I. Kaura, Rukesh, 1971– . II. Title. III. Series.
HF5548.32.C474 1998
658.8' 00285'4678--DC21   98-11200

Typesetting: Troubador Publishing Ltd, Market Harborough, UK
Printed and bound at the Athenæum Press Ltd, Gateshead, Tyne and Wear
34/3830-543210 Printed on acid-free paper

Preface

The last decade has bought about many changes, but perhaps the most profound is the impact upon the most basic of human activities – communication and access to information. Like most changes, they have ingrained themselves in our everyday lives before we know it. So it is with electronic commerce and business communications, now a critical element of corporate life and becoming increasingly so in the home through the rapid and unpredictable growth of the Internet.

From a corporate perspective, the marketplace continues to become more competitive, global in nature and changes occur in ever shortening cycles. Success in this new business environment depends upon having an awareness of what is now possible, and understanding how information technology can support business led process improvements that really make a difference in achieving competitive advantage.

For those in the forefront of electronic commerce initiatives, the fast pace of change has meant many new business opportunities. However, for others just starting, the growing convergence of various information technologies has left them without a clear understanding of these advances from a strategic viewpoint.

This book is a response to that need, providing a single source of both strategic and reference information for those embarking upon new electronic commerce and business communications initiatives. It is also intended as a useful point of reference for those studying the subject. In addition, the critical inter-dependence between business and information technology strategies is stressed throughout this book. For some organisations this requires the development of new working relationships between business managers and IT professionals, built upon a greater understanding and empathy from both sides.

Finally, the authors wish to acknowledge the contribution that electronic business communications has made to the preparation of this book, since they both work in separate organisations and are frequently in different countries. Put very simply, it would not have been possible to co-operate on this book project without such a capability.

Michael C Chesher
m.chesher@kingston.ac.uk

Rukesh Kaura
ricky.kaura@chase.com

Contents

Part C

Part A

1. *Business Context*

Introduction

Ever more business transactions are being conducted electronically, thanks to dramatic cost performance advances in IT. Organizations are subject to an unprecedented pace of change in the way they operate to meet the business challenges of the 21st century. Success is determined by the ability of the workforce to absorb change, and to work to exploit new and emerging technologies. The digital or information revolution is at the heart of these changes, comparable in impact to that of the industrial revolution of the 19th century.

Many organizations have been quick to realize the value associated with information, and the potential it holds to secure competitive advantage. This results in improved financial margins, shorter times to bring new products and services to market, an enhanced emphasis on quality, and significantly improved customer service.

The key is improved business productivity, together with customer oriented initiatives, through a combination of people skills and IT.

Three Introductory Scenarios

The impact of electronic commerce may best be illustrated through practical, every day examples. Part of what happens is familiar, while part is at present mysterious to the non-specialist.

Purchasing a Gift

Simple Description
The woman enters the store and goes directly to the information desk, having previously looked through the store's electronic catalogue on the Internet. Access to the Internet is made from home using her combined TV/personal computer. Her husband's birthday is just 24 hours away and she has almost decided what to buy him. "Do you still have stock of the Bosch cordless drill on special offer, as advertised in your electronic catalogue?" she asks. The store assistant moves to the computer screen to his left on the counter and enters an enquiry. Almost instantly he responds to the customer, "Whilst we currently do not have any in stock, a shipment of Bosch cordless drills will be delivered this afternoon."

Technical Description

There were several ways in which to establish a connection between their combined TV/personal computer and the Internet, but her husband had chosen a simple modem connection via their existing telephone line (public switched telephone network) to an Internet Service Provider that had been recommended to him. Once connected to the Internet, she runs a computer program (called a Web browser) that displays information from a frequently accessed Web site (a computer that offers access to information). A number of other locations (Web sites) that includes a DIY store have been conveniently added to a "bookmark" list. By selecting the DIY store from the bookmark, using a "mouse" connected to the keyboard of the combined TV/personal computer, the store's "home page" is displayed on the screen with the option to select their electronic catalogue. Once an item(or items) has been chosen from the catalogue, ordering and payment screens are displayed; but since she wishes to purchase the Bosch cordless drill that same day, she decides to note the address of the local store.

Responding to her question at the local store, the store assistant enters the enquiry using his computer keyboard, and that is sent first to the in-store computer, and then passed onto a regional server when no local stock is found (Fig. 1.1). The screen displays the local stock-out condition and outstanding order information from the regional server, which indicates an imminent scheduled delivery from the Bosch distributor, as well as identifying stock availability in another local branch. The regional server, with its knowledge-based system, recognizes that this is the third enquiry made within two hours for this product, and initiates a network connection to the Bosch distributor's order processing system. A real-time EDI transaction is created and passed over the link to be processed instantly by the Distributor's order processing system. The response is returned instantly in the form of an EDI advance delivery instruction, confirming ship-

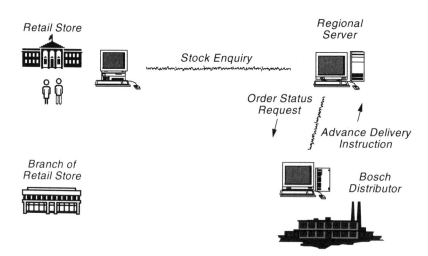

Fig. 1.1 The birthday present.

ments that afternoon to several stores, including the one in which the lady has now waited patiently for the shop assistant to respond to her simple question – which has taken just three seconds!

Sending Minutes of a Meeting

Simple Description

Due to a delay in the arrival of the in-coming aircraft, the businessman's flight is delayed by 45 minutes, which should give him just enough time to complete the minutes of the meeting held earlier that day with a prospective new client. He removes the laptop computer from its case and proceeds to expand upon the notes that he made earlier during the meeting. There are several follow-up items from the meeting which require immediate action. One such item concerns the need to establish exactly how much training is required for his prospective client to become proficient in the use of the new retail application, as well as including how much training is already a part of their standard contract. With the help of his mobile phone which is connected to the laptop computer, he establishes a connection to the service used by his company for information exchange and electronic mail (E-mail). Whilst this is used both internally and externally, providing customers with access to a wide range of product information, company-sensitive data related to clients is restricted solely to internal employees. In searching the database of existing clients from his laptop computer connected to the service, he soon finds one with a similar set of circumstances to that of his prospect. He notes the E-mail address of the sales manager involved, then attaching the minutes of his meeting, creates and sends a message requesting advice on the approach to be taken. Just before the flight is called he creates a distribution list for the minutes of the meeting, noting that the recipients have a range of different types of E-mail addresses. The minutes of the meeting are sent and as he finishes packing away the laptop computer and mobile phone, boarding commences. He can now relax on the journey home.

Technical Description

The businessman's mobile phone is using a digital cellular standard known as GSM (Global System for Mobiles) that was designed to replace all of Europe's analog cellular mobile systems and provide Pan-European coverage. In practice, many other countries outside Europe have adopted this same standard. With the help of his GSM cellular phone connected into the laptop computer via a PCMCIA card ("smart" pocket sized cards that plug into a slot in the laptop computer providing a range of interface functions, including data communications), he establishes a connection to a network access point by entering a local telephone number. His company have put in place an Extranet (Internet based service used for internal purposes and extended to include their own business community) based upon GE Information Services' Inter-Business Partner Service. This service is used for information exchange and E-mail. Once the "Dial-up" connection is established to the network access point, a TCP/IP session is initiated, over which an Internet browser application is launched to help locate the required client information. Once this is completed, he prepares a short message using the

E-mail client software integrated into the Internet browser application on his laptop, creates a MIME attachment containing the meeting minutes, and sends the E-mail message to the central E-mail server for mailboxing and delivery. The distribution list (a single address that expands to a number of separate destination addresses) used for the circulation of the meeting minutes, consists of seven recipients, several with different types of addresses, including Microsoft Exchange, Internet, X.400 and facsimile.

Small Business User

Simple Description

The Sunday driver has dropped into his local AutoHelp shop for a stop-light bulb. It seems just like any other small store providing spare parts to local garages and DIY enthusiasts. There is a slight smell of oil in the air, tools on shelves, together with racks of pre-packaged components, paints and car cleaning materials. On the counter, on top of the two cash tills, are two screens, each with their own printer attached. Cables disappear into the counter to be connected to a computer no larger than a video recorder, on a shelf and protected by a wooden panel. Another cable follows a pillar on the counter into the roof only to terminate at another computer with screen and printer in a small office 10 metres away. "It's a great system," the shopkeeper explains. "It allows us to check stock availability, price each product and create a customer VAT receipt if required." The capital investment was not very high when compared to the people costs in running the business, and the considerable benefits that the system had brought in, reduced ordering time, increased stock availability, elimination of paperwork and improved customer service.

Technical Description

The cables connecting the computers and associated equipment together forms the basis of a Local Area Network (LAN). This allows the computing resources within the store to be linked together and shared by users of the system. Whilst there are several different types of LAN, the shop is using an Ethernet-based LAN (defines the manner in which devices transmit over the LAN and the rules that apply when multiple devices transmit at the same time), which is simple and cheap to install. In addition, LAN software (computer programs) from Novell, a well known LAN software company, is used to manage some of the functions of the LAN, including access to a file server (a computer together with a large amount of disk space for storing computer programs and data). One of the devices connected to the LAN is a router, which provides the means, via an ISDN (Integrated Services Digital Network) line, to connect periodically to other LANs operated by regional wholesale distributors to the automotive after-market. ISDN lines are supplied by telecommunications companies in much the same way as telephone lines are provided (Public Switched Telephone Network), and can be used for both voice and data. Apart from handling in-store transactions, the system used by AutoHelp also creates replenishment orders based upon sales and stock information; once confirmed, these are sent electronically twice daily to several regional distributors based upon product sourcing information, with deliveries the same day for orders received before 11.30 am.

If you were unaware of such possibilities from these three examples or are unclear about the use of some of the terms being used, then do not despair, just read on. This book is meant for you.

Business functions are increasingly performed electronically, whether by placing an order with a supplier, sending a message to a colleague, accessing a data warehouse for product information, or passing business transactions directly from one computer application to another. This book, with its focus upon electronic business communications, is relevant to organizations both large and small. It explains the current state of technology and how organizations can achieve the business benefits of electronic commerce.

We consider the complex environment that organizations face today, which is having a profound effect on the way in which they operate, before looking in detail at electronic business communications. Changes over the last 30 years have been dramatic, and the business world has come to understand the value of information and how it can be exploited for competitive advantage, providing the stimulus for the emergence of a new industry centred around IT.

Think about your own organization or other organizations with whom you work. What is happening to them today? They are subject to a pace of change unrivalled in business history as they compete in the turbulent environment of the 1990s. Whether they collapse, survive or prosper will depend upon how well they are able to adapt to these changes. Acquisitions, mergers, fresh legislation, new products, geographic spread, new markets, outsourcing, economic outlook, competition, etc. are all symptoms of change, and all illustrate its diverse nature.

The "digital revolution" is bringing about structural changes within the economies of the more developed countries as profound as the industrial revolution seen in the last century. This is resulting in changing patterns of employment, with a decline in traditional manufacturing and a growth in the service sector. Automation has decreased the numbers required to support the manufacturing base and, due to labour costs, traditional manufacturing tends now to be transferred to the less developed countries. As more developed countries tend to base their economies around the growing services sector, the concept of the information age has emerged, based upon the rapid development and use of IT. It is contributing to the highly competitive environment being experienced across all market sectors.

The impact of computer technology can be seen in research, its inclusion in product design for the replacement of mechanical parts, automation to displace human intervention, and within human activity systems known as business processes. Many organizations started to show serious business interest in computers during the early 1960s but, for reasons explored in this book, there is an ever increasing use of IT within the newer business processes being introduced into organizations today.

People and Information Technology

While the world has seen incredible technological advances over the last 150 years, the human race itself has remained largely unchanged for some 150,000 years. The individual likes the way that it was and will frequently seek to defend the *status quo*. We do not attempt here to define the right corporate environment for change, but rather see it as vital to changing the way in which the company operates, and to successfully introducing a greater use of IT. Chapter 2 explores some of the techniques and programmes being adopted by the more progressive organizations as they seek to meet "head-on" the necessity for change, and evolve as leading players in their chosen markets. The challenge is to do "more" with less, to get "more" out of the organization for less input.

This phenomenon cannot only be seen in large organizations, but is fast becoming a feature of business life for all; it is equally applicable to small start-up companies, as well as to organizations in the public sector. Due to their scale of operation, large organizations are generally more able to justify the IT expenditures that may accompany business process change, and possess the people skill sets to carry them out.

In Europe, several initiatives are under way to encourage Small and Medium Enterprises (SME) into undertaking the transformation necessary to secure the benefits being achieved by many of the larger organizations. In the long-term, SMEs are likely to be the real beneficiaries of IT, and offer significant potential for the creation of wealth and capital.

These generalizations apply primarily to organizations that exist within more advanced or developed countries. Of the world's population, 50% are still waiting to make their first telephone call, and only 10% of the world's population have a basic voice telephone line. Of all telephone lines, 70% are found in countries that make up 15% of the world's population in total. But the situation is changing rapidly, and the spread of global telecommunications infrastructures is forecast to accelerate over the next 20 years, providing access for a greater proportion of people in the developing countries.

The growth of global electronic business communications and its extension to commercial trading between companies (not to be confused with trading in financial markets), increasingly referred to as "electronic commerce," is dependent upon the availability of basic telecommunications infrastructures. Governments of the world's leading nations are supporting a number of initiatives for the creation of so-called "digital information highways" based around the Internet. These initiatives and the impact of technology as an instrument for change are explored in Chapter 3.

The Business Manager

Today's business managers face increased pressure brought about by the changing environment, often requiring decisions of crucial importance to be taken within short time-scales. The quality of these decisions is often affected by the availability of data, the creation of information and access to knowledge. The emphasis upon information and knowledge is illustrated in the way organizations are being re-structured, with reporting lines built around the contribution individuals make to the business. This is different to the traditional hierarchical structure that accords power to individuals based upon their relative position within the hierarchy. Power in organizations today resides where information and knowledge are located, and knowledge is seen as the most enduring asset of any organization. It is hardly surprising that emphasis continues to be placed on computer-based applications, that deliver a wide range of information to meet the varying requirements of organizations and their extended organizations (e.g. customers, suppliers, shipping agents, etc.).

This implies organizational maturity drawn from experience gained in the development and introduction of computer-based applications; or for a smaller organization, a vision of what might be achieved and a practical understanding of computing by the management team. The successful exploitation of IT by an organization throughout its many business activities requires evolution over time. It would be difficult for an organization to embark upon the introduction of a fully integrated computer system, without having first already built up experience with a number of transactional applications.

The good news is that electronic business communications does represent a starting point for many smaller organizations, by providing the "transport" on which important "mail enabled" applications can be introduced.

Competition

Many organizations have been forced to look at their existing business processes, established over the years, to assess whether or not they are applicable to the way of working now demanded by the new business order. In many cases, it is clear that processes that were appropriate to the organization during the 1970s and 1980s are now irrelevant. This realization has resulted in some tough management decisions as companies seek to re-define organizational goals, calling for new levels of productivity and financial performance.

While the business world has rarely been characterized as a stable one, in past decades, organizations were allowed to develop marketing strategies that focused at competing upon price or various forms of product or service differentiation. In some market sectors, such as retailing, price still dominates the nature of competition, although when price parity is achieved there is a need to find new forms of differentiation, which the customer perceives to be of value. Even in those market sectors where it is possible to achieve value differentiation, price, while no longer the key competitive differentiator, still remains an important component of the marketing mix. This in turn places a pressure on margins and a need to control cost of sales if price flexibility is to be achieved. The ideal situation is where either the products or services marketed by the company have such a uniqueness or high perceived value to the purchaser that price is not a key factor, and the potential savings and benefits greatly out-weigh the price.

However, for many organizations, the arrival of competition means a reduction in the uniqueness of their product or service (Fig. 1.2), which in turn means that prices come under pressure and margins eroded. There is a limit to which it is tenable to continue price discounting, and therefore other forms of uniqueness are sought to which a purchaser attaches a value. These new forms of uniqueness are typically associated with differentiated services and heavily supported by IT innovation.

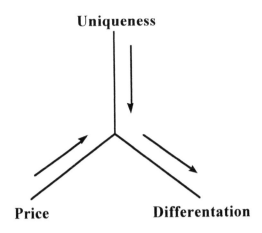

Fig. 1.2 Competitive dimensions.

CASE STUDY – WINCANTON LOGISTICS

Wincanton Logistics (Wincanton) is a distribution and warehousing company which embarked during the 1990s upon a major re-design of its internal business process, geared at a much greater control of costs. Wincanton operate from 100 locations throughout the UK with 12,000 employees, 9600 vehicles and 3M sq ft of warehousing space. They provide services to their parent organization the Unigate group, as well as to other major companies including Tesco, Somerfield, Unipart, Texaco and Shell, operating in various industry sectors including retail, manufacturing and petroleum.

Wincanton's revenues are in excess of £450M, and due to the highly competitive nature of their industry, where profit margins are extremely cost sensitive, it has developed a corporate culture centred around the control of costs. Costing information is developed in detail when making proposals to potential clients, and wherever possible, is very closely monitored in their day-to-day operation via direct cost allocation to individual clients. This information is used for competitive advantage, and is critical when negotiating the extension of contracts to ensure that the business remains profitable.

During 1992, Wincanton initiated a comprehensive internal review to establish ways in which information technology could provide greater support to the business, resulting in the development of a long-term IT strategy. By 1994, Wincanton reached the stage where it began to review how it could further improve access to financial information for control purposes, and embarked upon a project known as the Wincanton Information System Enterprise (WISE). The objective was to implement a new financial consolidation package which would collect and exchange information between a number of business applications, such as vehicle management, purchasing, warehousing and distribution.

Wincanton has data centres running IBM servers (RS6000, AS/400) together with PCs linked to local area networks and connected over a private TCP/IP Wide Area Network (WAN) based upon BT leased lines and Racal switching technology. In fact, over 600 personal computers (PCs) are geographically spread throughout the UK and connected to the network. In setting out the basis for the development of WISE, it was decided to use some existing legacy applications, to introduce new development methodologies and database tools and to place a heavy emphasis upon standard packaged software.

GE's Enterprise System, an EDI VAN gateway, was at the heart of developments being used to integrate the different legacy and new applications, some existing upon disparate platforms. Wincanton had been exchanging EDI data with some of its clients using PCs connected to GE's EDI*Express Tradanet Service. However, as part of the WISE project, work was undertaken to ensure that specific applications became EDI capable so that business information could be exchanged electronically with their clients.

WISE has proved to be highly effective, giving the following results:

- Cost reduction across the supply chain.
- Improved customer service – exceeded national average for on-time delivery – Wincanton 99.8% (national average 88%).
- Exceeded national average for vehicle up-time – Wincanton 98% (national average 87%).

The ability to integrate information across disparate systems, including new financial software packages and legacy applications, allowed Wincanton to meet its objective of using standard software packages (with minimal customization). As Wincanton has acquired new businesses or created fresh ones associated with new service contracts, the flexibility provided by the EDI VAN gateway has allowed the integration between applications to be achieved easily and within aggressive timescales. In addition, the system architecture allows Wincanton to split their financial systems into two distinct sets of accounts, primarily for convenience and ease of management, whilst retaining the ability to rapidly create a consolidation of accounts when required.

Wincanton see IT as a powerful weapon which has allowed them to remain extremely efficient, and more importantly, has helped them derive a competitive advantage, as more and more business transactions are being handled electronically, both internally, and increasingly externally, using EDI with their trading partners.

A major re-development of systems has taken place over the last few years and several new applications have been implemented. These include:

- Vehicle Management System, including Workshop and Maintenance Control.
- Sundry Purchasing.
- Warehouse Management System.
- Site/Vehicle-based data capture systems.
- Traffic Management system.
- Financial Ledgers, Vehicle Costing and Contract Accounting.
- Management reporting – utilizing business intelligence tools for database queries and EIS.

The EDI VAN gateway performs the routing and interfacing of transactions between the various applications, and external links with customers and suppliers.

The current business environment demands that organizations monitor and control their costs to achieve the desired financial performance, as well as being in a position to respond positively to market price pressures. Whereas organizations could compete on price alone in the 1980s, this no longer applies in the 1990s where discerning purchasers expect not only aggressive pricing, but high quality, superior customer service and speed in product innovation (Fig. 1.3).

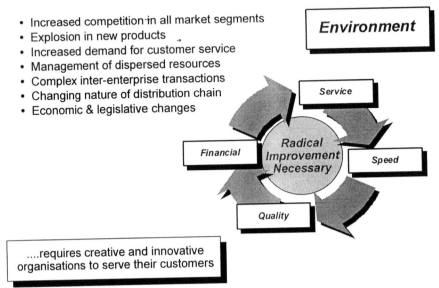

- Increased competition in all market segments
- Explosion in new products
- Increased demand for customer service
- Management of dispersed resources
- Complex inter-enterprise transactions
- Changing nature of distribution chain
- Economic & legislative changes

Environment

Service

Financial

Radical Improvement Necessary

Speed

Quality

....requires creative and innovative organisations to serve their customers

Fig. 1.3 Competitive pressures in the 1990s.

Speed/Time to Market

Things are happening much faster: distance and time are contracting; customer expectations for instant service are growing; all serving to increase the pace of business. Some of this is due to improvements in logistics, particularly in air travel; much is made possible through new IT infrastructures, commonly known as "information highways" now spanning the more developed countries.

With the pace of technology innovation and the emergence of the customer driven environment, product lifecycles are much shorter and obsolescence a continual threat. Alvin Toffler[1] comments on this fact when he says: "The forces that have made mass society have suddenly been thrown into reverse. The mass market has split into ever-multiplying, ever-emerging sets of mini-markets that demand a continually expanding range of options, models, types, sizes, colours and customisations, creating a totally new framework within which the production organizations of society will function."

Example – Financial Services

The Financial Services sector has energetically embraced IT, causing dramatic changes in the way that some of their services now operate. Traditional trading floors have been replaced by screens and keyboards to enable electronic trading to take place, together with links into back office systems to speed up the completion of the transaction. In foreign exchange markets, banks need to have a complete picture of their currency holdings around the world, and to set limits to such holdings that minimize risk and potential exposure by adverse fluctuations. The recent collapse of Barings Bank illustrates the dangers inherent when such systems are not in place. Another example is evident in the increasing use of Automated Teller Machines (ATM) and credit cards by the public and the subsequent reduction in visits to their banks. This in turn has enabled some banks to re-structure their operations causing the shedding of large numbers of employees or their deployment into roles providing more direct customer contact. In a commodity marketplace such as banking, this is a deliberate strategy aimed at winning business by focusing upon customer service.

Example – Fashion Industry

The fashion industry is heavily influenced by the need to bring new designs to the marketplace in advance of competition; the same trend also exists in the computer industry. There is an explosion of new products, where technical innovation and the ability to exploit speed of introduction, known as "time to market," can provide a head start on the competition (Fig. 1.4).

Example – Office Supplies

New management techniques such as Electronic Data Interchange (EDI) play a key role in making this possible by speeding up the process. Brun Passot, a French company in the office supplies business, is one such example. Through EDI and other direct customer ordering techniques, it has been able to respond far more rapidly to customer demand, to help reduce customer inventories and to build customer loyalty. The result has been to capture a significant percentage of the highly fragmented French marketplace for office supplies.

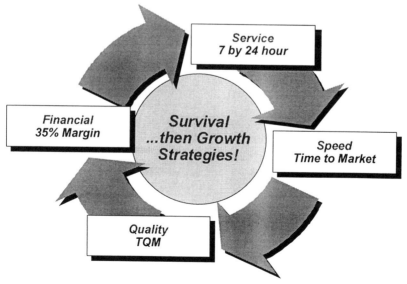

Fig. 1.4 Business strategies for the 1990s.

Quality

The quality movement of the 1980s has been diffused in the 1990s and, for some organizations, has become a corporate culture in which a Total Quality Management (TQM) philosophy has been developed. TQM is aimed at optimizing the internal working practices of the organization to eliminate inefficiencies and hence unnecessary cost. It encourages involvement and helps motivate individuals to work together, improving upon existing practices. This has led to a growing trend among companies to seek ISO 9000 accreditation, as a means of demonstrating to customers that they follow well established internal procedures and processes, to ensure that high levels of quality excellence are sustained. The 1980s saw a number of companies using quality for competitive differentiation, thus enabling them to secure high prices.

Customer Service

People and organizations have become more discriminate about the products and services that they seek to purchase, placing fresh demands on suppliers who wish to win both new and repeat business. While the 1980s were heavily influenced by the importance of quality, the current passion is for customer service.

Example – Domestic Insurance

A classic example of combining strong customer focus together with a highly competitive offering is Direct Line, a UK subsidiary of the Royal Bank of Scotland[2]; it offers instant quotations and insurance for domestic customers over the telephone. Set up in 1985, with its telephone-based and computer-supported customer contact, Direct Line insures over two million vehicles, making it the UK's largest private motor insurance company. In many respects, it has re-defined the manner in which private vehicle insurance is sold in the UK and, despite achieving a competitive edge for a period of time, it now faces strong competition from other insurance companies offering similar services. In effect, this method of selling private vehicle insurance has now become the norm, and it is a competitive disadvantage not to be able to operate in this manner. Having established brand recognition and by nature of its operation, Direct Line is able to offer competitive pricing without sacrificing quality of service. However, having lost the initial competitive edge, it is now seeking new ways of service differentiation to stay ahead of its competition.

Example – Automotive After-market

Another similar example is Kwik-Fit, which has built up a network of workshops throughout the UK, offering replacement tyres, batteries, exhausts, etc. with a very strong emphasis upon customer service, or what Kwik-Fit terms as customer delight in the service offered. This approach is complemented by a robust, but simple to operate, computer system that provides customer quotations of price and stock availability, as well as billing and payment. The address information collected from the customer at the time of payment provided the basis of a mailing list that enabled Kwik-Fit in 1995 to move into a new business venture of car insurance, using the successful formula already established by Direct Line and described earlier.

Business Productivity Improvements

Organizational change is needed to bring about improvements in business productivity. How can IT assist in re-directing employees' efforts into more "value added" activities? By their very nature, many industries command a uniqueness reflected in specific business processes. Most organizations use a range of business communications facilities for internal communications within and between departments, as well as with their trading partners. Since the mid 1980s, the use of electronic business communications has grown at a rapid rate, and is seen as an important management tool in the fight to achieve business productivity improvements.

Assuming parity of product or service, the ability for organizations to achieve an "edge" over the competition, combining a compelling marketing mix with innovative use of IT, will not continue indefinitely. The challenge is to extend the window of competitive edge for as long as possible, since over time competition will move to adopt the new practice, and it then becomes the "norm" for the industry. Those organizations that do not adopt it will suffer competitive disadvantage, but for the market leaders, the search goes on to identify new forms of competitive differentiation.

Notes

1.   Alvin Toffler, The Third Wave.
2.   Web site url: www.royalbankscot.co.uk

2. *Organizational/Cultural Changes*

From Downsizing to Rightsizing

Organizations face a tough business climate, with increased competition from newly industrialized countries and from local players, all against a background of changing demand patterns. Technological advances have been rapid, delivering completely new ways of doing business. The average time between these changes is ever shortening.

The challenge has been to become leaner: to cut the fat, slash the excess and add flexibility to the organization. This has meant a focus on financial cost cutting, and layers of management and workers have been shed. Companies are transforming themselves to meet tougher and more global challenges. The business world is seeing the most dramatic transformation in organizational hierarchies since the pyramidal command structure, developed centuries ago.

A conventional "job for life" is now seen as a corporate liability and the unwritten contract between the organization and its workers – counting on keeping your job as long as you worked hard – is being abandoned. The workplace is becoming Darwinian in its nature: the survival of the fittest for the employees, and the survival of the fastest for the organization.

Some statistics indicate the trend. In September 1993, US businesses were slashing jobs at the rate of 2000 a day. In 1992, US manufacturers dropped 275,000 workers from their payrolls[1]. In 1993, for the first time ever in the US, white collar unemployment exceeded that of blue collar unemployment. The trend is also visible in Europe, which has had to live with almost 11% unemployment within its EC member states. The job shedding situation has been further exacerbated by world economic boom and bust cycles.

We need to ask what effect this downsizing is having on the organization and its environment. There was an urgent need for organizations to remove "dead wood" that was slowing down operations, and impeding flexibility. The move towards a knowledge based society is also highly visible: the vast majority of new jobs created have been knowledge based rather than manually oriented. This has meant that fewer workers can achieve the same results, faster, with the aid of advanced technology, when compared to a decade ago.

Rightsizing was seen as an important priority for higher profits, and the wider costs of employee morale, loyalty and loss of experience were costs to be faced with a brave face. This was especially true in an environment of world recession.

Unfortunately, most organizations have not achieved the benefits that they sought from the exercise. A survey of 531 companies by consultants Wyatt and Co. outlined in a Wall Street Journal substantiated this view:

- three quarters of the organizations interviewed had cut their payrolls;
- 85% of the organizations sought higher profits but only 46% realized increased earnings;
- 58% expected higher productivity, but only 34% experienced it;
- 61% sought improvements in customer service, but only 33% achieved it.

These figures are worrying, but most startling was the fact that within a year after having made the cuts, more than 50% had *refilled the positions*. What went wrong, and how can we learn from the mistakes?

The initial perception is that too many organizations jumped on the bandwagon of the day: downsizing, de-layering, becoming lean (and several other euphemisms for laying people off) seemed the right way forward. This was the sensible way forward for some organizations, those that were removing people that did not fit within processes that had changed as business demanded. Too many other organizations followed the "fad of the day" without enough long term commitment.

Business Process Re-engineering

The tail end of the 1980s saw many organizations in the predicament outlined above. What was the appropriate response to increasing competition and varying demands? For some time, far sighted organizations had realized that their operations needed to change in order to compete within a new competitive environment, one where the rules had changed and were continuing to change at an astonishing rate. Business Process Re-engineering (BPR), the fundamental reappraisal of the way businesses operate, caught the imagination of thousands of organizations worldwide. In a survey conducted in 1993, 61% of 465 US companies stated that they were engaged in re-engineering their organizations[2]. Why the sudden interest?

Stepping back a hundred years or so, we experienced the industrial revolution; a period where industrial giants were being erected, fuelled by cheap labour and new technologies. Capital was scarce, labour plentiful. Management had a distinct role in these organizations: to do the thinking and instruct and monitor the workforce. In turn the workforce were allocated tasks that had been broken down into the smallest component, each carried out by a specialist. This scientifically calibrated view of work was engineered by individuals like Taylor (termed Taylorism)[3], where division of labour and efficiency was paramount. This fitted in well with the vertical, hierarchical enterprises prevalent at the turn of the century and utilized to great advantage by individuals like Henry Ford.

Today, organizations face a different climate that is not stable and will not sustain this view of the environment. Hence the focus on flatter hierarchies, more team working, empowerment and smaller flexible organizations. Those that have not realized the need for this type of organization are beginning to see its virtues from benchmarking studies and best practice cases. The question is how to achieve this change. Enter BPR, and the large amount of attention it has received from the management field.

What is BPR?

Managers have been subjected to many management fads in the past. Each promises to end all their ills, and quite beguilingly offers an important step to achieve competitive advantage. The 1980s were characterized by the focus on quality and its associated acronym: TQM. The 1990s are set to be dominated by re-engineering, also with its associated acronym: BPR. Both approaches promised much – they are not new but amalgamations of techniques that have been offered before. Like all great approaches, they offer something that is right, at the right time, but all too often they disintegrate into petty techniques that certainly do not resemble what their progenitors were advocating.

This has certainly been the case with BPR, being diluted in terms of what it can offer. In one study by Gateway Management Consulting, 54% of 121 senior executives admitted to an incorrect understanding of what the term "re-engineering" meant. In fact many have latched on to the term, and used it simply as what is perceived to be a dignified term for firing people. Others view it as an euphemism for downsizing or restructuring. Some consultants are selling the same old advice, masquerading under a new "sexy" name. What does BPR actually mean? The term was coined by Michael Hammer in a *Harvard Business Review* Article, and later refined in a book by Hammer and Champy (Hammer and Champy, 1993). They define BPR as:

> ...the fundamental rethinking and radical redesign of business processes to achieve dramatic improvements in critical contemporary measures of performance such as cost, quality, service and speed.

Furthermore, they claim that:

> Re-engineering isn't about making marginal or incremental improvements, but about achieving quantum leaps in performance...the alternative is for corporate America to close its doors and go out of business.

At the core of what Hammer is preaching is the transformation from functional specialization (such as marketing, production, finance, and so on) to process orientation. He argues that there are no more than six or seven core processes in any organization, an example being product development. The focus is on radical change; starting with a blank piece of paper and questioning everything, especially entrenched attitudes that always seem to begin with "we've always done it this way...". BPR does not leave room for any sacred cows.

The argument goes something like this: key processes, cycles of activity to achieve business objectives, have usually been built up over time on design principles of a past era. By applying engineering type concepts, it is possible to re-align these processes to take advantage of modern day technological and organizational improvements. Hence the heavy reliance on IT as the enabler behind BPR.

Old processes are out of date; especially those that had technology thrown at them in the late 1970s. Much of the attention that BPR is enjoying may be attributable to the realization that inefficient processes were automated, when perhaps they should have been obliterated, to use Hammer's terminology. Advanced technology has made many tasks obsolete, enabling one person to do many tasks at the same time. Old telephone operators are a case in point. New technology has completely obliterated the need for this task, with technology being able to do much more, faster and more accurately. The process has been re-engineered.

There is extreme frustration at the lack of productivity increase, despite the billions of dollars of investment that has been devoted to new IT-based technologies. White collar work productivity only increased a few percentage points in the 1980s. Inefficient processes were built at a time when artificial demarcations were erected between departments, making the organization unresponsive and unwieldy in today's market. We have all had the experience of being transferred from one department to another, at some time, whilst an enquiry is being dealt with only to be told that the file is "missing" or details are not locatable. It is particularly these types of inefficiency that BPR addresses.

To achieve this aim, BPR requires organizational changes. Teamworking, empowerment and shedding layers are all terms associated with a BPR project (discussed later). This is what BPR is about. It promises a more responsive organization, better equipped to deal in the competitive environment.

Cultural Change

The emphasis of this chapter is not about how to successfully implement a BPR project (the reader is directed to Champy (1993), Davenport (1990) and Johansson *et al.* (1993) for indicative reading), but rather on what it promises the organization; moving away from the evangelical vogue of the concept to a more pragmatic and critical appraisal of what BPR means in practice.

Core to successful transformation of any kind is a commitment from the workforce and a successful change in organizational culture. Changing culture is a difficult and creative process, and culture is a living thing within any environment, continually evolving and changing. It is difficult to manage, but can be influenced by the structures and philosophies emerging from senior management. This makes change a difficult process.

BPR is about organizing enterprises around continuous business processes. This has involved bypassing middle management and devolving responsibility and accountability lower down to multi-disciplinary generalists: empowerment of the workforce. Personal fiefdoms are disrupted and the *status quo* challenged. In summary, BPR is primarily the re-packaging of many traditional organization and methods techniques, but with some important distinctions:

- It is a top management business driven initiative.

- It is all about change within the organization: business processes, structure and culture.
- It relies upon expertise and knowledge within the organization, irrespective of level or position, to undertake the business process re-design.
- It is process and not functional driven: and does not respect fiefdoms.
- It is results and action oriented, and sets out to achieve quantum levels of improvement.
- Whilst the potential benefits are great, it can be a high risk exercise if the organization rejects the need or urgency of change.

IT and Empowerment

Empowerment of the workforce has a satisfying ring to it. It is deemed a good thing, and has been key to many initiatives to reshape organizations and practices. Multi-skilled teams, trained to high proficiency levels, are necessary if BPR is to succeed. The front line workers take on higher levels of responsibility, and rather than passing information and decision making up the hierarchy, they use knowledge to manage. The distinction between just working and just managing begins to blur. Managers are now increasingly seen as counsellors or coaches.

The level of autonomy afforded to workers varies with each implementation of empowerment. It can range from simply allowing a little lateral freedom in making more choices, to true empowerment where responsibility and power are truly devolved downwards.

With the large emphasis on the role of IT within BPR, the part technology plays in empowerment is changing: the technology can be promoted as a tool to enable a shift from hierarchical control to functional empowerment. Whereas computers were traditionally seen as individualistic tools, new developments in groupware and Computer Supported Collaborative Working (CSCW) are challenging this. Furthermore, advanced technology now raises questions as to who controls productive processes and in which way.

For instance, organizations of a past era were characterized by workers who were told exactly what they needed to do, and how to do it. Managers imposed a strict monitoring of work, for they understood the work and process better than their subordinates. Today this rule no longer holds true. Subordinates tend to understand their work and processes to a far greater extent than their managers; some do not even fully understand the technology being utilized. Technology has changed; processes need to as well.

The trend is visible as a new generation of manager proliferates through the organization, the sort of manager that is happy with, and understands, the technology, based on experience with use through earlier academic periods.

Computers are not neutral friendly devices that just free workers from boring repetitive jobs. They control the currency that most organizations trade on: information. Who is in control: management or workers? Should we resist the devolvement of control to lower levels and leave the real work to the workers and strategic control to senior management? Workers need to have accountability for their actions. Socially responsible decisions are unlikely if individuals are not held accountable. In many cases, organizations have asserted that they have empowered their workforce when they have achieved nothing of the sort. Delegating power down, whilst abdicating responsibility, is not what empowerment is about.

Initiating an empowerment programme is inherently political, and it is no accident that the term was traditionally used in political circles to signify the gain of power. Job roles are having to be re-defined and a new order of things will manifest themselves within the working practices of many. Some will have been perceived to have gained, whilst others may seem to lose out.

Success is derived from the effective management of other levers, such as reward schemes and redefinition of roles, where status was measured by how many people were below you, or what job title you held. New mindsets have to be created. The law profession is a good example where roles are not governed by job titles. You have associate, partner and a senior partner in law firms. Status is gained from doing your job well, progressing to harder and more influential cases.

IT has the potential to re-address the power matrix, allowing information to flow throughout an organization. New processes can only be sustained with the flow of co-operative work between traditionally fragmented sectors of the organization. This is going to mean some drastic changes in the way workers' roles are viewed and the role of middle management in the new order.

The emphasis on redesigning workflows has had significant repercussions on the role of the middle manager, who traditionally provided the "glue" that held old business processes together. New processes eliminate the need for the "glue", and a significant amount of the work required by middle management disappears, making them a main target for workforce reductions.

Where BPR Fails

Despite the euphoria about BPR, there have been significant numbers of failed projects, where anticipated returns have not been realized. BPR is risky and there are far more reports of failure than there are success.

Certainly some of the failed cases are due to organizations simply tinkering with the edges rather than aiming for radical change, or those that get sidetracked as change loses momentum. Radical change is a necessary starting point and although many zealots of BPR advocate that anything but fundamental change is not BPR, there is much value in "thinking big, and starting small."

Critics argue that an organization was never engineered in the first place, so cannot be re-engineered. There are very few cases of an organization completely re-engineering itself; the risks are too immense. Taking away the pillars may collapse the structure for good.

BPR In Europe

BPR has hit the US hard, and all signs indicate that interest in Europe has grown substantially. European companies that are crying out for change are looking at successful US implementations of re-design. Many factors, not least the single European market, have amplified the market forces organizations face, applying increasing pressure to reduce outdated processes and bureaucracies.

For BPR to succeed in Europe, the technique has to overcome some specific intrinsic characteristics that are not conducive to BPR:

- Europe is strong on social rights. One only has to look at Germany, where an average worker costs approximately 50% more to employ than an American counterpart. In its early stages, BPR necessitates substantial job re-organization and layoffs. One aspect that is not consistent with the US model is that many European countries support a strong union involvement. For instance, German unions possess powerful seats on the boards of organizations. For BPR to succeed, it is critical to have all parties united behind the effort.
- Some European Union members, such as Germany, are proficient at producing specialists: their praised education and training systems are geared towards this end. BPR requires flexible people whose skills are more general, with skill sets that can allow multi-disciplined teams to cross functional boundaries. Some would suggest that European firms are perhaps too ingrained and confident in their own managerial traditions;
- Some governments and industries are willing to save, and support bloated organizations, despite the need to make harsh change. The French government is a case in point, with Air France receiving substantial subsidies.

Buzzword or Strategy

Despite Hammer's claims that BPR is a revolutionary concept, it shares many similarities with other theories and models that discuss empowerment, customer orientation and teamworking. The term BPR was first used in the MIT research programme, "Management in the 1990s," which was started in 1983. BPR was located within a five step framework of IT induced organizational transformation.

What was revolutionary was the amalgamation of ideas, articulated at a time that was receptive to these ideas. The quality movement was becoming stagnant, and BPR seemed to be a logical step forward, and complementary to downsizing. The real question remains: Is there more to BPR than just another buzzword, that has successfully been propagated through business via management gurus and management consultants? Answers are not as easy as questions, but much can be gained by learning from the experience of others.

Notes

1. Robert Reich, US Secretary for Labor.
2. Stephen Towers, *Business Process Re-engineering – Lessons for Success*, Management Services, August 1993, pp. 10–12.
3. F. W. Taylor, *Principles of Scientific Management*, Harper and Row, 1947.

3. Information Society and Technological Impact

Background

Organizational use of Information Technology (IT) has evolved through several distinct stages over the last 30 years. Initially there was a heavy focus towards operational improvements centred around reduced costs, followed by a tactical emphasis upon achieving improved effectiveness, particularly for the individual. More recently, interest in IT has been dominated by the strategic contribution it can make towards gaining competitive advantage.

As new generations of employees, schooled with a strong reliance upon IT, enter the business sector, the digital or information revolution is giving rise to expectations of an Information Society. This concept is actively supported by many governments around the world through initiatives such as the building of information highways, to be used by both consumers and the business sector. A six layer model illustrates the telecommunications infrastructure required to support an Information Society, and how this links to the specific requirements of the business sector.

The steady increase in the use of electronic business communications is being helped by several popular IT trends; these include, end user computing incorporating Local Area Networks, distributed "open" computing, high performance networking and multimedia documents.

To compete in this new economic environment, companies will be required to extend their customer driven philosophies and adopt "best" business practices, making the most effective use of technology. This allows them to:

- Reduce support costs and improve business effectiveness.
- Use IT as an enabler to re-design business processes.
- Swiftly introduce new and differentiated products & services.
- Compete better on the basis of value, time, uniqueness and customer service.

Efficiency Improvements

Early business computing activities tended to focus upon automating well defined business processes, aimed at improving efficiency within the organization. Popular uses were in finance and production departments, where the computer's ability to process rapidly large quantities of repetitive information resulted in savings in time and effort. Both the technology itself, and the ability of organizations to use it, largely influenced the early uses of computers in terms of scope and impact. As part of the evolution, it became possible to achieve important new cost reductions, usually in staffing, simply by taking transactional and operational business processes and mapping these into data processing systems. It was accepted that as a precursor for computerization, the business processes themselves required re-structuring and that the claimed efficiency improvements, owed as much to the resulting simplification and streamlining as the use of the computer itself. This does not diminish the importance of the resultant applications that were able to support significant increases in volume with much smaller incremental levels of staffing.

Example – Hawker Siddeley Aviation

In the late 1960s, Hawker Siddeley Aviation (now part of British Aerospace) embarked upon an ambitious programme to design and implement a company production control system for use across its six UK sites. Significant productivity improvements were a direct result from the rationalization of paperwork and procedures that took place in parallel with the design of the system; but this process took time due to the need to gain consensus across the sites. The exercise converged on a common set of documentation including engineering process layouts, work order paperwork and inter-company transfer of work. The introduction of the production control system resulted in staff savings approaching 50%, excluding the re-deployment of staff to new roles associated with the maintenance of the new system. In addition, the production control system, together with the same level of staffing, was able to support increased volumes of work as the aircraft production rate steadily increased.

Personal Effectiveness

Advantages were soon realized: with ready access to information, carried by the transactions feeding the finance and production applications, accounts receivables could be sold to factoring companies and stock availability information could improve customer service. New IT capabilities centred around data communications evolved to serve the growing requirement of unleashing information, such that information could be distributed to those in the organization that could best use it.

The period that followed in the early 1980s was orientated towards the effectiveness of the individual, brought about by the personal computer. While revolutionary at the time, dramatic price/performance improvements in computer technology now offers increased processing power and information storage on the desktop never thought possible 15 or more years ago. This has given birth to a complete new industry in software products that aims to service corporate information requirements at the desktop, including, word processing, spreadsheets, E-mail and bulletin boards, together with the underlying operating system and network software that makes this possible. Companies such as Microsoft,

Lotus and Novell have emerged as significant players in this marketplace, and now exert a strong influence in much the same way that the industry was dominated by IBM (76% of the world market) in the late 1970s. IBM's acquisition of Lotus in 1995 demonstrates the power exerted by the software industry and the importance to a company such as IBM in securing its competitive position in the IT marketplace.

The most important advances in IT concern data communications and networking that allows computers, sometimes whole communities of computers, to be linked together. As organizations in the 90s seek new ways of conducting business, their ability to communicate with customers, suppliers, manufacturers, banks, etc. places greater reliance upon data communications facilities. The personal computer has evolved into a communications device providing access to information, whether held on a local file server linked to a Local Area Network (LAN), or on a corporate file server reached via a Wide Area Network (WAN). Information access is positioned alongside the traditional desktop applications such as word processing, spreadsheets, and communications intensive applications, such as E-mail and Electronic Data Interchange (EDI).

Competitive Edge

It is this combination of computing power and data communications that has allowed companies to develop new business applications that provide an "edge" over the competition. Typically, this is achieved by incorporating IT, with its speedy access to information, into their products and services, offering the opportunity for improved customer service.

Example – AA Sabre System

Classic examples go back to the 1960s when American Airlines introduced their SABRE system, an interactive reservation system. In addition to operational improvements, including lower staffing levels and increased aircraft loading (numbers of passengers per flight), by placing their computer terminals into the travel agencies, they immediately achieved an edge over the competition, by making it much easier to book a seat with American Airlines.

Example – American Hospital Supply Company

The American Hospital Supply Company increased their sales on average by 13% per year during 1978 to 1983 largely by an innovative use of IT. They connected hospitals directly into their on-line order entry system. The result was to eliminate the effort involved in ordering hospital supplies and achieve differentiation over the competition.

Example – Benetton

In the mid 1980s, Benetton introduced a system that allowed its agents around the world to transmit their orders electronically. This resulted in a reduced cycle time from 10/12 days to a few hours ensuring that their distributors received goods a lot sooner; it also enabled them to react much faster to market trends than the competition.

Example – DHL

The marketplace for global physical package/document delivery has experienced phenomenal growth. As an integral part of its service, DHL needed to put in place administrative systems which would cater for fluctuations in load and improve the quality of information in response to customer queries. This resulted in the development of a global package/document tracking system, that substantially improved communications between offices handling shipments, and also improved the tracking of specific deliveries, enabling a positive response to customer enquires concerning delivery status.

New Generation

Much of the process improvement achieved by organizations centres on the organization's ability to adapt to change and of finding new ways to tackle old problems. The situation continues to evolve as more and more people interact with computers as a normal part of their day-to-day lives, whether by paying at a store checkout, performing a transaction at a banking automated teller machine, making a flight reservation, sending an E-mail message to a colleague or preparing a letter on their home computer.

New generations of employees are entering the business world today having a strong reliance and knowledge of IT gained from at home usage, school and higher education. Their interaction with technology is natural and unbending, initially coming from computer games, then through education where their keyboards skills rapidly become the envy of the most proficient secretary. This generation in their mid twenties are rapidly more able to embrace IT and live with change. This contrasts with older members of the organization that find it difficult to understand the technology and learn its jargon, and who often feel threatened as a result.

Information Society

Changes taking place today within organizations in the more developed countries are revolutionary in character, and challenge many of the basic concepts on which organizations have operated over the last 100 years. This has come about through the "digital revolution". These changes have given rise to the concept of the information society, which for many goes far beyond the establishment of a technological infrastructure that supports a service economy. The Information Society should also create a business environment encouraging organizations to compete on an international basis, reduce unemployment and enrich the quality of life.

European Initiatives

During 1993, the Commission of the European Communities published a White paper entitled "Growth, Competitiveness, Employment – The challenges and ways forward into the 21st Century," which stressed that Information and Communication Technologies (ICT) had the potential to promote steady and sustainable growth and to increase competitiveness. This document was reviewed by the European Council in December 1993, who gave it their full support and requested that a further report be prepared by a group of prominent individuals on the information society, placing emphasis upon identifying actions to be taken. The resultant Bangemann group report entitled "Europe and the Global Information Society – Recommendations to the European Council," was submitted to the European Council in May 1994. It highlighted the need for an acceleration of the telecommunications liberalization process, placing initiatives with the public authorities to launch public interest, and laying the financing of an information infrastructure in the private sector.

The unexpected and spontaneous growth of the Internet since the mid 1990s, with an ever increasing usage by commercial users, demonstrates that the Information Society is on its way and that the concept of an information infrastructure or highway is a practical and desirable objective. The Internet, apart from confirming that the latent demand exists, has illustrated several of the inadequacies that need to be addressed in a final model of an information highway. These include the problems with security, reliability and anti-social usage.

Technology in itself is not the problem in achieving mass market demand. Technology is frequently in search of an application and its availability outstrips market demand. The objective is to identify the applications of real value to organizations, that use the uniqueness of the technology to achieve some form of competitive differentiation. A good example in Europe is the availability of Integrated Services Digital Networks (ISDN) which outstrips deployment in North America; it represents an opportunity for European organizations to develop completely new applications, offering facilities previously not thought possible by end users through the use of multimedia, (data, voice and image). Present ISDN services are progressively moving to even more powerful Broadband ISDN technology, based upon Asynchronous Transfer Mode (ATM), further increasing the capacity for multimedia based applications.

US Initiatives and the Internet

Discussion of the "information superhighway" started in the US in 1992 during the Presidential Election campaign waged by Clinton and Gore. After the election this turned into the programme known as the National Information Infrastructure (NII). During the intervening period a good deal of progress had been made, particularly by the private sector, with a focus towards the development of new market opportunities in home entertainment, including interactive TV and video on demand. Both in the US and Europe there are pilots underway, but it is difficult to forecast when the mass market for these services will emerge. While initiatives are underway in the home entertainment sector, it is in the "business to consumer" and "business to business" sectors that most interest is focused, with projects such as CommerceNet[1], MecklerWeb and Internet Shopping (described in a later chapter), where the long-term economic benefits and the impact upon society are potentially far greater.

The vision of the National Information Infrastructure (NII) as seen by the Clinton Administration provides for a seamless network, universal access, an open competitive environment, whilst addressing major applications of social significance (e.g. Healthcare) and making government accessible to all. There are a wide range of participants in the process, including: Federal and State government, equipment vendors, service providers, information providers, various associations and user groups. Apart from architectural design, there are numerous technical issues including interoperability, routing (particularly with mobile computing), quality of service, security, data organization, user interfaces and heterogeneous networks (e.g. Phone, Cable, etc.). As well as the involvement of many existing bodies in the process (some traditionally involved with standards), a cross agency group has been established known as the Information Infrastructure Task Force (IITF) to assist in gaining agreement on policy matters such as information (intellectual property rights and privacy), telecommunications (universal service and network reliability), standards and security.

During the Group of Seven (G7) Summit meeting held in July 1994 (Naples), President Clinton made a proposal for a Global Information Infrastructure (GII) and it was agreed to hold a G7 Special Committee meeting in February 1995 to agree the common rules on which the GII should be developed. Some of the issues that were addressed during this meeting covered intellectual property rights, interoperability, security and privacy protection. The ultimate goal for the GII is to contribute to an improvement in international trade and the world-wide economy.

The Clinton Administration took a further step in July 1997 with the release of a report entitled "A Framework for Global Electronic Commerce,"[2] that sets out the Administration's vision of the emerging electronic marketplace and very importantly, for the first time, outlines the principles that will guide the US Government's future actions to promote the new electronic age of commerce. It is both a recognition of the significant impact that the Internet and the electronic revolution is having in transforming people's lives – trading on the Internet alone is tripling every year – and an acceptance that, by their actions, governments can have a profound effect on the growth of electronic commerce. The document covers a set of principles, financial issues, legal issues (including security) and market access (including standards) to guide the evolution of commerce on the Internet. In addition, for the first time, it legitimizes the use of the term "electronic commerce" to describe the manner in which traditional paper-based commerce is rapidly moving to electronic based commerce and the importance of the Internet in this transition (see Chapter 4).

Initiatives in the Far East

Japan is already very well advanced in the re-cabling of its telecommunications backbone network with optical fibre, which is part of a project to link all Japanese businesses and homes by the year 2010, using an advanced broadband telecommunications infrastructure. Other countries in the region have also started projects aimed at the introduction of information infrastructures.

These moves all serve to demonstrate the commitment of many of the world's leading nations to play their role in safeguarding competitive forces in the marketplace, and respond positively to initiatives that make the "digital revolution" an economic reality.

Internet Shaping IT Strategies

Figure 3.1 shows a six layer model that has been developed to illustrate the link between the telecommunications infrastructure required to support an Information Society, with a specific emphasis to business users. The importance of standards should start to emerge as the model is described. Clearly, conventions/rules/standards need to be adopted if different parts of an organization or indeed completely different organizations, are to be successfully exchanging business information between their respective computer-based applications.

While there are many aspects that need to be addressed, international standards assume a new level of importance when information highways are to be extended from national to global usage. Many *de jure* (international) and *de facto* (industry) standards already exist that are entirely relevant to the various elements making up the architecture that supports the information highway. A comprehensive review of standards in electronic commerce is provided in a later chapter.

First, at the top of the pyramid, organizations are seeking to embrace IT into products and services to provide the opportunity for long-term strategic benefits,

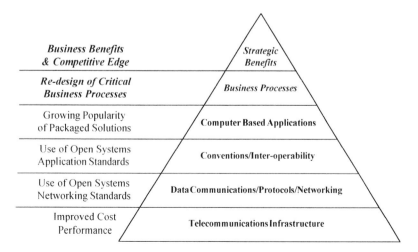

Fig. 3.1 The six layer model.

typically by seeking to disturb the marketplace in their favour. These are supported by the business processes that run through the organization and involve an increasing use of IT, naturally serving the varying requirements for tactical and strategic information.

Business processes usually involve the use of one or more computer based applications and if the information created by such applications, such as an invoice or a purchase order, is to be communicated to a business partner, then use of some common convention or standard becomes critical (EDIFACT is an example of a business document standard discussed later).

The strategic benefits referred to above are derived from business processes that have undergone review and, through an increased use of IT, are now able to offer a certain uniqueness in functionality that is of real value to the organization in marketing the product/service to its customers. By the term "strategic", this does not necessarily apply to those business processes supporting strategic management, in fact more normally strategic benefits are derived from business processes of a transactional or operational nature. As an example, by using electronic messaging technologies, to closely couple a supplier's logistics and warehouse operation, to the goods inwards and production facilities of a manufacturer, brings strategic benefits to both parties by reducing the boundaries between them.

Electronic messaging represents one of the basic services supported by two users connected over a network. For there to be co-operation between both systems and hence inter-operability, conventions, rules or standards have to be observed. In simple terms, this may mean using the same messaging system but this is frequently unrealistic if the sets of users belong to different organizations. Two primary open messaging standards or conventions have emerged to allow electronic mail (E-mail) to be exchanged between dissimilar E-mail systems to take place, known as X.400 and SMTP/MIME, (although SMTP/MIME has become more popular). At this stage, only try to focus on understanding the principle and do not be intimated by these acronyms, since they are discussed in detail in later chapters.

There has to be a mechanism that transports messages between the different sets of users and this is termed data communications. As with the messages, data communications also requires the use of conventions, more often known as protocols, that allow computers to be connected together. When a number of computers are connected together this may form a network. Communicating between two different sets of users most likely implies the interconnection of two separate networks, which would be impossible unless common and consistent protocols are observed. There are two primary sets of protocols or network architectures that are increasingly being supported by business, namely Open Systems Interconnection (OSI) and Transmission Control Protocol/Internet Protocol (TCP/IP). With the ever increasing popularity of the Internet, TCP/IP networking appears to be the dominant network protocol for Intranets (within an organization), Extranets (within a closed community) and, of course, the Internet (global open community). Other proprietary protocols exist but are only relevant within specific homogeneous environments that have no interaction with other communities; if this is not the case then gateways are used to provide the interfacing between the different network architectures.

Finally, there has to be a telecommunications infrastructure that provides the physical cables, optical fibre, microwave link, etc. perhaps even using the physical media to offer a service, e.g. Public Switched Telephone Network (PSTN). Some larger organizations have constructed their own private networks by leasing lines from Postal, Telephone and Telegraph authorities (PTT), known in some countries as Private Telecommunication Operators (PTO) following the re-regulation of telecommunication services in the late 1980s. In most countries, the Postal Service continues to be run as a monopoly separated from the PTO. A telecommunications infrastructure that is interconnected on a global basis represents a basic requirement for inter-company electronic business communications. In other words, a network protocol that securely transports containers of data (known as frames or packets), and indeed, the electronic messages so transported in the containers, requires a physical path connecting both sender and receiver before anything can happen.

Some of these terms might at first sight seem strange and for those readers keen to learn more, Part B provides the details. The key requirement at this stage is to understand the basic concepts. Telecommunications infrastructures are fundamental to the growth of electronic business communications, and require support and guidance from governments to ensure that they evolve in much the same way as the inland canal, railway and road networks have done in the past. All the same analogies apply: the need to avoid congestion, road works and sufficient capacity on the trunk routes to handle the volume of traffic.

Another important observation based on research conducted by the authors is the increasing trend by organizations towards the convergence of conventions/rules/standards and even applications, with a strong preference to those that are either open standards based or have strong market acceptance. The resultant "thick" IT architecture makes it easier to focus on the real use of technology, rather than worrying about interfacing issues. As an example, the Internet Protocol (IP) which defines the manner in which data is transported in containers over information highways, is being used within organizations (Intranets), between trading partners (Extranets) and as a means of reaching other organizations attached to the Internet. For the first time a homogeneous "open standards based highway" exists capable of being used by everyone, whether within the same building or across the world. This removes obstacles and brings much needed simplification to the use of information technology.

In Fig. 3.2 the first four layers represent the "thick architecture" referred to above and those standards highlighted in bold represent the winners that are supporting the phenomenal growth of electronic business communications.

Public information highways use existing telecommunications infrastructures, typically the telephone (PSTN) and packet switched (PSPDN) networks to transport a wide range of electronic business communications. This has yet to reach mass market proportions, but none the less will be inadequate to handle future multimedia applications that require greater speeds. Even for organizations that build their own private networks, they still need to connect to the "public" information highway to reach other organizations. It is expected that dramatic progress will be made over the coming years in the delivery of cost effective high speed services for both the "business to business" and "business to consumer" market sectors.

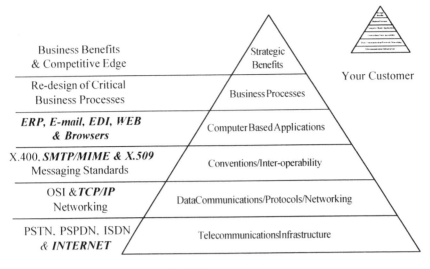

Business Benefits & Competitive Edge	Strategic Benefits
Re-design of Critical Business Processes	Business Processes
ERP, E-mail, EDI, WEB & Browsers	Computer Based Applications
X.400. **SMTP/MIME & X.509** Messaging Standards	Conventions/Inter-operability
OSI & **TCP/IP** Networking	Data Communications/Protocols/Networking
PSTN. PSPDN. ISDN **& INTERNET**	Telecommunications Infrastructure

Your Customer

Fig. 3.2 Thick architecture.

Information Technology Trends

It is important to understand some of the key IT trends and the impact that these have on new business applications and in particular electronic business communications.

End User Computing

The arrival of the Personal Computer (PC) started a movement away from central computing to place it directly in the hands of end users. Progressively, a number of applications which were originally served by mainframe host computers started to migrate to the PC. In some organizations where tensions existed between the central IT function and end users, this situation meant that the divide between the two groups became greater. This resulted in instances of inappropriate and uncoordinated development taking place within the PC environment. Whilst the standalone PC proved to be extremely productive for various desktop applications, by connecting a number of PCs together to form a Local Area Network (LAN) it became possible to share system resources such as printers and file storage devices, as well as run applications such as E-mail. The late 1980s saw a rapid growth in LAN implementations not only based upon geographic considerations such as a floor, building or site, but also along organizational lines such as client services, sales department, etc.

The need to interconnect LANs and hence provide a transparent path for end users across organizations, has given rise to a rapid market growth in LAN interconnection devices (bridges and routers). In the early 1990s, LANs came of age and were legitimized as important elements in an organization's IT strategy, rather than isolated and localized initiatives on the part of end users.

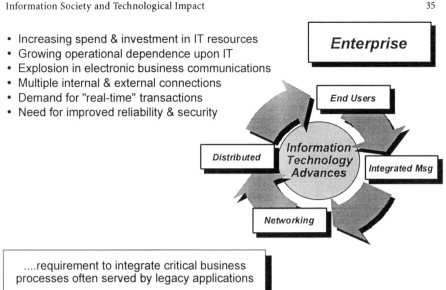

- Increasing spend & investment in IT resources
- Growing operational dependence upon IT
- Explosion in electronic business communications
- Multiple internal & external connections
- Demand for "real-time" transactions
- Need for improved reliability & security

Enterprise

End Users

Distributed

Information Technology Advances

Integrated Msg

Networking

....requirement to integrate critical business processes often served by legacy applications

Fig. 3.3 The Enterprise and Information Technology.

Increasingly, the power of the PC and its networking capabilities has almost brought computers and telecommunications into total interdependency and in consequence, has provided the motivation for close co-operation between end users and the central IT function.

Distributed Computing

The trend to end user computing as described above, has moved a class of application (known as desktop applications) from the mainframe computer to the PC. However, there is another class of application that supports the day-to-day operation of the business and is closely coupled with each business process. Such applications include order processing, production control, procurement, general ledgers, logistics, etc. During the 1980s, a new generation of computers emerged, physically more compact and often more powerful than their mainframe equivalents from companies including, Digital, HP, ICL, Sun Microsystems, Data General, Tandem, Siemens-Nixdorf and IBM. The movement from the mainframe to a distributed environment is primarily concerned with cost reductions; in other words, being able to perform similar functions much less expensively. A number of new technologies and approaches have emerged associated with "downsizing" projects, including client/server computing, open systems and relational databases.

During the initial period of its brief history, the computer industry was characterized by the market dominance of IBM. IBM and the other major computer manufacturers (known as the seven dwarfs including NCR, Burroughs, Univac, Honeywell, CDC and ICL), pursued a strategy of locking in their customers through deliberate technical differentiation. This situation made IT unnecessarily complex and expensive, hindered market growth and threatened the ability of different computers systems to communicate with one another. It was largely in response to this situation that the concept of open systems emerged, which is particularly well defined in the EPHOS Handbook as:

> *"Those systems which use standards to enable the operation of separately purchased solutions from independent sources of supply for all information handling needs."*

The new generation of mid-range computers that evolved in the 1980s generally met users' expectations of open systems, incorporating a powerful operating system known as UNIX, and are at the heart of the movement towards distributed systems. For this reason such computers are often simply referred to as UNIX platforms. In addition, bundled into these UNIX platforms is a powerful and open networking capability known as TCP/IP, that has been referred to earlier.

Networking

Networking has become a critical factor in the development of major applications that need to overcome geographic and time constraints. Electronic business communications is one important example of where networking is absolutely fundamental to its use, not just within an organization, but externally as well. Depending upon their needs, organizations use a range of networking capabilities as an integral part of their IT operation.

At the LAN level, it is usual for companies to construct a network to be run and operated by their own organization. However, once distance becomes a factor, the economics of constructing a Wide Area Network (WAN) means that many organizations turn to a service provider for assistance. Access is provided at a price to a telecommunications infrastructure that has usually been established by the Postal, Telephone and Telegraph authority (PTT), Private Telecommunications Operator (PTO) or service provider within the country.

While this used to be a monopoly service operated by the country PTT, with re-regulation and privatization in many countries, today, alongside the Private Telecommunications Operator (PTO), there will be other service providers granted licenses to offer value added network services. This is seen by government as important in encouraging competitive forces in the marketplace to help further establish the telecommunications infrastructure capable of handling much higher speeds and supporting the emerging Information Society.

Multimedia and the Web

As the use of desktop applications has grown together with the use of electronic messaging, several distinct trends have emerged. First, end users wish to exchange as attachments to their text message, the word processing document or spreadsheet that they have been working on. Assuming they have compatible software environments, once received, the recipient can then revise the attachment and return it to the sender with additional comments. A typical process might occur during the preparation of a contract or seeking approval of a budget. This possibility is largely available today, yet it is dependent upon compatible software (or conversion software filters) to access the attachment and the size of the attachment (influencing the time it takes to receive it). For large attachments consisting of mega bytes (million characters) of data, higher bandwidths/speeds become critical if end users are to be provided with a practical solution; hence, the continuing trend towards the deployment of cost effective high performance networking technologies.

A further trend is to create attachments, beyond traditional text and simple binary files used by desktop packages, which include full colour images, moving images (video) and voice. This requires a greater co-operative environment between the sender and the receiver, since not only are higher speeds required, but existing hardware and software environments for the end users may be inadequate to handle these attachments. Finally, in preparing a document, it is not unreasonable to wish to place within it an illustration or spreadsheet; indeed why not extend the concept to include a full multimedia document with voice annotation and video? Although some work still needs to be completed to ensure its success, the trend towards integrated and multimedia messaging is undeniable and will be explored further at a later stage in the book. The World Wide Web (Web), yet to be fully explained, is described as a "killer" application (one that has seen phenomenal growth and market acceptance) and delivered over the Internet. One of the Web's major attractions is its use of multimedia techniques to provide user friendly access to an unbelievable treasure trove of information.

Change and Information Technology

The organizational changes initiatives described earlier have set expectations on the ability of IT to serve the organization and its extended organization (e.g. customers, suppliers, shipping agents, etc.) primarily through the use of electronic messaging and information technologies. The trends in IT, as described in this chapter, clearly indicate that this expectation is a reality for many organizations in the way they operate today.

Figure 3.4 illustrates how organizational change may be viewed, first, through a focus upon business process improvements, rather than respecting the traditional boundaries erected by the functional organization; secondly, re-structuring and cultural changes that bring about fresh ways of working and acceptance of new corporate values; and finally, re-casting the external relationships away from adversarial, to integrate the extended organization fully into the overall functioning of the business. Electronic messaging and information technologies that embrace workgroup computing are ideal for this purpose, and can provide the tactical means for organizations to achieve the promise of a boundaryless operation with a free flow of information to those that need it. Organizations are realizing the critical contribution being made by their extended enterprise in being able to achieve identified business goals. At a practical level, this requires close integration of business processes between the par-

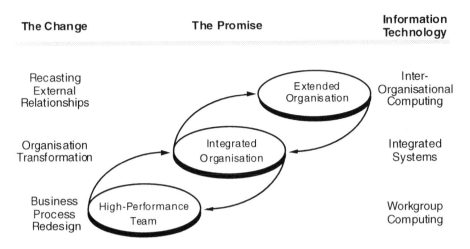

The Change	The Promise	Information Technology
Recasting External Relationships	Extended Organisation	Inter-Organisational Computing
Organisation Transformation	Integrated Organisation	Integrated Systems
Business Process Redesign	High-Performance Team	Workgroup Computing

Fig. 3.4 Competitive pressures in the 1990s.

ties, typically supported by sound business practices such as Electronic Data Interchange (EDI). As an example, a major retailer may well be extremely effective in its own operation, but without an efficient supply chain that closely integrates its suppliers with its own internal business processes, competitive advantage will be lost.

Notes

1.   Web url: www.commerce.net
2.   Web url: www.whitehouse.gov

4. *Electronic Commerce Evolution*

Introduction

The economic context in which organizations exist today places fresh stresses on the way in which they compete, and shapes the way in which products and services are brought to market.

While IT can make an important contribution to the introduction of improved business processes, it is a tool, and therefore it requires management to create the environment in which initiatives can bring about organizational change. The development of new computer-based applications must be aligned to the goals of the organization. This makes it possible to optimize the use of precious resources and directly contribute to improvements in critical areas of the business cycle.

Many organizations have been undergoing a continual process of change over the last two decades. Those that have survived the transition have established a "change" culture in their organizations, resulting in innovation and flexibility in the way they operate. Yet this process has not been easy, involving reductions in the number of employees, a flattening of the management hierarchy and a rationalization of business interests.

With management setting aggressive business goals to meet the challenges of the marketplace, many of the business processes created in the 1970s and the 1980s have ceased to be relevant. Organizations are changing the way they work and the resulting improved business processes have a greater dependency upon IT.

Growth in electronic business communications within organizations has been taking place since the arrival of the personal computer in the early 1980s, and has been further fuelled by the availability of third party messaging services and maturity of Local Area Networks (LANs). Electronic business communications takes many forms, as covered in Part B, and are becoming an essential framework for conducting business both within and between organizations, and indeed, across a wide range of business functions. It is this trend to trade electronically, that emerged first within the financial services sector, and that is now becoming the way business is conducted in a wide range of industry sectors.

What was termed "electronic business communications" is now becoming known by the more fashionable name of electronic commerce.

Throughout this book, "electronic commerce" is defined as any interaction between an organization and its trading community undertaken in an electronic manner. It is really a sub-set of electronic business communications that covers both intra and inter-organizational electronic messaging and information management.

The main factors attributed to the creation of the information revolution include:

- the economic context that has given rise to a highly competitive market environment;
- resultant action by management to change the way businesses are run affecting organizational structure, culture and staffing levels;
- the phenomenal pace of Information Technology (IT) development, its availability and continued improvement in cost/performance making it more affordable to greater numbers of organizations.

With the pervasiveness of IT, many of the new business processes being introduced by organizations contain a much richer IT content. In many ways, it is the application of IT by organizations that is making possible the drive towards improvements in business productivity, and resulting in the dramatic re-structuring of staffing levels across whole industries. This can be seen by examining performance indicators such as turnover per employee; for example, Tesco (a major UK retailer) increased turnover per employee in 1980 from £38,360 to £138,660 in 1994.

Example – Retail Banking

The nature of retail banking has changed rapidly in recent years, due in part to the emergence of a "cash-less society" and Automated Teller Machines (ATM) that now exist in most high streets and shopping centres. But retail banking is now in crisis, trying to redefine the business that it is in and find new services to market to its customers that will be seen of value. This has placed an even greater emphasis upon delivering services to business customers who continue to be a profitable part of the business. However, IT developments within retail banking have changed the habits of its customers. Home banking, typically offered over a bank's own private network, is likely to further change the face of retail banking in the coming years in much the same way that ATM machines did in the past. The Security First Network Bank (SFNB)[1] was the first US federally approved and insured Internet bank that aims to demonstrate that the Internet can provide a secure and convenient environment for conducting home banking. So unless there is some major business diversification or new initiative, it seems certain that this sector will continue to reduce staffing levels for the foreseeable future

The application of IT by organizations takes many different forms. The use of IT for internal electronic communications and external electronic trading, is explored more fully in this and subsequent chapters.

Birth of Electronic Commerce

Electronic commerce is an evolving concept that is coming to represent the spread of messaging and information management technologies across the whole of the business cycle. It recognizes the very significant increase in the usage of electronic communications by organizations as the primary means of conducting their commercial affairs.

Messaging and information management technologies form the core of electronic commerce, enhancing internal business communications as well as breaking down the boundaries between the organization and its trading partners. Trading partners might consist of suppliers, manufacturers, banks, freight forwarders, shippers, customs, laboratories, etc, forming an extended organization which, together with the organization itself, and with the aid of electronic business communications, creates a virtual and boundaryless entity.

In many senses, it is the increasing intensity in the use of information technology to support the world of commerce, displacing traditional paper based business processes, that is giving credence to the term electronic commerce. Forester has forecast that the total value of goods and services traded over the Internet will reach $8 billion by 1997 and will rise forty fold to $327 billion in 2002. There are numerous other sources of statistics, but whilst their figures may vary, all are unified in their belief that the market for conducting commerce over the Internet (Internet commerce) is huge. Equally the Internet, whilst becoming most important, is not the sole channel for conducting electronic commerce. For many years, the banks have conducted the transfer of funds electronically; over 200,000 companies exchange business documents (purchase orders, invoices, remittance advice, etc.) with their trading partners using Electronic Data Interchange (EDI).

In addition electronic commerce offers an important new way for organizations to conduct business by combining the re-structuring of business processes with the use of information technology. The resultant organizational benefits are many, offering the opportunity to:

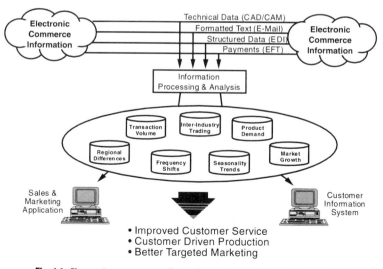

Fig. 4.1 Electronic commerce evolution (source: Gartner Group, February 1992).

- Reduce support calls and improve business effectiveness.
- Use IT as an enabler to re-design business processes.
- Swiftly introduce new and differentiated services.
- Better compete on the basis of value, time, uniqueness and customer service.
- Create exciting new applications that may extend the scope of the business.

The scope includes a range of business functions including departments communicating with one another, information access for customers, direct order entry, purchase order details sent directly to suppliers, automated payments against receipt of goods, advance ship notifications, manifest details sent to customs for clearance, simple status messages, etc. This phenomenon is referred to as electronic commerce and simply reflect the spread of electronic methods rather than paper as the basis of business transactions.

The potential for electronic commerce are limited only by the ability of organizations to accept new ways of doing things, a creativity at looking at old problems in new ways and continuing improvements in IT price/performance.

Messaging Technology

Since the early 1970s, messaging technologies have evolved from cumbersome file exchanges between two parties to sophisticated, easy-to-use systems capable of transporting a range of different "message" types. In the main, three primary uses have evolved to displace manual processes within organizations: Electronic Mail (E-mail) for people communications, Electronic Data Interchange (EDI) for communications between applications belonging to different organizations, and Application Messaging (AM) for interfacing applications within the same organization. Other usage variants exist which use the transport function of the messaging system, and these are discussed in a later section.

The principle is simple, using an agreed addressing convention, a message is composed and routed electronically to the recipient; it may help to relate this to the postal system analogy. Having placed the message in an envelope addressed to the recipient, the letter is entered into the postal system via a post-box, from which it is transported to a post office. At the post office it may be routed to another post office, or simply placed in a pile of mail to be delivered the next morning by the postman. It is then presented to the recipient via a letterbox where it stays until the recipient decides to open the envelope and read the message. Electronic messages follow a similar route, travelling from one E-mail server (Post Office) to another, and finally, entering a queue belonging to the recipient usually called a mailbox, which is accessed by the recipient when they wish to view their messages. Most desktop E-mail systems consist of two parts: the E-mail server that resides on a LAN and is shared by all E-mail users; and the E-mail client that resides on the desktop PC, through which messages are manipulated. In the case of EDI, the principle is much the same, but here the sender and recipients are applications which expect and recognize the exchange of specific business transactions that are translated into an EDI standard. With application messaging, no such standard exists because the transaction and flexible mapping techniques have been developed to translate between one format and another during the mailboxing process. The translation may often handle "in flight" other functions, such as calculations, table validation and database access.

Electronic Mail (E-mail)

From an organizational viewpoint, it is possible to introduce E-mail without having to effect major structural changes. However, since the process of internal communications changes from paper based to an electronic environment, a new culture needs to be established. Experience shows that E-mail has the power to:

- intensify existing relationships;
- create new relationships;
- facilitate work group and team communications;
- strengthen communications with other organizations.

Supportive management action is required during the implementation process and improvements in business effectiveness soon become evident. The implementation of E-mail throughout organizations can support more flexible and less formal relationships required for a rapidly changing environment and assist those organizations having geographically dispersed locations or implementing a strategy of decentralization. It can contribute to an increased pace of business, through faster decision making and ensure that these decisions are rapidly turned into action that is so critical for meeting the competitive challenge.

Example – GE

The GE Company, throughout its 12 main businesses, uses E-mail almost exclusively as the basis for internal business communications, as well as increasingly for external communications with its business partners. GE Information Services is both a heavy user and major supplier of global electronic commerce services including E-mail. Used internally since the late 1970s, it is impossible to imagine how the company could operate today without E-mail linking its employees in over 40 countries around the world.

In addition to E-mail, using IBM PCs or Apple Macintosh microcomputers, employees have had access to a range of information sources including products, competitors, sales materials, organizations announcements, etc. using a product known as Business Network, first introduced in the mid 1980s. Business Network, combining E-mail and information management in a similar manner to products from Microsoft and Lotus, was based upon a centralized service accessed over a wide area network and built around a mix of open/proprietary standards. However, during the 1990s many of the GE businesses introduced LAN E-mail systems for local messaging and only connected to the centralized system via gateways for external messaging to other GE business or to external business partners.

In the late 1990s, GE decided to implement a single integrated LAN E-mail system across all its businesses using Microsoft Exchange, based upon the

Internet TCP/IP network protocol. However, rather than use the Microsoft Exchange servers to satisfy the information management requirement, GE opted mainly to use Internet Web server technology. These capabilities have further improved internal communications, helped by the establishment of a global GE corporate directory accessible to all E-mail users. Customers have also benefited as GE is able to respond more rapidly to their requests for information or assistance.

In addition, GE needs to ensure that its products/services meet the requirements of the global marketplace and to do so typically brings together product commercialization teams based upon specific knowledge or skills sets, drawn from different locations around the world. The electronic business communication facilities made available to employees, including E-mail, information management and video conferencing, provide the key components to transform disparate team members into a highly effective work group.

Electronic Data Interchange (EDI)

By contrast, EDI places much greater demands on the organization up-front to review and in most instances, change existing business processes. This has proved to be an obstacle to the growth of EDI as the motivation or incentive to make these changes is not always present. It does not only apply to your organization, over which control can be exercised, but requires changes within your trading partners over which little or less control exists. As an organization commits itself to introducing EDI, there is a need to formalize activities, look to streamlining processes and introduce the concept of EDI standards. EDI standards simply allow user defined data from an application, specific to that organization, to be converted into an internationally recognized "Esperanto" format (known as an EDI standard) that can be understood by its trading partner.

The organization that is to become the central part of a new trading community, is referred to as the "hub" and its trading partners referred to as "spokes". For example, a large retail store group such as Auchan in France might have some 800 individual suppliers; in the traditional EDI model, Auchan is referred to as the hub and its suppliers as spokes. The advantage of this model is that while the spokes are all separate independent organizations, the hub is usually able to exert influence over these organizations that make up the electronic trading community. Aside from pointing to the economic benefits of electronic trading using EDI, the hub can simply mandate EDI as a condition of doing business with it; in these circumstances, very few of the spokes want to loose their on-going business relationship with the hub by rejecting this "request".

In summary, an organization embarking upon a successful EDI implementation must be aware of the evolutionary changes that will be needed both in the business process and structure, that it will involve:

- formalizing of activities;
- streamline of the business process;
- introduction of EDI standards.

However with strong management commitment throughout the process and the existence of a healthy culture accepting the importance of change, EDI implementations can provide many strategic as well as tactical benefits. Benefits include the opportunity to reduce the cost of goods sold, create customer loyalty, increase productivity, eliminate delays in the supply chain, respond more readily to changing demand patterns and speed-up the time to market. Naturally, the resultant EDI community becomes even more dependent upon IT; indeed both EDI and E-mail are very high visibility applications for the IT Manager.

CASE STUDY - HENKEL

Henkel is headquartered in Germany and manufactures chemical products for DIY, cosmetic and industrial markets. It has both sales and manufacturing operations throughout the world and its UK subsidiary is located in Enfield acting primarily as a sales outlet.

Henkel UK serves a number of major suppliers in the DIY market such as B&Q, Texas, Homebase and Safeways using two EDI VAN services to receive orders and Point Of Sales (POS) data, as well as to send invoices. There are a number of legacy order processing and financial applications that run on IBM System 38 (S/38) hardware, which connect with EDI VAN services, as transactions need to be received and transmitted.

In the mid 1990s Henkel UK initiated a process to upgrade its existing IT environment with the installation of a Unix based packaged solution from SAP. SAP is a major supplier of integrated Enterprise Resource Planning (ERP) packaged software for corporates that provides modules to support a wide range of business activities from order processing, through manufacture to financial accounting. The initial implementation of the SAP software was for the consumer products division (DIY), whilst the industrial products division would continue to use the original legacy applications running on the S/38.

As part of this business improvement programme, Henkel needed a new IT architecture that would integrate existing legacy applications with the new SAP packaged software and control the external communications with their business partners. As a result, a Unix-based EDI VAN gateway product, providing application integration, business document tracking and communications was installed. Due to the gateway's close coupling with the chosen EDI VAN service, orders and other data that were delivered by Henkel's customers were immediately routed to the gateway, which initiated various actions/processes based upon business rules associated with sending and receiving applications.

One such process was the translation of orders destined for the consumer products division received in a range of EDI formats (EDIFACT and Tradacom) into the SAP EDI interface known as IDOC; and then forwarding these directly to the SAP application running on a HP9000 Unix platform. This meant that a few minutes after the order was sent by the customer, the order was being processed by Henkel, without human intervention to hinder the process.

Another function of the EDI VAN gateway was to route EDI orders for the industrial products division to the legacy application on the S/38; that also performed translation from EDI format into the user defined file format required for the legacy application.

In addition, Point of Sales (POS) data received from Texas over a service inter-connection with the EDI VAN service chosen by Henkel, was routed by the server to another S/38. The incoming POS data was then processed by a forecasting application and various reports prepared.

The benefits of the electronic commerce environment to Henkel is primarily in speeding up business processes and avoiding errors by eliminating human interven-tion. As an example orders placed by B&Q each evening are now processed within minutes and means that Henkel is now "just in time" enabled. The necessary actions resulting from the processed orders can be completed over-night. This ensures that the ordered goods are made available for B&Q lorries to collect the following day, once they have completed their normal deliveries and the ordered goods from Henkel are back-hauled to their depots. Henkel is able to respond more readily to the demands of a major customer and B&Q is able to minimize its inventory costs, yet ensure adequate stock availability within its stores.

Application Messaging (AM)

Finally, there is Application Messaging (AM), the latest addition to messaging technology, which is being introduced into larger organizations that have a longer history of IT development. Application messaging appeals more directly to techni-cians, since it is essentially an IT infrastructure that eases the integration of sepa-rately developed applications that from time to time need to exchange information. Since the application messaging software sits in the middle between two or more applications, it has become known as "middleware".

Many organizations are continuing to re-develop their computer based applica-tions in support of the changing business environment and have the need to rapidly interface legacy (developed many years ago) applications with new and often packaged software solutions. With the increasingly frequent changes to applications (brought about by new business process requirements), custom developed interfaces between internal applications are seen as cumbersome and restrictive. Application Messaging seeks to remove these obstacles by using advanced mapping and translation techniques which may be built upon the archi-tecture of traditional mailboxing or use a transaction manager. Nevertheless, AM is not simply an interface technology, but can add real value to transactions by performing additional validations, initiating events based upon the presence of specific data and handling the requirements for real-time information processing.

Since AM uses advanced mapping and translation techniques, it can also inte-grate the internal processing of data between applications, with the need to intelli-gently route EDI data or other forms of messaging (E-mail and facsimile) to external trading partners. It is very much a technology that has evolved to meet the requirements of the electronic commerce era – widespread use of electronic communications across the whole of the business cycle. The Wincanton example described in Chapter 1 uses application messaging techniques as described in this section.

The very significant business benefits expected from electronic commerce is causing the IT industry to examine ways in which standards can simplify and converge current practices. E-mail and EDI are excellent examples of such convergence around globally supported open standards achieved by a combination of standard makers and market forces. It is therefore not surprising to find that a consortium exists, called the Object Management Group (OMG), that includes over 800 companies focussed at re-defining the way in which applications are developed in the future and how they more freely interact. The Common Object Request Broker Architecture (CORBA) is an important middleware project that addresses this requirement and is closely coupled with the use of distributed objects as the basis of new enterprise wide applications and the future vision of how these may be accessed via the Internet using the Internet Inter-ORB Protocol (IIOP). In particular aside from permitting for the first time the creation and deployment of distributed objects, CORBA enables platform independent software development to take place.

CASE STUDY - THE STATIONARY OFFICE

The Stationary Office (TSO) sources and supplies stationery, office machinery and printed goods to the public sector. Whilst now privatized, TSO is still the government's printing organization and a large scale publisher dealing with both private and public sector organizations, employing over 3000 people and having an annual turnover in excess of £360 Million.

With the increasing use of competitive tendering by government departments, TSO needed to provide competitive pricing of products and demonstrate an ability to offer improved customer service.

These requirements were originally highlighted in a 1987 review, that resulted in the implementation of a Total Quality Management program, together with a focus upon improved supply chain management techniques. In consequence, top management within TSO gave their full support to the concept of EDI, which also coincided with requests from some of their customers to accept EDI orders. It became clear that TSO required process and IT improvements that supported information flows not only internally, but also out to their customers and suppliers.

Based in Norwich, TSO installed a sophisticated Unix based EDI gateway to integrate disparate internal systems by handling the differing transactions formats, enhancing processes and providing an intelligent route to external customers and suppliers throughout the UK via an EDI VAN service.

The EDI gateway acts as the sole route for both internal and external communications providing a range of centralized functions including translation software, audit, security and control. As an example, through the validation of critical business information common to all systems found within incoming transactions, this allows errors to be detected earlier in the process. However, data validation is not duplicated between the gateway and the receiving application.

In this way EDI orders are sent electronically by customers principally through the EDI VAN service to TSO where the EDI gateway performs specific validation actions. One action involves access to an Ingres relational database to check supplier location codes that are substituted in the body of the in-coming/out-going transaction. Once orders are accepted these are routed to a Warehouse application that allocates stock and initiates shipment. In some instances stocks are not held by TSO, but sourced externally from outside suppliers; the EDI gateway then routes these orders to the appropriate suppliers.

The business productivity improvement program undertaken by TSO has allowed them to increase the number of business transactions served by electronic commerce; this has now reached over 400,000 orders amounting to £45 Million per annum. Despite aggressive moves by government towards a policy of open procurement, TSO has both retained and grown its customer base and believe that their IT strategy has been a key component in maintaining a competitive edge over the competition.

Characteristics of Electronic Commerce

From an organizational viewpoint, the establishment of an electronic commerce environment is closely coupled to radical changes in the way business is conducted, as well as a broadening of the scope of business activities. In consequence electronic commerce impacts multiple business processes over time and heavily relies upon IT for execution, due primarily to functional requirements, cost benefits and simply the pervasiveness of IT. Such a programme usually forms part of a top management vision for the organization and the setting of ambitious goals, together with an acceptance that radical changes will be necessary to achieve them. This implies a major re-distribution of internal resources with the creation of cross functional teams to bring about the required changes that will impact all stake-holders. In summary, electronic commerce usually:

- forms part of a top management vision for the organization and their commitment is critical;
- will be associated with aggressive goals;
- implies a major re-distribution of internal resources requiring cross-functional teaming;
- fundamental impact to all stake-holders including internal functions, trading partners and customers.

Electronic Commerce from an IT perspective

Viewed from an IT perspective, electronic commerce has a number of different attributes that help define its characteristics. First, it has a strong applications orientation, suggesting that from the use of electronic business communications,

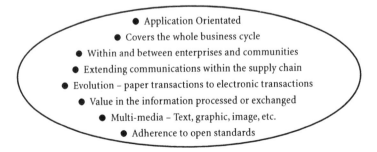

Fig. 4.2 Characteristics of electronic commerce.

process improvements are both realistic and achievable (Fig. 4.2). In addition no constraints are placed upon its usage across the whole business cycle. All functions can benefit and indeed many of the examples demonstrate how process improvements, made possible by electronic commerce technologies cutting across the organization, actually brings functions closer together and helps break down the barriers. A growing number of organizations have realized the importance played by their business partners in the achievement of their own business goals. This implies a need to couple the extended enterprise such as suppliers, customers, distributors etc, more closely with the organization itself using electronic commerce throughout the supply chain.

Another feature of this evolution is the movement away from paper-based transactions to electronic transactions that reduce the introduction of errors through human intervention, speed up processes and control costs. A by-product of electronic transactions is the information value that can be extracted as the transactions are processed providing opportunities for competitive advantage. Finally because of the many different business partners wishing to co-operate in an electronic commerce environment, there is strong support for IT open standards. This manifests itself in the need to work with and exchange transparently different media such as text, voice and image and indeed to recognize the growing interest in multi-media or compound documents that offer significant new ways to communicate information.

Teleworking

The age of electronic commerce is also affecting working practices within organizations, some quite radical in character such as teleworking. Teleworking is a way of working from home with the aid of a telecommunications network; the network providing the link to colleagues in the office or others working remotely in a similar fashion. With the steady growth in computerization of the office environment and the availability of cost effective, high speed methods of telecommunications such as ISDN, telecommuting is on the increase amongst certain groups of information workers. The authors remember seeing a slogan recently in the office of a large US software company which read, "Don't pollute, tele-commute". Experience suggests that there is a growing requirement for a more flexible working arrangement between both employers and employees and that teleworking can bring about considerable benefits to both parties. As the swing continues from employment in manufacturing to service industries, for many organizations the knowledge that their employees possess has increasingly become the most enduring asset of that organization. As a result, the means of improving employee motivation has become an important management goal, seeking to retain and expand the knowledge that the organization has at its disposal.

For the employer the opportunity exists to maximize skilled labour shortages, decrease the costs of office facilities and improve productivity, often due to less distractions and interruptions for the employee. For the employee, teleworking provides a means to change their lifestyle and avoid the monotony of working from an office, as well as saving time on the journey between home and the office.

In addition some employees are seeking a greater autonomy in their work and through teleworking, they possess more flexibility in meeting both private as well as business commitments.

While teleworking by information workers is a product of the Information Age, it is consistent with the following trends seen in the work environment:

- Lifetime working hours becoming reduced.
- Work times becoming more varied.
- Companies becoming more decentralized with fewer permanent staff members.
- An open market emerging with people bidding for work to match their knowledge and skills.
- Remuneration becoming increasingly based around the completion of a task and less related to the time spent on it.

In the long-term, information workers are unlikely to be constrained by national geographic boundaries, and the nature of certain tasks is such that it is feasible for organizations to follow the route to the cheapest labour costs, in much the same way the manufacturing industry has already done. Several of the computer software development companies serving clients in the London financial services market, have already established links to teleworkers in India, who produce high quality work at much lower costs than is possible in the UK.

This trend in teleworking is made possible by technological advances, discussed in more detail in later chapters, such as groupware which produces advanced forms of computer supported, collaborative working. In the past, individuals have been constrained by limited technology that drew a distinction between office, home and elsewhere. Telecommunications is eliminating this distinction such that collaborative working between people becomes a reality whether or not they are in the same building, city or country.

Outsourcing of IT Functions

Considerable pressure is now being placed upon organizations as they seek to develop their business processes, structure and culture towards an electronic commerce environment. The crucial skills are those of leadership and management of change, but there is a limit to what can be expected from the organization. Whilst it is critical to an organization's day-to-day operation, some top managers regard IT as a management distraction that can be best passed on to a third party to operate on their behalf. In practice, outsourcing can involve the use of specific IT services that are either uneconomical or just impossible to resource internally, to moving the complete operation of data centres to a facilities management company. It is rare for organizations to completely outsource their applications development teams, but there is a strong trend towards the purchase of packaged software and the use of internal developers as project managers for the implementation.

As technology continues to advance at such a rapid pace, outsourcing can provide a means by which an organization can reduce the risk of their IT capital investments becoming just as rapidly obsolete. In particular, telecommunications is a high cost investment, where the installation of a corporate network serving all forms of internal communications can represent a very significant allocation of both financial and people resources. In the early 1990s, the changing economics of VSAT (Very Small Aperture Terminals) and terrestrial based networks caused several North American organizations to write-off large sums of money associated with redundant and less cost effective technology. Those organizations that had outsourced their telecommunications requirements were simply able to move across to the more cost effective technology as their contracts came to an end.

Internet – Removing the Barriers

In the world of electronic commerce, access to information across the organization and between trading partners removes barriers previously created by paper based systems, bringing the parties closer together and eliminating inefficiency in the supply chain. This is also a starting point for an improved flow of information throughout organizations using electronic workflow techniques.

The logical extension of electronic commerce is to establish open messaging highways on which all forms of information can be transmitted within and between communities. This requires an infrastructure to be established based upon international standards and co-operation between the competing market parties. The trend is unmistakable; business practices, technology and standards are rushing together at a dramatic rate to create a new environment for conducting "business to business" and "business to consumer" electronic trading. This is already taking shape in North America, undeniably the world's most developed market economy and is being further re-enforced by active support from the US Government.

Naturally, an environment for conducting electronic commerce over the Internet, increasingly being referred to as Internet commerce, has to be completely secure. However, products supporting secure transactions over the Internet are now available, these, coupled with the bent up demand for additional ways for smaller organizations to improve competitiveness, are likely to fuel a dramatic increase in electronic commerce. It is likely that the larger organization with their existing EDI programmes will continue to use traditional EDI services in the medium term, perhaps experimenting with Web forms, until there is sufficient critical mass and experience to cause them to change. However, these same organizations are actively involved in the use of Internet Web technology to establish an Internet presence and extend information access to their trading partners. Many already provide the ability for customers to place orders via their public Internet Web sites and many of the market research organizations predict this trend towards electronic marketplaces to grow rapidly into the next millennium.

Convergence Between Domestic and Business Usage

The use of electronic communications is not just revolutionizing business, it is starting to have an impact on the domestic or home user. Many of the facilities used by businesses such as E-mail with access to information sources are increasingly being used by the home user. New services for banking, travel bookings and shopping are starting up from the home which will have a major impact upon domestic lifestyles in the long-term, in much the same way that businesses are experiencing change today.

This is likely to establish wider and different business relationships in the supply chain with the scope to remove some of the existing parties. In the travel sector, many organizations and people work through travel agents; but what will their future be once business and domestic customers alike have the ability to make a flight booking using a personal computer or an interactive television?

Value Added Network Services

As the term intermediaries suggests, there are many "go-betweens" that are helping to accelerate the growth of electronic commerce, and because most of the key players have a strong telecommunications orientation, they are often greatly influenced by government action. This is not surprising since the foundation of electronic commerce is based upon telecommunications, which as a global industry, is now equivalent to that of the automotive industry in size and importance.

The ITU (International Telecommunications Union) Telecom 95 exhibition and conference held every four years in Geneva provided an insight into the scale and scope of this relatively new industry. The 1980s have seen dramatic changes in the liberalization of telecommunications around the world providing the basis for this unparalleled growth, resulting directly from the highly competitive market environment created. Central to this industry are the traditional monopolies of the PTT (Postal, Telegraph and Telephone), affiliated to the ITU, that in many countries have or are being transformed into new organizations within the private sector looking to expand their services beyond telephone (PSTN public switched telephone network) and data communication (PSPDN packet switched public data network) services.

The European Commission (EC) Telecommunications Green Paper published in 1987 paved the way for re-regulation and liberalization of telecommunications products and services across Europe, aimed at increasing competition in this vital industry. The new PTOs (Private Telecommunications Operators) offer value added services such as E-mail and EDI, in addition to their traditional voice and data services. Examples of these new PTOs include, France Telecom, Deutsche Budespost Telekom, Unisource and British Telecom. In 1995, the EC published Part 2 of the Telecommunications Green Paper, which sets out a framework for the liberalization of the complete telecommunications infrastructure in Europe and identifies a number of key factors that need to be addressed as part of the implementation process.

The US market for telecommunication services continues to grow following the break-up of AT&T in 1982, prior to which there was limited competition to its telecommunications services and products. The re-structuring of AT&T with the emergence of Regional Bell Operating Companies (RBOC) controlling the "local loop" and the "long distance carriers" such as AT&T, Sprint and MCI providing the backbone and international reach has been a key factor in developing a competitive market in North America for telecommunications. The RBOCs are currently constrained through legislation in the geographic spread and nature of services that they can offer within the US, but this is likely to change over time. Similar situations exist in Europe where legislation is used to assist in the creation of a "level playing field" for competition or indeed, to eliminate potential dominant competition in new emerging sectors such as cable services.

For many years now, several companies with their origins in the US including AT&T, Sprint, Infonet, IBM and GE Information Services have been active in the service provider marketplace for value added services. In many countries, until liberalization and re-regulation in the late 1980s, such companies were only allowed to offer remote computing services (now referred to as value added services) and even then usually only with a license. Whilst a PTO generally operates at a national level, service providers are present in many countries throughout the world using a range of telecommunications services, to construct global data communications networks, that connect into their processing centres. This means that the global service providers can offer both national and multi-national companies, the possibility to outsource a number of different applications ranging from financial services, management reporting, marketing information systems, order processing to logistics, where the application resides on the service. Generally the core electronic commerce services of EDI and E-mail offered by service providers are interconnected so that users of one service can freely communicate with users of another service. Much of the infrastructure for service interconnections was put into place in the late 1980s and early 1990s, initially for E-mail, based upon X.400 and subsequently for EDI, based upon proprietary protocols. With the strong swing towards Internet technologies and its implicit open nature, much of this earlier work in establishing service interconnections has now become irrelevant.

With the growing interest during the mid 1990s from business users in the Internet, as distinct from the Internet's traditional users in the academic and research communities, most service providers have introduced a wide range of Internet services. This might involve setting-up and running an Extranet (closed community) for an organization and its trading community to use Internet E-mail and Web services. It might provide Internet Web forms data entry using a Web browser that is converted into an EDI standard by the service provider and routed to the recipient trading partner.

Internet Service Providers

However, a new breed of intermediary has emerged in this relatively new market sector known as Internet Service Providers (ISP), normally a small service organization within a country. As an example it is estimated that there are around 4500 ISPs in the US and perhaps as many as 240 ISPs in the UK. It seems that with the expected growth in Internet usage, that many of the ISPs will find it tough to compete on their own and may either cease to trade or be consolidated into larger groups. These larger groups include companies such as AT&T (US), America Online (US), UUNet (US), PSINet (US), EUnet (Netherlands) and PIPEX (UK), many also offering access outside their home country. The break-up of CompuServe, a pioneer in online services, with its extensive network going to WorldCom and its subscriber base going to America Online, serves to illustrate how the rationalization is also taking place amongst the "big boys". The user appeal for many of these services is the free and open access to an incredible amount of information (once the connection charges have been paid) stored on the Internet. Search engines such as Yahoo!, AltaVista, WebCrawler and Infoseek make it possible to readily locate the desired information rather than having to spend endless hours "surfing" the Internet to locate specific information.

World-Wide Web Creating Marketspaces

In the late 1980s two engineers working at CERN, the European nuclear research laboratory outside Geneva, developed an internal information system called the World-Wide Web (Web), that used hypertext to cross-reference to other parts of the database. From that point several other institutions installed the system on their computers, dubbed Web Servers. In 1993 a Web browser called Mosaic was written, followed in 1994 by Navigator from Netscape, both significantly easing the process of working with the Web and credited with the exponential growth that the Web has seen with the number of sites rising to well in excess of 1,000,000.

The application uses of the Web can be broken into several parts:

- First, static information that needs to be referenced from time to time, such as historical information, guide to the Internet, business libraries in Europe, etc.
- Information about organizations or companies which largely exists as a sub-set of static information; that helps to build-up an electronic presence in a new type of marketplace.
- Information that is more dynamic in character that reflects a status at a given point in time such as flight arrivals; or for a specific corporate application such as order tracking.
- The electronic marketplace, where the emphasis is on the business customer/consumer ordering directly from companies/shops that display their products electronically.

Based upon Internet technologies, the electronic marketplace for both business customers and home consumers is predicted to grow significantly into the next millennium. For an organization that currently uses a mail order catalogue as a means of selling its products, the use of Web technology represents a logical exten-sion of their current services. It has the power to dramatically change consumer buying patterns and for certain market segments, it will alter the supply chain by eliminating sales resources and thus avoid the order processing and distribution costs associated with traditional retailers. Internet Web technology combined with catalogue systems offers exciting new possibilities to market products and services, replacing physical marketplaces by electronic information marketspaces.

Notes

1.   Security First Network Bank url: www.sfnb.com/
2.   The Forrester Report, July 1997. Url: access.forrester.com

Part B

5. *Traditional Business Communications*

Working with Information

A fundamental feature of business today is the need to obtain, store and communicate information, so that individuals have access to the necessary facts from which decisions can be made and actions taken. However, there are several behavioural models that apply when people work with information inside organizations. First, there are those people who regard information as power that reinforces their own position, and thus should be disseminated sparingly. Then there are others who give little thought to who really requires information and discharge it throughout the organization like a "scatter-gun", risking the problems of information overload and loss of productivity on the part of the recipients. Finally, there are those who are more discriminate in their use of information, distributing it selectively and making people aware of where it can be obtained when needed.

Sending a message irrespective of the method used involves a "push" approach. Being presented with a situation demanding specific information and knowing where to obtain it, is termed the "pull" approach. It is these two principles that are so difficult to cater for using traditional methods, and which are having such a deep impact upon the way electronic messaging is evolving into timely information exchange, which is built around the use of E-mail, information servers (bulletin boards and databases) and clipping services along with intelligent agents. But more about this later, for in this chapter, popular forms of business communications are explored from several points of view, namely, the parties involved, the media, the mode and lastly the communication method that can be chosen.

Media Choices

Whether the need is an informal communication about a future meeting, a form concerning a salary review, the placement of an order with a supplier or merely information to aid decision making, there are a number of different media choices available. Interestingly enough, it would seem from research that efficiency is not an important factor in media choices when formulating a message to be communicated. Indeed, it appears to be related more to whether the subject is simple and well defined, or by contrast, complex and ill-defined, in that questions are more difficult to formulate.

When the subject matter is relatively simple, a written communication is likely to be more appropriate than say a "face-to-face" meeting, which could better serve a more complex and questionable situation where direct interaction is required.

There are range of media possibilities for the individual to choose from which will best aid the success of the intended communication, the written word being perhaps the most explicit in avoiding misinterpretations, while voice bringing a greater intimacy required for urgent, sensitive and immediate communications. The use of image/graphics often increases the speed of comprehension; a picture is worth a thousand words. Television and video have increased people's exposure to moving image and this is also being used in various forms by organizations for applications such as training purposes or to communicate product concepts to potential customers.

Business communications within organizations are usually considered to be largely people dependent. However, with the growing use and availability of IT, people interact and use applications for access to routine information previously held in a non-electronic media, sometimes stored within an individual's mind. Most business communications take place within the organization directed at the day to day management and operation of the company. Once facilities are provided that speed up the process of preparing internal communications, evidence seems to suggest that the volume and intensity increases. In addition to internal business communications, the proportion of external traffic taking place by organizations with their trading partners is also continuing to increase and with it a demand for greater efficient in the methods used. The reason for this external growth is varied, but includes re-structuring of the supply chain and distribution channels, outsourcing of functions no longer considered part of the core business, as well as greater international sourcing and trading. Under these circumstances, new requirements have emerged for "business to business" communications that involve computer-based applications that specifically exclude people in the process, where traditional forms of business communications have proved to be inadequate and required adaptation.

Historical Perspective

The importance of effective business communications to the efficient operation of a company is well understood and has developed extensively over the last 150 years, primarily through technological innovation, from quill pen to biro (invented in 1944) and from typewriter to word processing. It was only 1878 when Remington patented the first upper and lower case typewriter, a rarity in today's modern office; it has since been displaced by word processors and personal computers. At the same time, the growth of organizations has often led to a proliferation of new office procedures and associated forms, used for its administration. Characteristically, business communications are closely associated with office procedures and business processes, each of which has evolved over time and can lead to the overlapping and duplication of functions. Therefore improvements in business communications cannot solely be achieved by moving from manual to electronic methods; other actions are necessary to create the right culture that reviews and restructures business processes.

Factors Impacting Media Choices

In examining the nature of communications that take place within and between businesses it is helpful to consider a number of factors (Fig. 5.1):

Methods – the proposed communications process to be used, whether postal, telex, telephone, facsimile or electronic business communications.

Media – the medium used for communicating namely textual, voice or image.

Mode – this can be viewed as a classification of the information being sent or received as either a message, transaction or file driven by the business process involved.

Originator/Recipient – this describes the relationship or status of the sender and receiver whether these are people or computer-based applications. Their relative physical location is also important whether they both reside within the organization, or one party is external to it.

There is a good deal of confusion around the terms image and graphic. For simplicity, an "image" can be thought of as describing a high quality picture. In electronic messaging terms, the high resolution image would be stored on an electronic medium using a "bit" representation. Moving image describes a sequence of digital images which is better known as digital video. However, a "graphic" can be considered as a diagram or a graph, the schematic or presentation usually created by an associated desktop application (which is usually required if changes are to be made to it). For the purpose of this section, image also encompasses graphic objects.

For inter-personal communications, there are a number of possible methods

	The Media			The Mode		
	Text	Voice	Image	Message	Transaction	File
Person to Person	Electronic Mail [E-mail]	E-mail Attachment and/or Voicemail	E-mail Attachment and/or Facsimile	Simple Text or Structured Desktop Application	Business Form	Report using Structured Desktop Application
Person to Application	Mail Enabled	Voice Response or Informational	Electronic Catalogue & Directory Services	Order Entry & Simple Enquiry	Complex Database Enquiry	News Clipping Services & Electronic Publishing & Directory Svcs
Application to Application [Intra-Company]	Application Messaging	Unlikely	Technical Data Interchange [TDI]	Structured Non-EDI Standard	Transposition & Processing	Flat File of Structured Non-EDI Standard
Application to Application [Inter-Company]	Electronic Data Interchange [EDI]	Unlikely	Technical Data Interchange [TDI]	Unlikely	Structured EDI Standard	Interchange or File Transfer

Fig. 5.1 Information choice matrix.

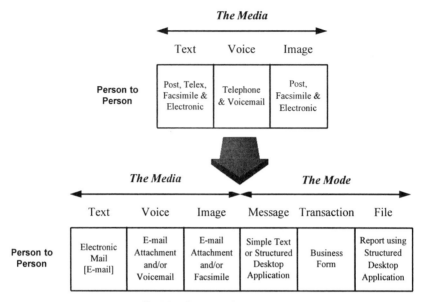

Fig. 5.2 Information choice matrix.

that can be used, aside from electronic messaging. However, electronic messaging tends to broaden the scope still further, enabling the interaction between people and computer based applications. When one considers person-to-person communications, it is very simple to visualize the possibilities and decide whether text, voice or image is the best media, and what associated communications methods are possible.

Clearly the context of the communication from the originator will influence the method chosen, for example:

- Is it necessary to communicate directly with the recipient?
- Is some immediate response required?
- Are the communications for informational purposes only?
- Is the recipient accessible?
- Are both originator and recipient in the same country and time zone?

Generally, we differentiate between the "person to person" type of business communications as compared to the "application to application" processes which are explained in a later section. Some 80% of business communications still flows within an organization and traditional hard copy memos have been replaced by electronic mail (E-mail) in many organizations. However, external communications are still dominated by post, telephone, telex and facsimile. Telex has seen a heavy decline, except in some industries and in various parts of the world that are lacking in modern telecommunications infrastructure.

The growing trend towards E-mail within organizations is starting to extend to external communications as telecommunications infrastructures are now in place, with administrations and service providers to handle electronic business messages. This is a natural evolution of the ubiquitous Packet Switched Public Data Networks (PSPDN) that have been established since the early 1980s and the steady growth of the Internet in the 1990s, which is being used more and more by the business community. The growing need to enhance traditional text messages to include voice clips and images, demands higher bandwidths (greater capacity) of the digital highways, yet without price increases. This in turn has a "ripple-on" effect upon the power of the desktop personal computer and software required to support multi-media or compound documents.

Patterns of Business Communications

Let us now examine the patterns of business communications in terms of the nature of the communication required and the method employed (Fig. 5.3). For simple freeform messages, a number of methods are used today including the post, telex, telephone, voicemail, facsimile and an increasing number of E-mail users. However, for external business communications, facsimile has achieved mass market penetration since the late 1980s and its volumes far exceed those of E-mail for inter-company business communications. Reports, forms and documents tend to use post, facsimile or electronic means for communication, whilst business documents such as invoices, purchase orders, payment advice, etc., are exchanged between trading partners using Electronic Data Interchange (EDI).

Taking an A4 page of text, consisting of 250 to 2000 characters, the amount of electronic storage required to represent it as a word processing document or facsimile, increases significantly. Forecasts and trends in practice indicate that businesses will, in future, transfer many more documents of an image/graphics nature

Nature/Mode	Method	Reason
Free Form Message	Post, Telephone, Voicemail, Telex, Facsimile or Electronic	Ad Hoc or Application
Structured Report	Post, Facsimile or Electronic	Application
Completed Form	Post, Facsimile or Electronic	Ad Hoc or Application
Business Document	Post, Facsimile or Electronic	Application
Enquiry Request	Telephone or Electronic	Ad Hoc or Application
Business Document with Image/Graphics	Post, Facsimile or Electronic	Application

Fig. 5.3 Patterns of business communications.

electronically than at present. This type of document is known as a "compound document" and can include several different media (text, voice and/or image) within it and as a result is sometimes also referred to as a "multi-media document". This is having a major impact on the IT infrastructure services needed by organizations, requiring greater electronic storage and network architectures supporting much higher speeds.

As the options are broadened from "people to people" communications to include computer based applications many possibilities already exist and others wait to be discovered, particularly in the use of voice communications between people and applications. The growing maturity of IT in many organizations has been accompanied by an unprecedented period of change. The impact upon so many internal business processes demands integration and linking between applications (as described in Chapter 4), and this process is known as application messaging.

The external communications infrastructure supporting business communications itself has changed dramatically, from traditional services such as post and telex that have dominated business life over the last century, to the introduction of data networks and value added services over the past two decades (Fig. 5.4). As a result, standard bodies around the world have agreed to an international convention for the interconnection of networks and computers to these Packet Switched Public Data Networks (PSPDN); and indeed many of the larger multinational organizations have constructed their own private networks by leasing circuits from the telecommunications administrations responsible for these services in their country. The Internet, a parallel but separate initiative, has demonstrated even greater possibilities for the interconnection of networks and computers on a world-wide basis. These moves are essential to the continuing growth of electronic commerce and business communications.

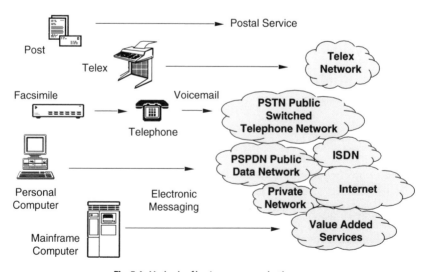

Fig. 5.4 Methods of business communications.

Post

Postal services still continue to be an important factor in business communications used within and between organizations, as well as for the domestic consumer. The principle in all cases is the same, some form of infrastructure is required to collect, transport and deliver letters, documents and parcels. It is called the mail room within an organization and for external purposes, it is known as a post office. It is the linking together of post offices with the collection/delivery services that forms the infrastructure required to offer a postal service; this analogy is used to represent the model of the global electronic messaging environment described later.

In many countries around the world, the trend to liberalize telecommunications services by governments has meant that postal services have been sectioned off as independent units and continue largely under the protection of state monopoly. However, they have not been totally insulated from the competitive pressures of marketplace developments in physical delivery services. More specifically the growth of courier services offering overnight delivery to major cities within a country and extending these services to major cities around the world has been damaging to the administrations that run postal services. With the increasing pace of the business world, courier companies have been quick to seize the market opportunity to guarantee fast and secure delivery of important shipments. Organizations needing rapid shipment of small quantities of high value products have been prepared to pay a price premium for these types of services, rather than use other alternative postal services.

To achieve differentiation in their services and secure competitive advantage, courier companies have invested heavily in IT to develop tracking systems to provide prompt and efficient delivery status of the shipments they are handling. The success of the courier companies (such as DHL, Federal Express, TNT, etc.) has had a serious impact upon the parcel business of the postal administrations and as a result, several co-operative agreements have been put in place whereby the postal service acts as the country agent for a global courier company. In addition, by working together, postal administrations have developed several projects aimed at regaining more of this business.

Recognizing the inevitable direction towards the information age and electronic communications, postal administrations are attempting to re-assess future strategies; indeed, several have introduced electronic messaging services including E-mail and EDI to compete with those services from the telecommunications administrations and service providers. Most of these market developments influence the business community, where the growth of E-mail is predicted as having a long-term adverse effect on hardcopy delivery volumes. Within the domestic marketplace, albeit much smaller in size, little impact has so far been felt from these developments and hardcopy delivery (letter post) continues at much the same levels.

In their search for new services, some postal administrations are now offering hybrid mail services to their customers, which combines computing technology with traditional postal services. Organizations such as utility companies wishing to provide their customers with bills, pass copies in electronic format (either in magnetic tape or transmitted directly) to the postal service, who then print, envelope and deliver the bills via the post in the normal manner. This is highly cost effective in the domestic marketplace and is also being used by businesses to handle promotional mail shots.

Telex

The popularity of telex, (evolving from the telegraph that offered the telegram service) with its slow speed of approximately 100 words per minute, is rapidly declining in developed countries in preference to facsimile and electronic messaging. However, in the developing countries of Africa and South America, it continues to thrive and has shown modest growth. Telex still holds the title as the most pervasive form of business communication in the world with a heavy emphasis towards inter-company traffic.

Early telex exchanges were similar to the telephone exchange in that the user simply dialed the telex number required, to establish a switched connection between both machines for the duration of the transmission. Indeed, telex exchanges tended to become computerized before telephone exchanges mainly because telex signals already contained digital codes and were therefore more suitable for computerization than the analogue telephony.

Through case law, Telex has established precedence for the status of a business transaction conducted between two or more parties as being legally binding. This is re-enforced by telex machines being designed to provide an "answer back" message to the sender, which authenticates the receiving machine as the correct and intended destination.

There are several industries around the world, such as shipping with its freight forwarders, that still continue to be heavy users of telex services despite its slow speed, unfriendly presentation and high cost. Although other forms of improved business communications continue to grow, it will probably be some years before telex services will totally disappear.

Telephone

The telephone is still the most popular form of personal communications used by business and it is experiencing a renaissance with the mobile telephone which is starting to achieve mass market growth rates. It is now easy to envizage a time when greater numbers of people will have their own highly compact mobile phones providing them with personal communications on a global basis at minimal cost.

However, from some recent informal surveys, a number of interesting facts have emerged: whilst three in every four calls are answered, 60% of the communications are of minor importance and 50% are of an informational one way basis only. Another interesting aspect of the survey indicated that having reached the person, three out of four times the person was already occupied on some other task and would have preferred not to have been interrupted. So whilst the telephone has some very definite advantages, in being able to introduce a more

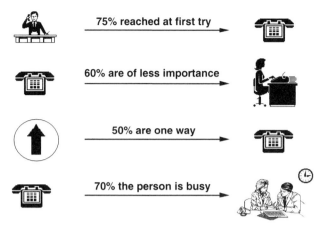

Fig. 5.5 Telephone communications.

personal note into communications, there are practical deficiencies, some of which have been addressed by the introduction of services such as voicemail. The above example also illustrates a phenomena known as "telephone tag", where progressively two people wishing to communicate with one another, continue to leave messages, "that they have called" or "returned a call". This situation, which can be most frustrating and counter-productive, is particular true when the two communicating parties are in different time zones. Electronic messaging can help ease and overcome this situation. Where an E-mail culture has been established that encourages electronic messaging as the primary form of business communications (such as in a groupware environment), such communications take place irrespective of distance. This also avoids another form of needless missed communication, where a visit to the work-space of a nearby colleague finds him absent or otherwise engaged.

Telephone communications are clearly a very critical form of business communications, indeed several new business opportunities have been created, combining the immediacy and intimacy of telephone with the speed of computer-based applications, e.g. domestic insurance, reservation and booking systems, etc.

Voicemail

Voicemail systems have emerged in response to some of these issues and can significantly improve productivity and responsiveness. The originator can leave a message indicating the reason for the call, the urgency and how they can be contacted. The owner of the voice mailbox can then listen to the messages at their convenience and not interrupt work in process, and then respond as necessary or even forward the voice message with annotations to another colleague for information or action.

While voicemail is potentially an effective business communications tool, it can also bring a very impersonal image to an organization, if people are continually passed from voicemail box to voicemail box. Indeed, for some organizations, it is a matter of policy that for those functions dealing directly with customers, voicemail is not permitted. A good practice in a voicemail environment is to have users alter or vary their greetings on a daily basis, thereby giving a greater impression of personal contact.

Facsimile

The use of facsimile dates back to the 1920s, from which time it has been used to send pictures within the newspaper industry with the resultant received copy being of exceptional quality. It is probably the oldest additional service associated with the telephone. However, it was not until the 1970s that facsimile emerged in the business world with less-expensive and more reliable machines, available for use over a dial-up public switched telephone connection. By the end of 1980s, it's total acceptance in the business world was achieved by dramatic improvements in quality, ease of use, faster transmission times and competitive pricing, making it a popular means of business communication. This has resulted in a spectacular growth in the use of facsimile, such that it has become the most widely used modern messaging system in the world today. This can be clearly demonstrated by examining business cards, where very few people would think to omit their facsimile number from them. Indeed, there is no choice; the business world has mandated its use and expects facsimile to be used as a basic condition of doing business. As more and more people include their E-mail addresses on their business cards, it is interesting to speculate when E-mail will attain the same business status achieved by facsimile.

- The most widely distributed modern messaging system
- Can handle text and graphics
- Problems with transmission quality
- Has to be re-copied (thermal paper)
- Easy to use with simple addressing concept
- Internal distribution becomes a problem for larger organisations
- Poor security
- Frequently has to be turned back into electronic form by the recipient

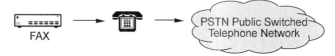

Fig. 5.6 Facsimile/Fax.

Facsimile is not just a method of communication; it consists of a sophisticated protocol that can be used between the "point-to-point" facsimile devices, including personal computers equipped with the necessary interface cards and software. Based upon the quality of the connection and capabilities of the two facsimile devices, the protocol allows speed and compression options to be negotiated and agreed between them before transmission takes place. The ITU-T has classified facsimile systems into four groups, of which the latter two are of more interest.

Group 3

An analog system and the most popular standard in use by business today, that can establish interworking with earlier groups. While originally quoted as taking approximately 1 minute to transmit an A4 sheet of paper, improvements in compression techniques has reduced this dramatically.

Group 4

Designed to work over digital networks and not very common in use within business today, due in part to the popularity of Group 3 facsimile and the lack of use of switched digital networks such as ISDN. It is likely to become far more popular in time, offering very high quality transmission of an A4 page in a matter of a few seconds.

The real strength of facsimile lies in its ability to handle both text and graphics, plus its ease of use with a simple addressing scheme that everyone can understand, namely a telephone number (Fig. 5.6). However, there are some disadvantages:

- problems with transmission quality;
- if on thermal paper, it needs to be re-copied for record purposes;
- internal distribution can be a problem in a large organization, although the number of available machines tends to be far greater than telex;
- security is poor;
- frequently the recipient turns the hardcopy facsimile back into electronic form for editing purposes.

Corporate Messaging in Evolution

The 1980s saw a substantial increase in the use of electronic messaging at both a corporate level, initially through mainframe computers, and towards the end of the decade at a departmental level as many computers and PCs became popular and affordable due to price and performance factors. In these circumstances it was not uncommon to find large organizations operating several disparate E-mail systems in different geographic locations. The recognition that a need existed to interconnect these disparate "islands of electronic messaging users" within an organization if the maximum benefits of business communications were to be achieved, resulted in several initiatives to address the problem, which are explored in the next chapter.

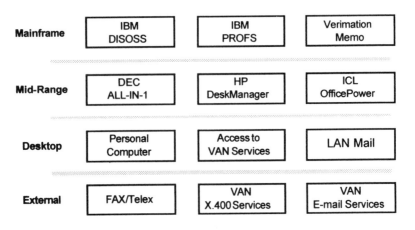

Fig. 5.7 Islands of electronic messaging.

As Fig. 5.7 shows, E-mail systems of the 1980s were dominated by mainframe and mid-range multi-user systems, based upon the proprietary messaging standards of the hardware suppliers, who saw it as an opportunity to increase their hardware sales. The variety of E-mail systems in use within a single organization was due to:

- lack of corporate IT strategy;
- mergers and acquisitions;
- decentralized management control;
- numerous national and international geographic locations.

However, the effect was the same, specifically a need to integrate the various E-mail systems, achieved using gateways that mapped messages between the various E-mail systems. This resulted in fresh problems, as a feature on the sender's E-mail system might not exist on recipients' E-mail systems. What should the gateway do in such circumstances? Due to some of these difficulties, the use of Value Added Network Services or Service Providers that provided fully integrated global electronic messaging services (and even connectivity to these islands of electronic messaging) became popular by the larger organizations.

The growing strategic importance of electronic messaging, lack of general X.400 market acceptance, growth of LAN E-mail systems and lastly the phenomenal success of the Internet, provided the stimulus for a major shift in electronic business communications in the late 1990s.

Note

1. Lea, M. (1991) Rationalist assumptions in cross-media comparisons of computer-mediated communication, *Behaviour and Information Technology*, 10(2), 153–172.

6. *Introduction to Electronic Commerce*

Background

Messaging forms the nervous system of any organization. Hardly any business activity can take place without messages being exchanged; progress reports, requests for help, arrangements for meetings, instructions to co-workers, purchase orders, delivery notes, invoices and so on ...

Until relatively recently, most businesses operated at a leisurely pace within close and well defined geographic boundaries, and messages could be written or typed on pieces of paper and distributed by internal or external postal services. For urgent messages, or for communications where a degree of interaction between the parties was necessary, electrical devices have been available for about a century. The telegraph and its descendant, the telex, provided for expensive, rapid, long distance delivery of short written messages, and the telephone enables two people to communicate, providing they are both available at the same time and have a language in common. The remarkable degree of co-operation between national telephone companies allows telex and telephone messaging to take place, simply and without the intervention of operators, on an almost worldwide basis. Mintzberg wrote in 1972:

> *One can perhaps visualize the organization of the future with teletype terminals in the offices of each senior executive. Then, true to the managers' information needs, the transmission of instant communication would be automated. The transmitter of information would simply choose which managers were to receive a current bit of news. He would then key in the code to open the proper channels, and would enter the message which would appear simultaneously in the appropriate offices.*[1]

However, during the past 25 years, this cosy world has changed:

- Business has become much more international in nature; for example, a product may be designed in Europe, assembled in Taiwan using components bought from a dozen countries around the world, and then packed with additional components into a complete system in Europe, ready for worldwide distribution.
- Competitors are no longer just the companies up the road; they are often from other continents and intent on extending their markets across the world.
- Customers have become more demanding, expecting immediate response to their requests, whether for goods or for information.

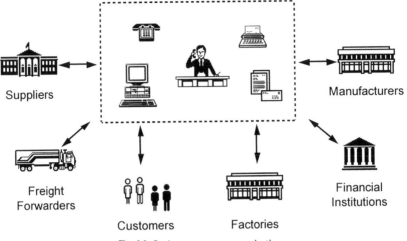

Fig. 6.1 Business *means* communication.

- The regulatory environment has changed – and will continue to change – as governments seek to encourage competition, and as consumer protection and environmental issues become more important.

To keep pace with these changes, messaging systems have had to adapt. The laboriously typed letter or memo, carried from place to place by the postman, has given way to electronic or digital messages, created in a computer and distributed by electronic means to other computers, and thus Mintzberg's prophesy has indeed come true. Some messages are still typed by, addressed to and read by humans, but another class are created, addressed, received and interpreted entirely automatically.

In this chapter, consideration will be given to both types of message, as well as to their integration within information management and directory services, enabling electronic business communications to be used as naturally and easily as traditional means. In addition, a new form of messaging, known as "application messaging", which is used within organizations to provide a powerful bridge between applications, adding significant new functionality in the process, will be described.

Electronic Mail for People (E-mail)

After mainframe computers gained the ability to service communities of remote users, each with a simple terminal, users soon realized that the computer itself could be used to provide a personal messaging system. All that was necessary was for the sender to type a message and leave it as a file with the recipient's name attached. At some later time the recipient could retrieve the message and, if need be, re-label the file to pass the message on to another reader or initiate a response to the original sender.

Such an informal mechanism will work perfectly well for a small, close-knit group of users who can agree upon a simple file naming convention for message addressing, but can descend into chaos when the user community grows. The result was the creation of simple electronic mail systems which are built around a "rack of electronic pigeon holes" or mailboxes. Each user is allocated a mailbox by a central administrative function which can prevent duplication of names and handle message counting and billing activities. Simple security mechanisms were added to prevent users from peeking into other peoples' mailboxes, and the outcome was the direct precursor of the "private" or in-house electronic mailing systems available today from computer vendors and third party software suppliers. IBM's PROFS, Digital's ALL-IN-1™ system, Microsoft Exchange and Lotus Notes are but four well-known examples.

A message is created simply with the aid of computer terminal using a simple text editor, which usually forms part of the E-mail package. The subject, destination and copy addressees are added, then it is sent. The message is then immediately deposited into the recipient's mailbox and becomes available for retrieval.

The next step forward came about 15 years ago when the regulatory environment changed, first in the USA and subsequently in many European and other countries. In Europe, a major milestone was the publication by the Commission of the European Community (CEC) of their Telecommunications Green Paper in 1987. The new rules relaxed PTT monopolies on certain telecommunications services and permitted "service providers" to offer commercial electronic mail services. Within a few years a host of such services were available, some aimed at the inter-site internal mailing requirements of major corporations, and others at inter-company mail. GE Information Services' QUIK-COMM™ system is representative of the first group, and British Telecom's GOLD™ Service is representative of the second.

The 1980s saw the increasing growth of E-mail using systems provided by the suppliers of computer equipment, external services and independent software companies marketing software packages. This growth has been fuelled by dramatic improvements in the telecommunications infrastructure and the popularity in Local Area Networks (LAN) towards the end of the 1980s.

The Standards Issue

The success of these "second generation" mailing systems demonstrated that businesses had a real need for the flexibility and power of electronic messaging systems to complement conventional telephone- and paper-based methods. At first, growth was simple; user communities grew by adding more and more "dumb" terminals to the supplier's data network. The widespread availability of desktop and portable microcomputers was handled by providing software packages which enabled the micro to act like a dumb terminal, albeit with sophisticated message creation and display facilities.

This resulted in a wide variety of different E-mail packages in use within organizations, together with the establishment of separate E-mail communities associated with each of the external services providers. "Islands of electronic messaging" were created. This presented major problems of integration and strange situations where E-mail users were required to subscribe to a number of different internal and external services to reach their business associates. This was like having a number of different telephones on the desk corresponding to each of the E-mail communities to which they needed to communicate.

This division between in-house and third party electronic mailing systems has continued, and has been accompanied by a considerable increase in the number of products and services available to end users, each claiming superior features and functions. The computer industry and the related service companies have made a virtue of "own brand" solutions since their beginning in the 1960s.

The primary difference today is that, while the "look and feel" for the end user is different from product to product and from service to service, considerable progress has been achieved in getting these products and services to work with one another (inter-working). This has been made possible by the growing insistence of end users that the suppliers of products and services adhere to international or *de facto* industry standards: they must conform to open system principles. This implies conformance to X.400 and its associated series of recommendations, or to those of the Internet and its associated set of standards. The nature of these standards are reviewed in a later section, and it is sufficient at this stage to recognize that they provide the basis for a consistent set of rules and conventions between electronic messaging environments.

There has also been a trend by larger organizations, as part of their IT strategy, to reduce the variety of E-mail systems in use. This both simplifies the scale of the integration problem and reduces the need for diverse end user training. It is a further example of the tendency of many organizations to establish a "thick IT architecture" as described in Chapter 3.

Electronic Mail to Telex, FAX and Postal delivery

While traffic volumes are declining, telex still represents the most universal and extensive form of global electronic messaging. Earlier in this century many of the larger organizations persuaded the local 'phone companies to rent them point-to-point teleprinter circuits, which were used by the postal services for the public telegram service, that provided hard-copy delivery. As time progressed it became generally accepted that telex, when used between organizations, and even without an authenticating signature, could be viewed as a legally binding message. Indeed, to reinforce this status as the switched services started to evolve, the concept of an "answer back" code was introduced. This allowed the originator to identify precisely the receiving machine beyond solely the telex number.

It is natural that many users wish to both send and receive telex messages from their desktop computing environment, and an E-mail message should be able to include telex destinations. There are many ways in which organizations can achieve this: first, a telex gateway can be installed in their mainframe or LAN environment that is connected to the Telex Network; alternatively, there are several companies, known as telex re-filers, who will receive a file of telex messages in an agreed format to be entered into their telex re-filing systems. Based upon the country destination, by adding a three digit prefix to the telex message, the telex re-filing system will either enter the telex message directly into the Telex Network or transfer it to another re-filing node, ideally in or close to the country of the telex recipient. Within the country of the telex recipient, the same process applies and the telex message is released into the Telex Network. Upon successful delivery of the telex message, the appropriate notification is returned to the originator via the telex re-filer. An incoming telex is usually a little more difficult to organize, and either requires a unique telex number to be associated with a messaging user (via their E-mail address), or the telex originator needs to include the recipient's E-mail address within the telex message according to some pre-agreed format, i.e. the E-mail address will always be contained in the first line of the message.

E-mail users sending to or copying telex destinations need to be aware that a telex line is 60 characters in length and is received in upper-case with a limited character set, so some special characters cannot be used. To be more specific, telex uses the Baudot code which is a 5-bit character set (a code consisting of 5 bits is used to represent a single character), which, with each bit either representing 0 or 1, gives 32 possible combinations or characters. Partly for these reasons, as well as cost and speed, telex has never been seen as a particularly user-friendly environment, and in many organizations, the telex machine has often been co-located with the telephone Private Automatic Branch Exchange (PABX) equipment, making it somewhat inaccessible.

The development of teletex (not to be confused with teletext, a service provided by television channels) was aimed at addressing some of the problems with telex, and can be considered as a superior form of telex. It handles an 8-bit character set known as T.61 (an ITU-T recommendation), and is ideal for supporting international textual communications. Teletex was an early service made available in some countries over the packet switched public data networks that evolved in the early 1980s, but which has never really established itself as a full international service. The teletex terminal is much like a normal computer terminal, and once connected to the destination machine via the Teletex Network, can send messages at speeds up to 9600 bits per second (compared to 100 bits per second for telex). Provision is also made for interworking between the Telex and Teletex Networks. The advent of personal computers with dial-up modems using the Public Switched Telephone Network (PSTN), together with various messaging options, has effectively curtailed the market growth and acceptance of teletex.

Facsimile is not a new concept: its origins date from the 1920s, but it has only been from the mid/late 1980s that this form of business communications has grown significantly. There are many reasons for its phenomenal success, but high on the list are the low cost of equipment and its ease of use. Part of facsimile's ease of use is its addressing scheme, the telephone number, which is included by most people on their business card alongside their normal telephone number used for voice communications. Due to their relatively low cost, facsimile machines, unlike telex machines, tend to be spread around organizations, and have become an effective way of sending text and graphics from one point to another. The most popular standard for facsimile machines in use today is known as Group 3 FAX, which uses a very sophisticated protocol, including compression and allowing for speed negotiation. While it is clear that the popularity of facsimile has slowed down the take-up of electronic messaging, this competition has forced many of the E-mail suppliers to be more attentive to the demands of users for greater simplicity in the operational aspects of electronic messaging.

In many instances, as the document being sent by facsimile has been produced on a personal computer, and once received is then input into a personal computer, it is not surprising that good progress has been made in converging these technologies. One of the initial steps in this process was the development of the FAX card that, once installed in a PC, allows a document created within that PC to be sent directly to a facsimile machine. This was closely followed by the packaging of the FAX card with the PC Modem card into one unit, together with the necessary software. Clearly, in a LAN environment, it would be inefficient to equip each machine with a FAX card, and therefore a FAX Gateway is usually installed which becomes accessible to all users on the LAN.

As with telex, E-mail users are able to send messages from their desktop computing environment to facsimile users by simply including the addresses of their destinations according to a pre-defined format in the address fields. Owing to the pre-defined format, the E-mail system recognizes the nature of the destination and ships it to the FAX Gateway for delivery. Usually, delivery status messages are returned and a re-try mechanism used if the destination facsimile machine is busy.

Most of the FAX cards referred to above have the ability to be placed into a "receive mode" offering point-to-point communications, such that they can receive incoming facsimile transmissions. Once safely stored in the PC, there are software viewers that allow the user to read the facsimile message that has been received. However, in-bound facsimile brings with it some difficulties in being able to transpose the document that is received as an image (represented by bits according to a greyscale) and identifying those sections of the image that are text. Such a mechanism would be necessary if it was intended to place the electronic form of the facsimile into a user's mailbox. Once identified, or indeed if the originating document being sent via facsimile was text only, it is necessary to convert the image into a normal character set representation through a scanning and transposition process. This can be laborious, and does not guarantee that the final text document will be 100% accurate, usually requiring some further intervention by the recipient.

One preferred option is to preserve the nature of the message as facsimile and to include it as an attachment to an E-mail message. In this way, the addressing issues are overcome and it can be simply deposited into the recipient's mailbox. The user can then read the document with a software viewer, but it is generally not in a form that can be readily amended.

Universal Mailbox

Prompted by the growing expectations of end users for a far greater ease of use in their electronic business communications, there is a movement by some messaging suppliers towards the concept of the "universal mailbox". This is made increasingly possible by a convergence in the basic telecommunications infrastructure, transporting the various media types of text, voice and image. The concept is very simple; from the desktop (or laptop and possibly even palmtop)

the user has access to their mailbox containing all the various message types –
E-mail, facsimile, voicE-mail, news clippings, etc. These can be serviced in the
same way that the individual media types are serviced today, but the big difference is that they are serviced from one single messaging environment. Coupled
with the availability of video-conferencing software for PCs run over telecommunications services such as ISDN, the universal mailbox heralds a new era in electronic business communications for the user.

Electronic Mail Enabled Applications

There are numerous applications that rely upon the supply of information from
distributed locations. For example, consider an organization with a number of
sales offices spread across a number of European locations. Monthly, the sales
offices need to pass on to the organization's head office details of performance
over the last month, usually expressed in financial terms. At head office, this
information is channelled into a financial consolidation application from which
various reports, including financial statements for the company as a whole, can be
prepared. As each sales office prepares the required head office reports, which
may be directly output from a computer application existing in the local environment, the file is passed across an interface to the E-mail environment, where a
message is automatically created, addressed, the file attached to the message, and
finally the message sent. The recipient is in effect an application that polls a specific mailbox periodically, and extracts the message with the attached file, which
is passed into the financial consolidation application. A sports footwear manufacturer might equip his sales people with laptop personal computers that may be
used to enter customer orders when meeting with the store owner or buyer. At a
later stage, using the transport mechanism provided by E-mail, these orders are
transmitted to the company's ordering department for processing. Both of these
scenarios are examples of mail-enabled applications, not directly person-to-
person communications, but using the same transport mechanism to exchange
information between loosely coupled applications. Mail-enabled applications are
more generally used within an organization, since inter-company business communication demands a more rigorous coupling between their respective computing environments, through the use of agreed conventions and standards.

Electronic Data Interchange for Computer Applications

Electronic Data Interchange (EDI) has its origins in the early 1980s when the first
of the electronic trading communities started. These companies, sometimes
forming part of an industry group or association, saw the potential that electronic
communications could bring in reducing costs and gaining time by linking their
computer-based applications. Initial progress with EDI was frustrated by the
availability of cost-effective IT at the time, and the increasing realization that
it was difficult to undertake EDI without both organizational impact and the
redesign of business processes. More specifically it was necessary to:

- formalize and document activities,
- streamline and adapt business processes, and
- agree common sets of rules and standards.

While management commitment was necessary for the success of E-mail, this became even more critical for EDI, as the processes were not solely under the control of the one organization, but many. It was under these circumstances that several competing service companies emerged to act as the intermediary for the exchange of electronic business documents between community members.

For those companies engaged in EDI, it is necessary to develop an organizational culture focused upon change and an acceptance of increased dependency upon IT. While there are real tactical benefits from EDI, such as reducing costs, there are also strategic benefits to be obtained by using the technology, primarily through the business relationships that become established between co-operating organizations and the scope for using the information thus exchanged more effectively, leading to increased competitiveness.

Using a similar analogy to the creation of E-mail messaging islands referenced above, electronic information cannot be successfully exchanged between computer-based applications belonging to two separate organizations unless some pre-agreement exists on its format, which implies some level of standardization effort.

Benefits of EDI

At the beginning of this chapter, we saw how electronic mail is evolving from a myriad of little local user communities with a need for a certain amount of inter-community messaging, into the global X.400 and increasingly more popular Internet communities. While this was happening, a second form of electronic messaging came into being and followed a roughly parallel path. Electronic Data Interchange was invented as a means for business documents, such as requests for quotations, purchase orders, invoices, acknowledgements, etc. to be passed

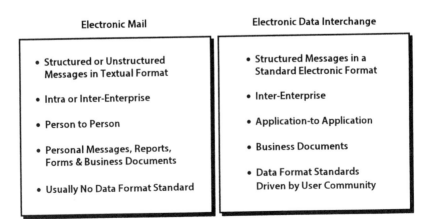

Fig. 6.2 E-mail and EDI characteristics.

directly from the sender's application to the complementary application in the recipient's computer.

The driving force was a need to reduce costs and improve customer service. By transferring a purchase order, for example, through some form of electronic messaging system, several benefits would arise:

- The order would be available to the vendor's computerized order entry application within a matter of minutes rather than the several days taken by conventional mail.
- Opportunities for orders to be misdirected or simply lost would be virtually eliminated.
- With the order already in computer-readable form, the expense, delay and possibility of introducing errors, all inseparable from keying the order into the recipient's computer, would be eliminated.
- The customer would receive better service, and, over time, the frequency of ordering could be increased without significant addition to overheads.

The last of these is, perhaps, the most important since it has permitted the introduction of "Just In Time" inventory philosophies. This allows wholesale buyers/purchasers, such as automobile assemblers or the large "high street" retail stores, to phase out their goods inward stock-holdings, and move incoming goods direct to the point of use or point of sale, with replenishments on a daily or even shorter cycle. Successful implementation of such systems provides for order-of-magnitude improvements in end-user service, enormous one-off savings, improved flexibility in production planning (i.e. giving the ability to make what is actually needed rather than what a planner thinks might be needed), and improved cash flows.

Differing Characteristics of EDI

EDI was first used on a large scale in the automotive assembly industry and has spread to virtually every industry sector, as well as to areas such as customs documentation and payment services through links with clearing banks. From the outset it was clear that, while some of the underlying mechanisms of interpersonal messaging might be used for EDI, EDI messages had some additional characteristics needing special treatment.

The recipient is not human but a computer program and, unlike humans, computer programs are highly inflexible. If a paper purchase order is received, it is possible for the individual keying the information into an order processing application to do so in the required format, whether a name is at the top or bottom of the form, or even running up the side. The individual can unscramble an order line in whatever sequence the information is presented, and can even make sense of one which reads: "Please send six dozen cans of spray lubricant in the economy size, with the red tops, since those with yellow tops won't fit into the spray guns."

It is necessary to take an order in the format in which it is presented by the replenishment application and, having relayed it to the supplier's order processing application, persuade the latter to read and understand it. Some years ago, when these problems were first presented, it was virtually impossible to find any complementary pair of applications capable of accepting one another's output. It was unreasonable to expect all of one's customers to re-code their applications to present orders in the format used by the supplier (and, even if they would do so for one supplier, they could hardly do it for twenty), so the need for standards soon became apparent.

EDI Standards

No international bodies were ready and waiting with proposals for global standards, so each industry invented its own, predictably with different forms in different countries, and a new electronic Babel sprang up in just a few years. Within each "island of users" this did not matter much, since each user merely had to translate outgoing documents from the internal format into the industry format, and translate incoming documents back into (usually a different) internal format. However, the manufacturers of commonly used products, such as paint, sold to every industry, and it soon became clear that proper cross-industry standards were necessary.

In the United States, the American National Standards Institute (ANSI) developed their X12 family of standards, and the Transportation Data Co-ordinating Committee (TDCC) developed a different family for communications between shippers and carriers. In Europe and the Far East, a number of independent standardization bodies developed more or less compatible standards under the Global Trade Data Interchange (GTDI) banner. It soon became evident that universal standards were necessary and the Joint EDI (JEDI) Committee was set up to produce harmonized standards for global use. There are now a large number of these that have been agreed, or, are on their way through the agreement procedure, which are known as the UN/EDIFACT (EDI for Administration, Commerce and

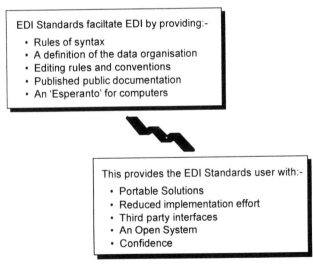

Fig. 6.3 EDI standards.

Transportation) standards. In 1994 ANSI agreed to a transition from the X12 to EDIFACT standards in the USA, but this message seems to have been lost on industry in the United States, which continues to actively support ANSI ASC X12.

ANSI ASC X12 and UN/EDIFACT are by far the most popular EDI standards used in North America and Europe, respectively. In Asia Pacific there is a fairly even split between the use of both standards. However, the reader may well have come into contact with others, including ANSI ASC X12 subsets/implementations such as VICS and UCS:

- VICS is used extensively in the North American retail sector.
- UCS is used in grocery and public warehousing.

Similarly, UN/EDIFACT subsets/implementations include EANCOM, AECOM, EDIFICE, EDIPAP, ODETTE and IMPA:

- EANCOM used mainly in the retail sector and very popular in France.
- AECOM developed by AEOC that represents the European Article Numbering Association (EAN) in Spain.
- EDIFICE is used in the electronics sector.
- EDIPAP is used by the paper industry.
- ODETTE is used extensively in the European automotive sector.
- IMPA is used by the ocean shipping industry.

In addition, other well known EDI standards include:

- AECMA 2000M, which is a European specification popular within the defence industry covering provisioning, codification, procurement planning, order administration, invoicing and consumption data exchange.
- SEDAS is a proprietary EDI standard used primarily in the retail sector in Germany.
- TRADACOMS is another proprietary EDI standard developed by the Article Number Association (ANA) in the UK, and widely used in the retail sector.
- VDA is a proprietary EDI standard used by the automotive sector in Germany.
- SWIFT is the Society for World Interbank Funds Transfer, and its EDI message definitions are used by the banking industry worldwide.

Despite the existence of these proprietary EDI standards, nowadays most companies can exchange a large number of types of business document by translating internal formats to and from a single, universally agreed format based upon the UN/EDIFACT standard. The data re-formatting process is normally undertaken by a software package known as a mapper/translator. When planning to use such a facility, it is good practise to first prepare a "desk map" that defines the flat file format of the data coming from an existing application and the format of the intended EDI message to be created (Fig. 6.4). This helps identify which information goes where, whether any information is missing and the processing logic that is to be incorporated, e.g. perhaps the quantity and unit price are to be multiplied together to give an extended price that will be placed in a new field.

It remains only to relay the EDI-standard format document to the intended recipient.

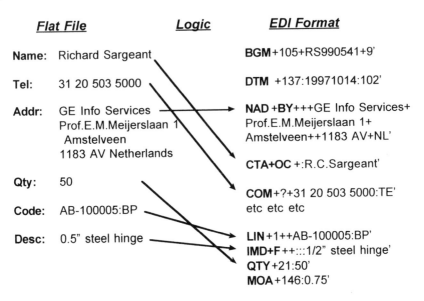

Fig. 6.4 Desk mapping process.

Transmitting EDI Messages

There are two commonly used mechanisms for transmitting EDI messages (Fig. 6.5):

- Using a mailbox mechanism like that used for inter-personal messages, which has become the most popular way that EDI is conducted between trading partners.
- Direct machine-to-machine transfers have not been popular until recently, owing to the incompatibilities between computers making inter-working problematic, and the difficulty of scheduling message exchange sessions. This mechanism has been viewed as appropriate only in situations where small numbers of trading partners have regular high volume interchanges.

A number of service providers, including GE Information Services, began to offer message transfer systems specialized to the requirements of EDI users. These differ in some respects from inter-personal messaging systems, and the differences are important if we are to understand the issues which arise when we try to extend the X.400 and Internet messaging mechanism to embrace EDI messages. First there is a broad area of "security", which we may break down to include:

- *Trading Relationships.* It is clearly vital that a pair of trading partners do not start trying to exchange EDI messages until both are ready to do so (i.e. they have their internal systems and message translators in place); some EDI messaging systems refuse messages unless the recipient has previously signalled that he is ready to receive messages of that type, thereby preventing messages from being delivered into an electronic "black hole".

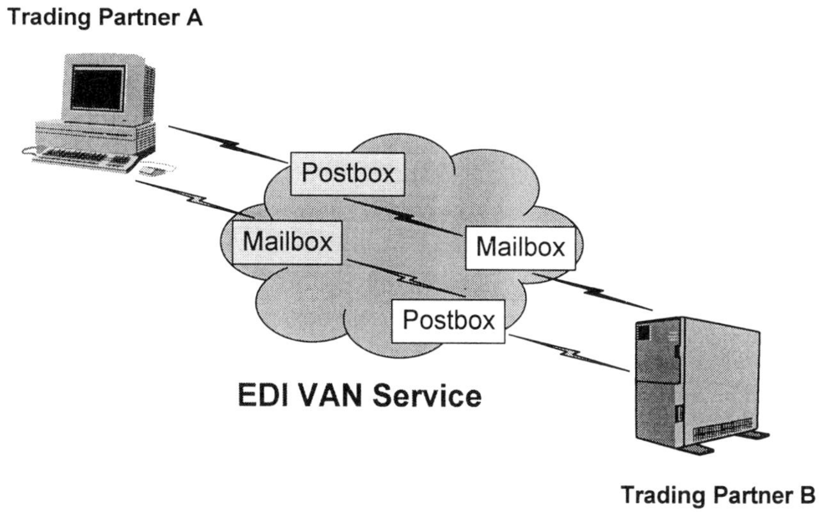
Trading Partner A
Postbox
Mailbox
Mailbox
Postbox
EDI VAN Service
Trading Partner B

Fig. 6.5 EDI using VAN service.

- *Exclusion of interlopers.* The integrity of a business depends upon messages being delivered intact to the intended recipient. It should be remembered that, unlike inter-personal messages, many EDI messages have a real monetary value, and incorrect delivery could result in loss of trade (for a retail store) or loss of output (for a supplier). Third parties should be unable to tap into a message stream and, for example, extract messages and throw them away, or change messages and re-insert them or simply replay them time and again. This area is receiving considerable attention as EDI methods are adopted by payment systems and the messages act as electronic cheques or money transfers.
- *Message Integrity.* The system must not alter or truncate messages, and if this does happen as an artefact of the transfer process, it must be detected and either damaged messages must be re-transmitted automatically or they must be marked as suspect and the parties to the transaction informed immediately.
- *Message Acknowledgement.* The sender cannot feel secure until he has received a positive acknowledgement that each individual message has been received by the intended addressee; a second level of acknowledgement indicating that the message has been read and understood is also needed in some cases (a purchase order needs to be acknowledged line by line, while there is little requirement for, say, an invoice to be acknowledged except as a message).

A second group of EDI service facilities extend the message transfer, offering to include a level of sorting and batching of messages. Thus, a sender might make up a bundle of messages of many different types, but all to a single addressee, and send them as a batch. The addressee will usually have a number of different applications involved in EDI transactions and wish for incoming messages to be bundled by type, each bundle including inputs from many different sources.

A third type of service provides for automatic *en route* translation between different EDI standard formats (or, indeed, between private internal formats and EDI standard formats). The need for this additional service has diminished as the number of different types of EDI standards in use have reduced and sophisticated mapping/translation facilities exist at the periphery.

Finally, some services permit a wide range of payment options, ranging from "sender pays" to "equal shares for sender and recipient" or flexible terms agreed by each pair of trading partners.

Application Messaging and CORBA

Within an organization, there is often a need to share information between different applications. Such information flows are certainly not informal in nature nor so well structured as an EDI standard. However, when information is exchanged between applications in this way, it needs to be in a pre-defined format to make it possible for the receiving application to understand and use the information within the "message". For many organizations, the progressive use of IT has meant that a heavy investment now exists in applications of varying ages, and it is impossible to imagine that, as new business processes evolve, the supporting legacy applications can all be replaced at one time.

To address this need, a number of software products have emerged which receive and route transactions from the one application to the other. Apart from the routing function, these gateway or "middleware" products, transform the incoming business transactions into the required format for the destination application, based upon pre-determined business rules. In addition, they may also create multiple transactions for several different destination applications in the appropriate formats. Finally, they offer sophisticated audit features which provide a central point of control for managing and tracking transaction traffic flow.

A typical example might be where a stock management system is used to generate replenishment orders that need to be passed into the purchasing system. The stock management system may be an older or legacy application, whilst the purchasing system is part of a new suite of packaged software recently introduced into the organization. Clearly, there is nothing new in the practice of integrating applications, where transactions or messages are passed from one system to another. What is new is a greater frequency of change in business processes and hence applications, demanding the extraction of additional and timely information from messages during their movement between applications. This needs to be performed in a speedy and flexible manner. Responding to this requirement are several new approaches, some linked into advanced relational databases, others an extension of traditional EDI mapping and translation techniques, which are typically used to create formatted messages according to a recognized EDI standard from files created by the application and referred to as "any to EDI standard message".

In the case of application messaging, the need is to create a message in one format and transpose it into another format, which is sometimes referred to as "any-to-any" message transposition. The need to transpose the information content of the message may not be the only requirement: consider the earlier example of a replenishment order being passed to a purchasing system. It may also be necessary to verify whether the product code being ordered is still current and to add the product description, possibly even to create an additional transaction that will be passed to a financial application to build up an early record of accounts payable. It is most likely that the purchasing system will generate a series of EDI standard messages, using traditional mapping and translation, that can be passed via the organization's corporate server to its suppliers, via one or more external EDI value added network services.

EDI tends to be used between organizations, Application Messaging within organizations and E-mail both within and between organizations. Described in this way, Application Messaging means that a minimal amount of change needs to be made to the applications exchanging information, and all that is necessary, is to be able to simply understand the nature of their interfaces. However, in the message exchange process, considerable added value can be introduced beyond simple re-formatting, principally by concentrating the logic at the centre, which can then be easily modified, leaving the co-operating applications to appear coupled in an unrestricted manner. Consider an organization implementing several new financial software packages, each requiring information feeds from a series of existing systems. It is no longer necessary to embark on customization of the software packages as well as the existing systems, but simply to use application messaging techniques to couple the different environments. Where both new and old systems need to co-exist for periods of time, such an approach eases the transition by offering a step-by-step evolution. Of particular interest to many organizations is the opportunity to revitalize older applications for which technical knowledge has ceased to exist, limited documentation is available and yet the system itself is critical to the operation of the business, but becoming less so, due the limited possibilities of undertaking further improvments. Simply by understanding the application interface, its lifecycle can be extended through enhancements made externally using application messaging techniques.

Enterprise Resource Planning (ERP) software such as SAP, Oracle Applications, Baan and PeopleSoft represent a new breed of integrated software packages that are built in a modular manner and cover all the normal business functions undertaken by most medium/large sized organizations. They are usually built around a relational database with a large level of parameterization to assist in the customization of the implementation to meet the specific requirements of most clients. Application Program Interfaces (API) provide the hooks through which more specialized business functions, perhaps associated with a particular industry sector, can be developed and grafted onto the system. However, ERP systems are often not EDI enabled, but provide an interface standard through which transactions may be presented to a gateway for transformation and routing to trading partners, either directly or via an EDI VAN Service. Taking an invoice as an example, SAP defines a corresponding intermediate document format (IDOC), which needs to be converted by the gateway into an EDI standard, if it is to be passed to a trading partner using an EDI VAN service. This task is performed by the EDI VAN Gateway that sits between the SAP system and the external EDI VAN service.

When considering the ability that different applications have to talk with one another, a standard called Common Object Request Broker Architecture (CORBA) is an important development. CORBA lays the foundation for different applications to freely interact, irrespective of their hardware platforms. It uses distributed business objects that may be accessed over the Internet using the Internet Inter-ORB Protocol (IIOP). As more implementations of CORBA compliant applications emerge, so the need for traditional middleware products is likely to diminish.

Information Management (Notes, Exchange & Web)

The need for information in the "day-to-day" operation and management of an organization is nothing new; managers turn information into action. However, trading in the 1990s has placed new emphasis for managing improved business processes and their associated information flows. This involves breaking down traditional hierarchical organizations with a functional bias, into those where the business process determines the structure and departmental boundaries are no longer respected. These new business processes and the associated computer-based applications are being created in such a way that information is available throughout the cycle.

The challenge is therefore to make information available to those that need it, ideally in a form that is easily digestible and relevant. The philosophy of E-mail in which information is directed or "pushed" from one person to another, can be extremely efficiently integrated into an information management concept. Rather than overusing E-mail, identify the information that requires periodic access and make this readily available for "pulling" to those that need it, via an information server (a database that can be readily accessed from the user's desktop personal computer).

The sort of information accessed in this way might be stored in a hierarchical structure (as in a bulletin board, such as pricing information, a report, article or other reference document) or in a threaded structure (series of correspondence related to the same subject). There are several dominant competing technologies today for accessing corporate information of this type from the desktop. Lotus Notes software (server software) is deployed by many companies to successfully store information used widely across the organization. Facilities also exist to view this information not only from the dedicated desktop software (client software), but also using Web browser technology (Domino). Another competing technology is Microsoft Exchange, which is similar to Lotus Notes in as much as it integrates a number of desktop functions (E-mail, Calendering, etc.) together with access to public and private folders, viewed using a range of client software. Finally, with the popularity of Internet technologies, the use of World-Wide Web servers capable of hosting information in much the same way as Lotus Notes and Microsoft Exchange servers, but capable of attractive and imaginative visual displays using a mark-up language called HTML, has become the cornerstone of corporate wide TCP/IP networks (Intranets).

Directory Services

Most people will operate with a simple address book that represents a small sub-set of the people they know, but most likely represents 90% of the people they routinely wish to contact. When they need to contact someone who is not in their local address book, at first they might examine their hard copy directory provided by their telephone company, and then if this is not adequate, access a directory enquiry service. For the electronic messaging user, a similar structure is likely to exist with a local public directory, accessible to "all" local users associated with a geographic location typically served by a Local Area Network (LAN). In addition, each individual user will create a private local address book on their personal computer that will contain a list of frequently accessed E-mail addresses, partly populated from information extracted from the local public directory – other sources being from correspondence, telephone conversations and business cards.

Organizations have found it difficult to establish an accurate corporate public directory service that represents a central depository of directory service information replicating the local public directories. In many respects, it does not make sense to replicate local public directories. The need is merely to link them together such that they form the composite corporate directory from which addressing information can be obtained. Indeed, if this is pursued to a logical conclusion, then the global directory service would be comprised not only of just one physical directory, but also of one logical directory made up of a very large number of distributed physical directories.

The corporate directory needs to satisfy three essential requirements:

- That it serves the whole organization, and all employees/members may access it and take the fullest advantage of it.
- It should provide full details of all employees/members, as well as all departments/divisions making-up the organization.
- It should support several applications because it achieves synergy between the various means of electronic business communication (E-mail, telephone, facsimile, conferencing, etc.) and can assist in navigation to any kind of corporate information.

For organizations trading in an electronic commerce environment, whilst the electronic address of the trading partner is important, there is probably a lot more information that is required, including their "invoice to" and "deliver to" addresses, physical location within a building, digital signature, telephone and FAX numbers, business transactions to be exchanged, transaction format to be used, etc. The concept of a comprehensive directory service, capable of handling a wide range of business information, is included within the ITU-T X.500 series of recommendations.

When directories or directory services are mentioned, most people tend to think of the white pages (residential and business telephone numbers listed in alphabetical sequence) and yellow pages (business details organized in alphabetical sequence of business categories), as well as operator service provided by the telephone companies. As it happens, there are no global postal or telephone directories, or indeed, readily accessible external directories for people working within organizations. However, the traditional hard copy internal telephone directories created and published by organizations are being progressively replaced by their electronic equivalents, to provide critical information to companies, concerning electronic, telephone and physical delivery addresses of their employees. In many instances, each of these categories still remain separate and in different formats. From an organizational perspective, there is usually a need to extend the information stored within the electronic directories to include details of products and services that could be usefully accessed by prospective customers given access to the directories.

With the establishment of corporate Intranets (networks embracing Internet technologies but used by a single company), many organizations are using browser technology to distribute corporate information, including the internal telephone directory. For E-mail users, hard copy directories are largely irrelevant, due in part to the rapid ageing process of directory information, and since by definition, each user has a networked personal computer, it makes more sense to access directory information electronically. Although convergence is taking place, integrated directories within E-mail systems handling E-mail address information all too often sit alongside Web browsers providing access to directories for telephone numbers.

Most electronic messaging users have a rather limited requirement from directory services: simply the need to identify the electronic address of the individual with whom they wish to communicate. There is a great deal of other information about the individual that would be extremely helpful to access from time to time, including their physical work/home addresses, work/home telephone numbers, job title, favourite drink, name of partner, etc. This raises one of the main issues related to directories – how much information should be included, and to what extent should this information be restricted or made available in the public domain.

Usually, a directory service, however limited, is provided as part of a message handling system. For EDI the nature of the information stored in the directory may differ to that of the E-mail user, and include the types of documents to be exchanged between the trading parties, details of communications protocols, physical network addresses and X.509 public-key certificates. For the E-mail user, there is typically a local public directory associated with that particular community, system or LAN. Such a directory is updated as amendments are made and, in the case of the popular LAN E-mail products, a process exists to synchronize the public directories to ensure complete consistency. In the same way that individuals maintain an electronic personal organizer to store a sub-set of the address information they wish to access, it is common for each E-mail user to have their own personal address book on their personal computer.

Whilst this works well within the same E-mail environment, with multiple systems, compatibility between proprietary directory service implementations becomes a major problem. Take as an example an engineering company engaged by a major petroleum company to build an oil rig. It requires close electronic communications with the petroleum company as well as its alliance partners and contractors involved in the construction of the oil rig. Many organizations have been slow to implement a corporate directory, in part because there is really no "killer" application driving the requirement and there are many other pressing priorities. The closest "killer" application is E-mail and many of the LAN E-mail and LAN Network Operating System suppliers already provide directory services, mostly proprietary, but many now based upon open standards or very similar. The question still remains: how do all the parties gain access to directory service information to facilitate the flow of electronic communications? An obvious approach is the use of the X.500 recommendations for a global directory, that is independent of network architecture; together with the Lightweight Directory Access Protocol (LDAP), which is described in detail in Chapter 14.

Organizational Considerations

Whilst the introduction of electronic mail implies few, if any, organizational changes, there are many cultural changes that occur, since it intensifies existing relationships, extends to new relationships and assists in work groups or team communications. Whilst E-mail can be a very effective and convenient way of conducting business communications, care has to be exercised that the medium is not abused and that individuals cease to use more appropriate forms of business communications as demanded by the situation. Clearly, when exchanging business transactions electronically between organizations, basic changes will be required in business processes and their supporting IT applications. This in itself is complex, and implies a much greater scale of change than with E-mail. The requirement to turn business transactions into a "format" that the receiving system can recognize, and subsequently process, adds even greater complexity to Electronic Data Interchange. Considerable effort is being applied to find ways to make EDI simpler to perform, so that smaller organizations can also start realizing the benefits.

For electronic messaging to be successfully introduced within and between organizations, the business community ultimately needs to mandate that this is the way in which business communications are going to be conducted, almost as a condition of community membership. As an example, individuals no longer have choice as to whether they use facsimile or not; the corporate community has mandated that this is a necessary condition of doing business, and it is no longer a question of individual choice. The increasing presence of E-mail addresses on business cards, adjacent to the now familiar telephone and facsimile numbers, is a testimony that E-mail is rapidly reaching a similar status. Suppliers to the major high street retailers have no choice; it is a condition of doing business that they exchange business transactions electronically using EDI. Current indications point to the growth in Internet commerce as a likely catalyst that will place a similar dependency upon small to medium enterprises in the future.

Notes

1. Henry Mintzberg, "The myths of MIS", *California Management Review*, Vol. 15 No. 1 (Fall 1972) p. 97 (University of California – ESS P68).

7.   Internet Dominance of Electronic Commerce

What is the Internet

The Internet is the subject of numerous books and continues to attract a great deal of publicity and worldwide interest. At one level it represents a similar environment to X.400 for global electronic messaging, but its traffic patterns are much greater, and in addition it offers a far wider range of other services, some of which are not currently included in the X.400 environment. Its origins are from the US military, spreading into the academic and research communities with government funding. As colleges and universities around the world set up their own computing environments the Transmission Control Program/Internet Protocol (TCP/IP) architecture became a popular choice. It was not long before campus networks based upon TCP/IP suite were being interconnected or internet-worked – hence the birth of the Internet.

In 1969 the US Department of Defence (US DoD) established a 'wartime digital communications' project to understand if it would be possible to design a network that could rapidly re-route data traffic around failed network nodes. The Defence Advanced Research Projects Agency (DARPA) launched the project, and by 1975 declared the resultant DARPA Internet to be a success. Its management was then taken over by Defence Communications Agency, and by 1980 the major protocols, still in use today, were stable and progressively adopted throughout ARPANET. The US National Science Foundation (NSF) started the Supercomputer Centres program in 1986, as until that point supercomputers such as Crays were largely the playthings of large, well-funded universities and military research centres. NSF's objective was to make supercomputer resources available to those of more modest means by constructing five supercomputer centres around the US and building a network linking them with potential users. NSF decided to base their network on the Internet protocols, and NSFNET was born. For the next decade, NSFNET would be the core of the US Internet, until its privatisation and ultimate retirement in 1995.

The creation of the World-Wide Web (WWW or simply Web) has been one of the Internet's most exciting developments that propelled the Internet into the public eye and caused the business world to take Internet technologies seriously. The idea of hypertext had been around for more than a decade, but in 1989 a team at the European nuclear research laboratory (CERN) in Switzerland developed a set of protocols for transferring hypertext via the Internet. In the early 1990s it was enhanced by a team at the National Centre for Supercomputing Applications

(NCSA) at the University of Illinois, one of NSF's supercomputer centres. The result was NCSA Mosaic, a graphical, point-and-click hypertext browser that made Internet usage easy.

Aside from the Internet's technical progress over the last three decades, its sociological progress has been phenomenal, becoming a prominent feature of business life, as well as having an increasing presence within the home. It seems headed for even greater prominence in the next millennium.

Overview of Internet Technologies

The Internet architecture has at its core five standards that are collectively known by two of them, namely Transmission Control Protocol and Internet Protocol (TCP/IP). For those readers requiring further details, these are described in a later chapter (Chapter 10). The objective in this section is focus upon the ways in which users interact with the Internet so that its evolution into the business world can be fully appreciated. Whilst the Internet architecture provides the networking framework for a global electronic community, innovation continues to evolve new and better ways to exploit the technology.

Much of this innovation is centred around extending the use of Web technology, which has so captured the imagination of the business world. The Web is based upon two concepts: first, the use of the hypertext mark-up language (HTML); and secondly, it employs a client/server framework. Information is arranged into pages and stored in an HTML encoded format on a Web server and accessed with a Web browser (client). Using HTML, pages can be created that provide a rich combination of textual and multimedia content (voice, graphics, image and video), together with links to other pages that may exist on separate Web servers.

With the requirement to promote universal accessibility, it is important that the Web browser implements minimal functionality and derives the required level of functionality from the Web server to which the end user requests to be connected. The Web server not only provides the co-ordinating function between databases

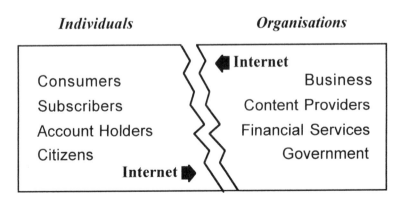

Fig. 7.1 Consumers and business.

containing HTML encoded information, but also can be linked to applications. In addition, it provides another useful purpose as a means for downloading applications, e.g. new versions of Web browsers, or files to be used with other desktop applications, e.g. Powerpoint or Excell files.

Whilst a large number of Web sites provide access to static content (i.e. HTML encoded information that does not change), a standard interface known as the Common Gateway Interface (CGI) provides one way for dynamic information to be included in Web pages. More specifically, CGI is a specification for transferring information between a Web Server and a CGI program. A CGI program can be written in any programming language, such as C, Visual Basic or Perl, and is designed to receive and return data that conforms to the CGI specification. When a Web browser displays an HTML page containing a form, frequently it is a CGI program that processes the data once it is submitted to the Web server. This is the basis of the popular Web forms capability described later in this chapter. In addition, with CGI, dynamic information can be extracted by an application from a database, the extracted information encoded in HTML and forwarded to the Web server for display by the Web browser.

The high level communication (running over TCP/IP) between Web browser and Web server uses the Hypertext Transfer Protocol (HTTP), which simply: establishes the connection, transports the request from the browser to the server, returns a response (a page) to the browser, and both browser and server disconnect, such that the transaction is ended. Each Web page has its own unique identity known as a Uniform Resource Locator (URL), which provides the powerful feature that enables "surfing" the Web to take place, by readily moving from page to page. Many organizations quote their URL in their promotional literature, and employees even include it on their business cards, usually using what is termed the home page, e.g. http://www.kingston.ac.uk/ as the starting point for exploring that particular Web site.

Another important development has been the ability to further extend the functionality of the Web page by embedding powerful scripting languages such as Java and ActiveX, which mean that documents now become both interactive and dynamic. The Java scripting language offers programming logic that allow mini-applications or "Java applets" to be invoked from within the Web page to perform functions such as data validation, calculations, animations, etc. The use of Java applets (or Active X controls) essentially lets users run computer programs through their Web browsers, and offers far more attractive screen displays, richer functional features, and provides a competitive advantage for those Web sites embracing the technology.

Intranets and Extranets

Acceptance of the Internet by the business world, particularly for electronic mail (E-mail), as well as access to information via the Web, has caused many organizations to consider applying this same model solely for internal usage. In this way, organizations are able to harness the Internet's "ease of use" and other benefits, yet avoid security issues that figure highly in the list of concerns with open

Internet access. Very simply, the term "Intranet" has evolved to describe the use of Internet technologies within an organization for enhancing connectivity and communications. Previously, this may have involved the use of proprietary LAN E-mail systems together with bulletin boards or textual databases tailored to the specific needs of the organization. By definition, establishing an Intranet means that it will be based upon open Internet standards, making it easier to purchase software, support users and extend its reach to trading partners at the appropriate time.

The infrastructure, where specific trading partners forming part of the extended enterprise are given selective access to the organization's Intranet, is known as an "Extranet". Providing entry to corporate information via an Extranet introduces security issues requiring action to be taken to restrict unauthorized access to specific applications and information (normally only made available to employees) using some or all the following measures:

- system passwords;
- router filtering;
- challenge/response authentication;
- firewall techniques.

The primary motivation to implement Intranets is to improve the flow and timely access to information within an organization, as well as to facilitate collaborative working on corporate projects. Use of Internet technologies offer cost savings over competing alternatives, as well as reducing the training time for implementation. One-to-many publishing applications can significantly reduce the cost of producing, printing, shipping and updating corporate information. Two-way transaction driven applications can improve information quality and provide a highly efficient alternative to paper-based business processes. Finally, many-to-many interaction facilitates the exchange of information between interested individuals, perhaps forming part of a newsgroup or workgroup.

Whilst an Intranet serves the internal organization, and the Extranet extends the capability to major trading partners, it is quite likely that at some point open access to the Internet will be required. At this stage the software "firewalls" mentioned above become even more critical in preventing access by many millions of Internet users to precious proprietary corporate information. Additional security is needed when transiting the Internet to "public" Web sites to enter sensitive information, or when sending a business transaction over the Internet to a business partner, via an E-mail attachment. These aspects are discussed in detail in Chapter 13.

Various Examples

GE's Intranet includes access to information sources such as, human resources, employee benefits, hot news, travel agency, GE values, internal training, ideas forum, their public site as well as access to the individual Intranets of the separate GE businesses.

Ford developed the Mondeo (the world car) by establishing a worldwide team, whereby, when one team slept another continued the work using common information sources, based upon an Intranet infrastructure.

Federal Express provide customers with browser-based access to their internal tracking system for shipment status enquires, which improves customer service, increases customer loyalty at reduced operational cost.

British Midland provides customers with on-line flight booking facilities using browser access that offers greater customer convenience at reduced costs.

Texas Instruments use Web Form-based EDI for low cost customer data entry, which is converted by a server into a standard format that can then be processed by their internal application.

CASE STUDY - BT

In the early 1990s, BT (British Telecommunications plc) began to suffer from chronic internal problems due to paper overload. This coincided with a period when BT's business was becoming global in character and the pace of business accelerating due to an increasingly competitive marketplace. The need to transmit information as well as support paper-based business processes resulted in major processing delays and rising costs. E-mail helped alleviate the situation, but only at the expense of major IT investments providing increased network and electronic storage media. Many electronic documents distributed as attachments were replicated and stored electronically many times over. This resulted in a Document Management System project being initiated in 1994.

In the same year, BT began large-scale experimentation with the Internet's World-Wide Web technology, and by early 1995 had concluded that this was the best means of improving internal access to information. In addition, the same browser technology could provide a consistent front end to many of internal applications, at the time each requiring their own different client software interface. A decision was taken to proceed with a full implementation of an Intranet and after 18 months the community of users reached over 60,000 (E-mail and Web access). BT senior management regard the Intranet as a business critical application that has major operational consequences for BT should it be unavailable for any reason. BT's 1995 business case for the Intranet projected an annual saving of £60 million, yet in its first year of full operation these savings rose to £305 million and have since grown to £663 million per annum, mainly due the productivity improvements so far achieved. BT's Intranet includes access to:

- Internal Directories
- Job Specific Pages
- Sales & Marketing Information
- Service Planning & Provisioning
- Fault Resolution
- Total Human Resource Support
- Facilities Management
- Voice/Data Integration
- Group Working
- Company News
- Executive Information Systems
- BT Policies
- Tracking Enquiries

The benefits cover increased speed of working, less paper, timely information, move from "push" to "pull" information mentality, less duplication, virtual/distributed team working and better morale. However, opening up the Internet connection from the Intranet can result in "cyber skiving", access to improper information and security issues, that require appropriate company policies and firm management direction.

CASE STUDY - TYSON FOOD

At Tyson Food the prime motivation for implementing an Intranet was to achieve efficiency improvements that would bring about internal cost reductions. As an example the company estimated that to publish each of its 50,000 staff with an employee reference manual on an annual basis could cost as much as £7 per manual. That is well over a quarter of a million pounds, just to distribute one document. Tyson Food also use their internal Web servers to publish company information by department, competitive analysis, etc.

Internet Commerce Evolution

Electronic commerce has been defined earlier as "any interaction between an organization and its trading community, undertaken in an electronic manner". Indeed, the term Internet commerce is coming to mean much the same thing, but implying the use of Internet technologies to govern the interaction between the trading parties.

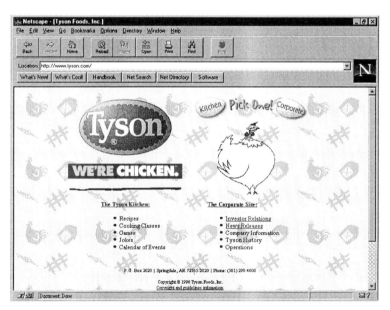

Fig. 7.2 http://www.tyson.com

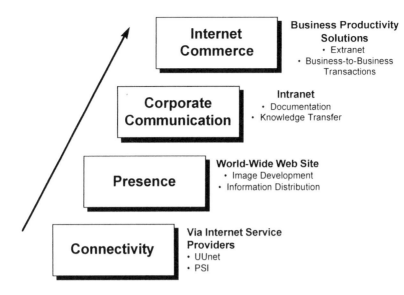

Fig. 7.3 Internet commerce evolution.

A pattern is emerging to illustrate how organizations start their involvement with the Internet and progressively extend this activity to conduct electronic commerce over it (Figs. 7.3 and 7.4). Frequently during the initial phase, connectivity is established using an Internet Service Provider (ISP). In this way, nominated employees are able to access the Internet's vast quantity of information, perhaps for research or competitive analysis purposes. The ISP connection also enables the corporate E-mail switch to be used to process incoming and outgoing Internet E-mail (SMTP/MIME based) between employees and external trading partners.

The next phase in the evolution is to establish a presence on the Internet by setting-up a "public" Web site, primarily as a marketing communications exercise to promote the image of the organization and make available "public" information such as products and services (see Fig. 7.2). Since the "public" Web site can be accessed by anyone with Internet access, it is usual to place this outside the corporate "firewall", either using a separate Web server or by renting space on the ISP's public Web server. The development of an external Web site, to provide information to potential customers and other interested parties in support of marketing or operational initiatives, is usually undertaken before the implementation of an Intranet.

In the next stage a decision is taken to set-up a corporate Web site for internal usage. This is not a trivial exercise, as it requires a culture change within the organization to support the free exchange of business information in electronic form and a complete rationalization of existing methods/processes used to support the current means of information dissemination. More importantly, procedures need to be put in place to ensure that information is continually maintained up to date, otherwise the Intranet is doomed to failure. This stage may herald a further rationalization of E-mail usage in the organization and a migration to a common

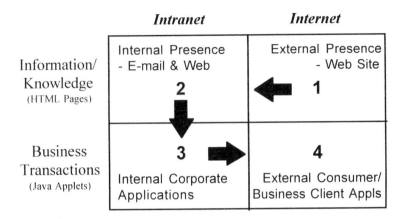

Fig. 7.4 Internet commerce evolution.

client/server E-mail environment. End users may be offered E-mail features that are integrated into their Web browsers and accessed via their desktop personal computer (e.g. Netscape Navigator or Microsoft Internet Explorer), or use a separate E-mail interface (e.g. Microsoft Outlook) that still has a Web browser "look and feel" about it.

An Intranet implementation also provides the opportunity to extend corporate legacy applications by offering a browser-based interface, that gives the same "look and feel" as normal Internet Web access. This is particularly well suited for an administrative support system, or where forms-based data entry is required, using the Web technologies described earlier. Other application examples include financial accounting, procurement and logistics applications, each providing a consistent interface to the end user.

The final phase in the Internet commerce evolution is described in the next section, where internal applications, including on-line ordering and quotations systems, are deployed (together with appropriate security measures) on the Internet for use by consumers, business customers and suppliers.

Electronic Marketplaces and the Web

Basic Model

The conventional way of conducting business tends to be centred around finding customers either by mailings, the telephone or face-to-face meetings, where the salesperson seeks to match the latent needs of the customer with the product/service from the supplier. This process implies the use of intermediaries such as wholesalers, agents and dealers, so that the broadest possible coverage can be achieved by the seller in reaching the business customer or home consumer.

Conducting commerce over the Internet introduces a fourth channel (in addition to mail, telephone and personal contact) for operating a business, and in doing so reverses roles by placing customers in the position to select suppliers from a very large number that are accessible via a Web browser, than by bringing the goods to them in the conventional model. This reversion of roles seems to indicate that the electronic marketplace model emerging on the Internet, as well within closed communities such as securities trading in the financial sector, is less like the seller "selling" and more like the buyer "buying". Another way of describing this phenomena is to think of it as an extension of the self-service purchasing trend that has emerged since the 1970s.

An electronic sales environment places fresh challenges on the seller, who can not reach out and touch the buyer, to create a compelling sales proposition at the point of sale, namely the computer screen. Internet Web technology, delivered via a browser, provides the medium to make this possible through its attractive presentation style, ease of use and sophisticated functionality using computer languages such as Java and Active-X. As described earlier, the tremendous success of the Web browser has caused many organizations to establish the Web browser as the "footprint" on the desktop, and thereby provide a consistent presentation interface to all their computer applications.

Business to Consumer (e-commerce)

Computer-based applications supporting electronic commerce initiatives are becoming progressively more critical to business success as the emphasis swings still further towards the customer and the emergence of electronic marketplaces. Electronic marketplaces allow the organization to establish an electronic pres-

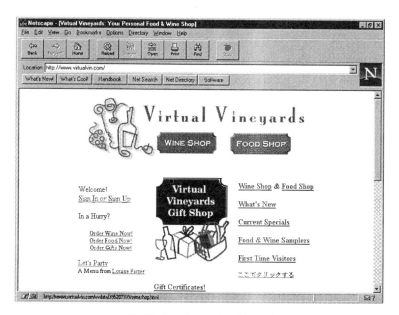

Fig. 7.5 http://www.virtualvin.com/

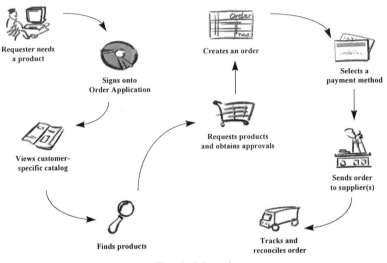

Fig. 7.6 Order cycle.

ence in an "electronic shopping mall" that its customers may prefer to use rather than conventional shopping. In this respect the "electronic shopping mall" becomes an important new source of orders, and must form an integral part of both the IT infrastructure and associated business processes. There are several success stories, including Virtual Vineyards who sold over £700,000 worth of wine in their first year of trading, all of which came from their Web site in the first month of usage, Daytona Go-Kart Racing, who picked up £48,000 of bookings from their Web site, and a group of ladies from the Orkney Islands, who marketed their hand knitted jumpers on the Internet and within a few weeks received 2000 orders (sufficient to keep the inhabitants of the Orkneys knitting for months).

Electronic marketplaces will have a major impact upon the supply chain, particularly in retailing, where for a manufacturer a high proportion of product cost lies in using a retailer to reach the marketplace. As it becomes feasible to reach the end customer in sufficient numbers using electronic marketplaces as an alternative to conventional retailing, then clearly elements in the supply chain can be eliminated, resulting in important cost savings and improved customer service (Fig. 7.6). A further significant evolution in the use of messaging and information management technologies is being predicted to create direct business to customer relationships, which naturally need to be factored into the organization's business processes.

Consumer interest in e-commerce is driven by a belief that existing goods are available at lower prices, new products and services add greater convenience and customer service is improved via "self-service". The Web's interactive capabilities, availability, and abundance of "live" information are all unique. Indeed, a consumer has extraordinary access to a wide range of sales materials, giving the buyer an unprecedented level of control in a sales situation, where there is virtually no pressure to purchase. As with most successful sales, it is necessary to reduce the consumer's perception of risk and uncertainty. In this respect, Web based sales are no different from any other type of sales, but the novelty of the Internet can only add to an underlying doubt that occurs to any buyer in an strange context. Removing this concern will be key to the success of electronic marketplaces in the future, helped by the development and deployment of cheap, easy to use presentation orientated services that are taken up by the consumer on a mass market basis.

The Internet is proving to be an interesting and useful experiment, but of the estimated 24 million users worldwide approximately 4% (but growing rapidly) are private customers, the rest being from the research or academic communities. In addition, they rather represent an elite as far as computing skills are concerned. Another success criteria for electronic marketplaces must be to minimize computing skills, perhaps through the adaptation of familiar devices around the home such as the television or the telephone. With the changing worldwide telecommunications regulatory regimes more services are being introduced into the home, typically through the new common carriers (NCC) such as Energis and Worldcom and, these are likely to play an important role in stimulating this new marketplace in the future.

CASE STUDY - *SLATE*

In Spring 1998 the online magazine *Slate* only became available to subscribers (approximately $20 per year or 40 cents per week) and both *Dow Jones* and *The Economist* are expected to follow this move by charging for their Web based editorial content. This illustrates a trend in the publishing industry to move from an environment where digital media has been made available at no cost, to gain experience and build communities of "readers", to a new age of "click and pay". Many market research organizations (e.g. Gartner and Forrester Research) already have mechanisms in place to charge for reports that are accessible by subscribing to their services. However, the success of magazines such as *Slate* ultimately depends upon a culture change both in accepting digital news magazines/papers in place of their hard-copy equivalents, and a willingness to pay.

Business to Business (E-commerce)

While forecasts vary between the different market watchers, today's business purchases over the Internet is estimated at around £550 million rising to over £45 billion by the turn of the millennium. This is believed to be a much larger marketplace than the business to consumer marketplace. Interest from organizations in E-commerce is being driven by a belief that it can increase revenues, whilst lowering operating/capital costs and in its present stage of evolution can offer new opportunities for competitive advantage.

In an earlier chapter, the trend away from a traditional EDI approach, using an EDI value added network (EDI VAN) service, to the use of direct connections between trading partners over the Internet was described. Several EDI VAN

Internet & Business-to-Business

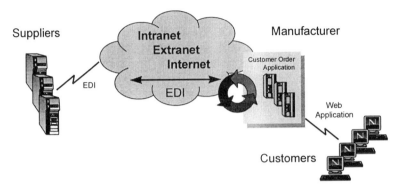

Fig. 7.7 External selling and supply chain.

services have introduced new services that allow smaller trading partners to take fullest advantage of the Internet. TradeWeb from GE Information Services is an example of such a service that is based upon EDI Web forms, and which allows subscribers to this service to become members of the world's largest trading community of more than 40,000 trading partners. All the traditional back-end EDI requirements, such as mapping and translation services, are hidden and are transparent to the subscriber, who simply work with a Web browser which displays a business document as a form for completion. Services such as TradeWeb are expected to penetrate a significant proportion of the EDI market, and contributed to extending traditional EDI beyond the larger organizations to Small/ Medium Enterprises (SME).

In the current competitive business environment, organizations are looking to extend and improve the way in which their business customers interact with them. This is giving rise to a new range of Internet centric applications which increase customer intimacy through the use of information technology. Many organizations have developed computer-based applications that allow customers via remote PC workstations to place customer orders and track status. Figure 7.7 illustrates a new breed of sophisticated application build upon Web technology, that can behave as a front end to the customer ordering module of an enterprise resource planning systems such as SAP, Oracle Applications or Baan.

The business process used by a customer is similar that shown in Fig. 7.6 and illustrates the "self-service" characteristics described earlier. The key components are the use of a simple Web browser environment, intuitive functions to minimize training, catalogue based to speed-up product choice and a shopping cart analogy for comfort and ease of use. An organization operating this type of sales front, could in theory be a virtual wholesaler, where orders are sent electronically to suppliers using EDI and it is the supplier that maintains the inventory and actually fulfils the customer order.

Internet & Business-to-Business

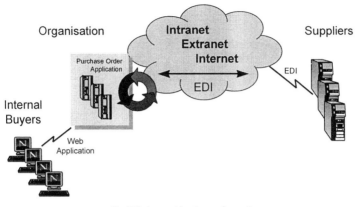

Fig. 7.8 Internal buying and sourcing.

A variant on direct customer ordering using a "selling"application is external purchase ordering using a "buying" application. This arises from internal buying requests that are raised within an organization, and results in the placement of purchase orders upon suppliers. Many organizations have realized that improvements in their internal buying process, coupled with direct links to suppliers, offers great scope for cost reductions, by more effective purchasing, yet increasing customer service to the internal buyer. Preferred suppliers are usually chosen on the basis of product availability, best price and delivery performance, and provide the information to populate the internal buying application. Direct EDI links to these suppliers may also exist, as shown in Fig. 7.8, once internal approval has been given for the purchase order to be placed.

In late 1996, several leading Fortune 500 organizations within the US, together with their key suppliers, formed the Internet Purchasing Roundtable. Their goal was to provide access to easy-to-use, open, standards based Internet purchasing solutions for the procurement of high-volume, low cost indirect goods and services. Through discussion and close consultation with both technology providers and financial institutions, the Roundtable participants developed the Open Buying on the Internet (OBI) standard. This is based upon current Internet standards including SSL for secure communications, HTML as the user interface, SET for credit card transactions and X.509 for digital certificates. Once the initial version of the OBI standard had been completed, a nonprofit making users' consortium was created. Whilst the OBI Consortium aims to improve and promote use of the standard, it is also keen to develop other standards and share business practices for conducting business-to-business Internet commerce. GE is a member of the OBI Consortium, and the following case study provides a practical example of "business to business" purchasing using the Internet.

CASE STUDY - GE LIGHTING

GE Lighting, one of General Electric (US) 12 businesses, has its corporate headquarters in Ohio, USA where the global sourcing team is responsible for co-ordinating the centralized sourcing for GE Lighting's 45 plants worldwide. By mid-1995 GE Lighting had over 25,000 global suppliers, and whilst the sourcing system had been re-developed in recent years, the system was still too labour and cost intensive to support the demands of the business, particularly the evolving global operations.

GE Lighting classified its purchases into five discrete segments consisting of: finished products, raw materials, packaging, MRO (maintenance, repair and overhaul) and indirect/machine parts, the latter representing high volume purchases of low vale products and the most troublesome of the five sourcing segments. The buying characteristics of the indirect/machine parts had remained the same: low value products purchased in high volumes. The 300–500 requisitions received each day represented over £26 million in annual purchases. The buying process was entirely manual, involving the accompanying blueprints to be requested from storage, transported, photographed, etc., before being sent out to suppliers with Request For Quotation (RFQ). Because the process was so time consuming, sourcing were unable to send out RFQs to more than two or three suppliers at a time. By the time the suppliers' RFQ responses were received , bids evaluated and business awarded, some 18 to 23 total days had elapsed, leaving sourcing with little opportunity to focus upon cost-cutting activities.

During the early 1990s, as GE Lighting moved to consolidate its purchasing in Ohio, USA, several process improvements were made, including the implementation of a Purchasing Management System (PMS) for electronic purchase order generation. While this eased the purchasing process, it still relied heavily upon manual

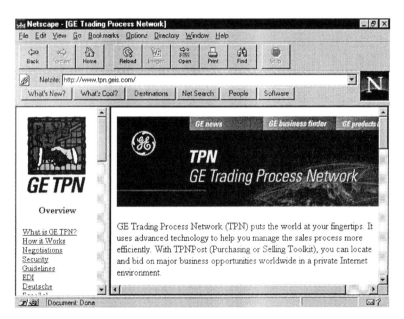

Fig. 7.9 GE Trading Partner Network.

intervention for the preparation and shipment of blueprints. Because of the high cost associated with purchasing of indirect/machine parts, it was decided that further process improvements were necessary. This resulted in an automated purchase order capability being added to PMS, which covered part requisition that met certain purchasing criteria and sourced from the same qualified supplier. This had the effect of reducing requisition processing by approximately 60%. The next step occurred in 1994 when a quote module was to added to PMS.

By 1994, GE Lighting had also implemented EDI for the electronic exchange of purchase orders and material releases with suppliers, and had decided to outsource some of its more manual tasks. At this same time, a company was retained to manage and begin the task of electronically scanning each blueprint to focus upon the very costly bottleneck that remained. In 1995, GE Lighting started to experiment with an electronic bidding solution and, whilst not a success, the experience convinced them that the principle was right and important for future growth.

Having seen progressive enhancements to its PMS system, use of purchase order to Fax, automated purchase orders, EDI, quote system using Fax and a chance to see suppliers fight in an electronic bidding marketplace, the time was right to make a   significant process change in search of productivity gains. GE Lighting decided to proceed with the implementation of a fully automated sourcing system based upon Internet technologies. Having reviewed the option of implementing such a capability themselves, GE Lighting decided that it would be too costly and joined forces with GE Information Services to base its future vision on TPNPost, an Internet based electronic RFQ distribution and bid receipt system, part of the GE Trading Partner Network.

GE Lighting decided to start with the purchasing of indirect/machine parts on a pilot basis, before implementation of TPNPost across all categories. Implementation started in 1996, and soon demonstrated many of the expected improvements. Initially working off-line, GE Lighting simply select the requisition system on their desktop PC, create a customized requisition project and choose the suppliers from the community supplier database to receive the RFQ. They then connect to a Web

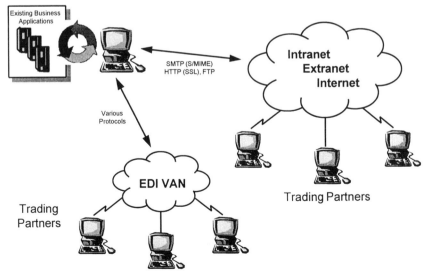

Fig. 7.10 EDI using the Internet.

server that hosts the Trading Partner Network and post the bid package to the selected suppliers around the world, the system automatically retrieving the electronic blueprints and attaching them to the electronic requisition form. All data is encrypted and entirely secure. The RFQ process that used to take more than seven days is now reduced to less than two hours. Suppliers are notified of incoming RFQs by either E-mail or Fax, and use a Web browser to access the RFQ information and respond within seven days. GE Lighting then retrieve the bids, evaluate them and award the business the same day. The entire requisition process that used to take between 18–23 days (and sometimes a lot longer) is now reduced by well over 50%, and combined with overall cost savings of between 5% and 20%, has made this a highly successful project for GE Lighting.

EDI over the Internet

Whilst the Internet is reliable, low-cost, highly accessible and is technically mature, there have been some concerns relating to its use for EDI. These concerns revolve primarily around security, message tracking, audit trials and authentication. Indeed, the need for encryption, necessary to achieve high levels of message security, is of a general nature and not specific to the Internet. However these security issues are rapidly being solved by using a collection of new standards and agreements on best practices. This aspect will be covered in greater detail in later chapters, but suffice to say at this stage that the Internet Engineering Task Force created the Electronic Data Interchange Internet Integration (EDIINT) Work Group to address these concerns. EDIINT provides a set of recommendations and guidelines that combine existing EDI standards with the Internet protocol suite to ensure that EDI transactions can be exchanged in a secure manner between trading partners.

The Internet provides an opportunity for smaller businesses to become EDI enabled and to realize the benefits only afforded to larger organizations in the past. In part, this is made possible by lower costs of getting started, as well as lower on-going running costs when compared to traditional EDI that involves the use of EDI VAN services. In addition, the Internet provides access to an on-line global marketplace which operates on a 24 hour basis, with millions of customers and thousands of products and services. It provides organizations with new, more cost effective and time efficient means of working with customers, suppliers and development partners; plus, the opportunity to purchase products and services from new supply sources in other parts of the world that hitherto they would not have thought of approaching.

Internet commerce together with EDI will enable companies to:

- shorten procurement cycles through use of on-line catalogues, ordering and payment;
- cut costs on both stock and manufactured parts through competitive bidding;
- reduce development cycles and accelerate time-to-market through collaborative engineering and product implementation;
- gain access to worldwide markets at a fraction of traditional costs;
- ensure product, marketing information and prices are readily accessible.

In simple terms, EDI transactions may be sent over the Internet using the same transport mechanism used for E-mail but with extensions to cover the rather special requirements of EDI described above. A variant on this may be to simply send an EDI Interchange (envelope with a number of EDI transactions contained within it) as a file using FTP (the Internet service for file transfer) over a "secure" link. Or finally, to use Internet Web browser technology to display a form that can be completed by the sender and, in due course, be translated into an EDI standard for onward transmission to the recipient. Again, at this stage it is important to focus upon the principles, as further details can be found later in the book.

EDI Web Forms

EDI is still not widely used by many Small/Medium Enterprises (SMEs), but remains in the domain of larger organizations that have the resources to address the many issues associated with a successful EDI implementation. For a SME with scarce resources, EDI requires the purchase of particular software packages, as well as developing an understanding of EDI standards. It is primarily these technical complexities and associated costs that have deterred SMEs from using EDI, and it is estimated that less than 1% of all businesses in Europe use EDI. Even for large retail organizations with their developed EDI supplier communities, there are frequently smaller companies that fall into the SME category that still request paper or Fax based business transactions.

Internet commerce offers an opportunity for SMEs to participate in EDI, using a Web forms capability, without the complexities mentioned above. This is achieved by using the Web browser to present the end user with forms that closely resemble their paper-based equivalents of a purchase order, invoice, etc. The necessary information is submitted to the Web server and processed using a CGI program to create a file that is input directly into an EDI mapper/translator. The translation process creates an EDI transaction in the required EDI standard for onward transmission to the trading partner. This EDI Web forms capability is offered by most of the valued added network service providers as a low priced option that is integrated with their EDI VAN Service. Work has also started to agree standard layouts for the EDI Web forms, since a supplier participating in several supply chains does not wish to be working with completely different forms for each retailer.

Several other Web related initiatives are underway, focused at considerably simplifying the EDI process for SMEs, particularly the mapping effort, where the use of the XML language (richer functionality than SGML) appears to be a natural fit for EDI and is receiving a good deal of attention. The objective is for smaller organizations to use Web technology to openly exchange structured business transactions in a secure and meaningful manner, but with reduced emphasis upon a separate EDI mapper/translation function.

Security

Naturally, conducting electronic commerce over the Internet has to be completely secure, and above all else, this has represented one fundamental reason that has kept both consumers and business users away, a perception of a non-secure environment. Much has been achieved to address this issue, which is described in a later chapter. In respect of EDI, CommerceNet, an industry association launched in 1994 and based in California to promote Internet commerce, recently announced that a number of software vendors had successfully completed formal interoperability testing that demonstrated the secure exchange of EDI transactions over the Internet. These interoperability tests are based upon the Internet Engineering Task Force EDIINT Workgroup recommendations for secure EDI over the Internet. The 14 tests included successful exchange of digital certificates, signed messages, encrypted messages and signed receipts (non-repudiation of receipts) for EDI and general electronic commerce data over the Internet. Since products supporting secure EDI over the Internet are now available, these, coupled with the pent up demand for additional ways for smaller organizations to improve competitiveness, are likely to fuel a dramatic increase in Internet commerce.

8. *Business Strategies for Electronic Commerce*

Extended Enterprise

Organizations are continuing to extend their use of IT in support of new business processes which not only affect internal sharing of information, but impact on the electronic exchange of information and business transactions with their trading partners. In the past, conducting business electronically referred exclusively to the use of Electronic Data Interchange (EDI) for the exchange of transactions such as purchase orders and invoices with trading partners. However, the world has changed – new ways, *electronic* ways, of conducting *commerce* between companies have resulted in a much wider adoption of messaging and information management technologies than just EDI. However, to be successful, organizations need to develop appropriate business strategies for electronic commerce that direct internal resources appropriately, ensure consistency with corporate goals, serve to strengthen business relationships, and secure that elusive competitive advantage.

The interest in and growth of electronic commerce is primarily due to the highly competitive environment that has evolved during the 1990s, and the resulting search for new forms of market differentiation. This has engendered a new style of organizational leadership, capable of facilitating the necessary corporate transformation for these new business opportunities to be fully exploited. It is this determined search for new innovative ways in which to drive the organization forwards, towards achieving new levels of performance, that brings about the identification of process improvements. For those organizations competing in growing and enlarged marketplaces, getting it right means significant and worthwhile rewards, including survival. However, for some organizations there is an added urgency for change when competing against new entrants, naturally drawn into growing marketplaces. This is because many of the new entrants are not constrained by the same legacy systems and organizational structures as are the traditional players.

While the scope still exists to secure internally focused efficiency improvements, invariably it is the external processes involving the extended enterprise that can really make a huge difference. Senior management recognize the importance of sound business practices, under-pinned using electronic commerce technologies, in reducing costs, improving customer service and in remaining competitive. The traditional "win-loose" relationship that has existed between supplier and manufacture/retailer illustrates the dramatic manner in which

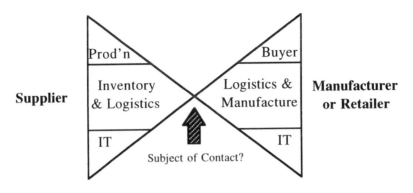

Fig. 8.1 Traditional organizational model.

attitudes are changing (Fig. 8.1). In the past, once all of the basic product factors had been satisfied, the primary subject of contact came down to price/delivery, with the assumption that there was a winner and a loser as an outcome of the negotiations. Several of the more innovative retailers have seen that by a greater integration of their supply chains, a "win-win" relationship can be established with their suppliers. As closer long-term strategic relationships become established, there is a greater willingness to exchange information and co-operate more fully, resulting in efficiency and productivity improvements that can be shared between both parties. This is referred to as the *strategic* or *extended enterprise model* (Fig. 8.2). In the retail sector, supply chains compete, not retailers. This is in recognition of the vital contribution towards the success of the retailer, made by how well business processes along the whole of the supply chain are managed.

In summary, there is a growing realization that profitably producing and selling a top quality product (or service) at the best possible market price is not solely a function of the organization alone, but is increasingly dependent upon the effectiveness with which the extended enterprise is managed. Therefore, business process improvements need to extend beyond organizational boundaries to

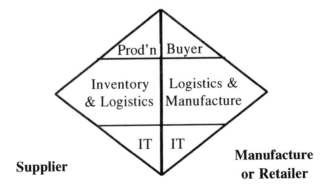

Fig. 8.1 Strategic or extended enterprise model.

envelop and integrate with those of their trading partners. Electronic commerce strategies play a critical role in making this possible.

Strategic Management and Information Technology

Ultimately, corporate business strategy captures the vision of the chief executive and his or her top management team to provide the overall direction for an organization to follow, and hopefully satisfy the various interests of its stakeholders. The desired corporate direction will usually be set down in some form of mission statement, from which a series of specific objectives can be derived for onward communication throughout the organization. Finally, each manager, assigned the responsibility for specific objectives, is tasked with developing action plans that describe the activities necessary for their attainment. For some organizations, the dynamics of the marketplace coupled with short-term pressures frustrate attempts to develop business strategy. However, Information Technology (IT) strategies, and more specifically, the development of strategies for electronic commerce, need to be business led if the outcome for the organization is to be successful.

Having created a business strategy (the process is outside the scope of this book), it is important to appreciate the key contribution that IT can make in the achievement of the specific objectives set out in the strategy. Indeed, IT's contribution to adding value to a product or service can be such that new opportunities to broaden or change the scope of business activities emerge. IT applications that have the ability to impact on the business in this way are termed "strategic computer based applications", or simply "strategic applications". Naturally, every organization would like to believe that included in their application development portfolio are applications of this nature, not just contributing to improved efficiency and productivity, but really capable of making a significant competitive difference. However, in most cases few organizations formally evaluate the potential business outcome of IT applications in these terms, and certainly do not go back after the implementation to measure whether the stated goals were in fact achieved. In developing corporate strategies for electronic commerce, it is worth considering some of the tools and thinking that are available to assist organizations in both the alignment of business and IT strategy, and to identify those strategic applications that should be given the greatest level of support and priority by top management.

Information Systems Development Framework

How do organizations integrate business and IT strategies? What is the process used to identify and develop strategic computer-based applications? While considerable attention needs to be given to the way in which change is successfully introduced within organizations, as far as the IT contribution is concerned, experience shows that there are generally four main stages in the information systems development framework (Fig. 8.3).

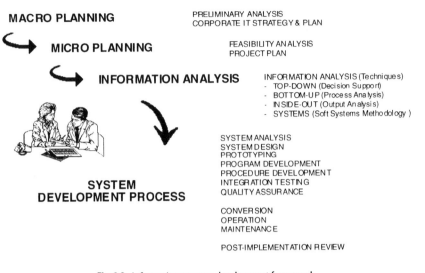

MACRO PLANNING

PRELIMINARY ANALYSIS
CORPORATE IT STRATEGY & PLAN

MICRO PLANNING

FEASIBILITY ANALYSIS
PROJECT PLAN

INFORMATION ANALYSIS

INFORMATION ANALYSIS (Techniques)
- TOP-DOWN (Decision Support)
- BOTTOM-UP (Process Analysis)
- INSIDE-OUT (Output Analysis)
- SYSTEMS (Soft Systems Methodology)

**SYSTEM
DEVELOPMENT PROCESS**

SYSTEM ANALYSIS
SYSTEM DESIGN
PROTOTYPING
PROGRAM DEVELOPMENT
PROCEDURE DEVELOPMENT
INTEGRATION TESTING
QUALITY ASSURANCE

CONVERSION
OPERATION
MAINTENANCE

POST-IMPLEMENTATION REVIEW

Fig. 8.3 Information systems development framework.

Macro Planning

This stage ensures that a good understanding of the business requirement exists, including the outcomes required. Together with close involvement of the management team, it sets out to define the likely application development portfolio to support the achievement of the business strategy. Since many of the internal stakeholders carry organizational baggage and are not viewed as being impartial, external business consultants are frequently used during the initial stages of macro planning. If the situation is not so well defined, information analysis techniques can be used to gain a clear view of what is required. These techniques include several approaches: top-down (decision analysis), bottom-up (process analysis), inside-out (output analysis) and systems (soft systems methodology). This initial information gathering exercise is frequently referred to as a "preliminary analysis".

As described earlier, strategic applications are those few IT projects forming part of the portfolio that are critical to the organization in achieving its business objectives. Ultimately, the corporate IT strategy should be a direct by-product of this process, bringing together those resources required over time to meet the business requirements. Any actions arising from specific electronic commerce initiatives are complex, since these initiatives tend to serve both the needs of the organization and its extended organization (used here to describe suppliers, customers, freight forwarders, manufacturers, etc.). While IT serves to blur organizational boundaries, great care has to be given to ways in which the extended organization can be influenced to co-operate in the process of change. Achieving successful change within the same organization can be tough, but between different organizations it presents fresh challenges. The ultimate success of an electronic commerce project will be heavily dependent upon how well this co-operation has been established, as well as ensuring that a realistic level of resourcing by the parties involved. The organization and its extended organization create what is also referred to as the "virtual" organization, which may include outsourced functions (perhaps, not considered to be part of the core business).

Micro Planning

This step involves moving into the individual feasibility and planning phase for each specific project forming part of the application development portfolio. If the outcome of the feasibility study is successful, then a deliverable from this phase will be an outline project plan, which becomes the basis for allocating resources, namely money and people. It is quite likely that at this stage, sufficient information about the project becomes available to start classifying the project in terms of its strategic contribution to the business, and in consequence, its relative priority. A later section examines the potential tools available to assist in its prioritization relative to other projects competing for resources, also known as the "rack and stack" process.

Information Analysis

The information analysis phase is important in defining the information requirements that the computer-based application needs to satisfy, and starts to re-shape the associated business processes. A number of techniques exist that can help increase the successful outcome of a project, and indeed, Business Process Re-engineering (BPR) as a change initiative uses many of these same techniques. A *top-down* (decision analysis) approach is best used for those organizations where a clear direction has been established by top management, and that a reasonable level of stability in the business environment exists. In the context of the specific business process identified for improvement, an exercise involving successive managerial layers of organization seeks to understand the tasks/goals to be achieved, and the supporting information requirements. Indeed, there are many similar methodologies that have been developed by the main management consultancies based upon this analytical approach.

Bottom-up (process analysis) exercises tend to be used by those organizations where management leadership or communication is lacking, and no clear top level business objectives appear to exist. This could be due to rapid changes taking place in the business environment which makes a formal goal setting process exceedingly difficult. However, a bottom-up approach can be used to test whether there are similar information requirements to those already derived from a top-down approach, resulting from working upwards through the organization. It typically involves the evaluation of information obtained via surveys and audits. While very effective for specific departments/functions, there is a tendency with this approach to achieve sub-optimal solutions of a localized nature, since the information gathering exercise does not fully recognize that processes run across an organization.

The *inside-out* (output analysis) is really taking a very innovative and creative approach, thinking outside the box and testing ideas through prototyping or small scale trials.

Finally, *soft systems methodology* is used to simplify a complex environment and better understand the relationships between the people involved and their interaction with the various business processes that form a human activity system. When used in its own right, such an approach rarely defines information requirements. "Soft" systems methodologies are sometimes used as a front-end exercise for one of the "harder" methodologies described above.

Some of these same techniques can be used in a slightly modified manner to assist when undertaking a preliminary analysis, conducted during the macro planning phase.

System Development Process

This final activity concerns the execution phase, where functional users and IT professionals are formed into project teams to work closely together in the detailed design, development and implementation of the computer-based applications. If the functional requirement is best satisfied by an Enterprise Resource Planning (ERP) system such as SAP, Oracle Applications or Baan, then the development effort is better described as customization. Successful implementations not only require that applications meet the original specifications, but also that they readily form an integral part of new business processes.

Approaches to the Integration of Business and IT Strategies

Ideally, the outcome of a business led approach to the determination of IT strategy ensures that the focus of business process improvement is directly related to the establishment of an IT infrastructure that makes the achievement of business goals possible. With the continuing pressure on containing costs and a finite budget for IT spend, it is crucial that funding goes to those projects that will really make a difference to the organization's ability to achieve competitive advantage. As described earlier, projects classified in this way usually form part of the "strategic applications portfolio". For the reasons discussed in earlier chapters, such projects are increasingly assisting organizations to conduct their commercial business activities in new ways, through the use of electronic commerce concepts.

However, since electronic commerce still represents a relatively new concept for many organizations, what are the approaches/methodologies that have been developed to assist organizations identify and prioritize projects in this way? The following summary is not exhaustive, but should serve as an overview and basis for further reading on approaches for assessing the potential strategic contribution projects can make, and their resulting prioritization within the application development portfolio (Fig. 8.4).

Value Chain
This approach, developed by Porter (1985), examines the activities performed within an organization to establish how they interact, and where improvements could be a source of competitive advantage. Porter's earlier work also examined

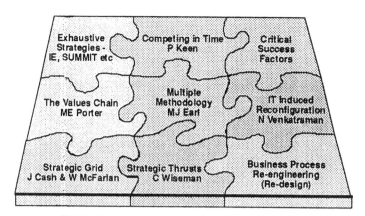

Fig. 8.4 Approaches to integrating business and IT strategies.

the competitive forces within an industry, and can be used as a basis for determining ways in which IT can be used by an organization to destabilize the equilibrium of a marketplace in its favour. The value chain of an organization and its extended organization can be mapped together to identify areas of potential process improvement. For example, using IT to closely couple the information flows between the inbound logistics function of the manufacturer and the outbound logistics function of the supplier, materials/parts can be called off with certainty of delivery, thereby achieving considerable savings in stock holdings and warehouse space. Such an approach is more generally known as "Just in Time" ordering within the manufacturing sector and "Quick Response" ordering in the retail sector. Aside from the obvious savings achieved by closely coupling information systems in this way, a strategic and important new relationship becomes formed between the organization and its extended organization. The value chain model helps identify those areas where IT can make an additional contribution, in both adding value to products/services, and eliminating those activities that add cost, but no value.

Multiple Methodology

This approach by Earl (1989) is based upon the supposition that no single methodology to determine the strategic application portfolio will work, and therefore several need to be applied in parallel to serve as counterchecks between one another. Earl suggests that such a complex approach is necessary because of the inherent complexity of organizations. In practice, it is necessary for an organization to perform:

● top-down analysis (decision support) to clarify business needs in IT terms;
● bottom-up analysis (process analysis) by evaluating current IT systems;
● inside-out analysis (output analysis) to apply innovative thinking to identify new strategic opportunities made possible by IT.

The resultant areas identified for process improvement form candidates for the strategic applications portfolio.

Strategic Grid

Developed by McFarlan (1984), the strategic grid considers the contribution made by IT to the business now and into the future by reference to four categories of IT development, in which candidates for the strategic application portfolio are allocated. Ideally, those applications located in the strategic segment of the grid and critical for future success should receive the highest priority for funding. A simple but effective model to assist management integrate business and IT strategies.

Strategic Thrusts

Originally described by Rackoff (1985) and extended by Wiseman (1985), this approach is based upon the belief that organizations determine a focus or target for their strategic intentions such as suppliers, customers or competitors. Having decided the target, it is necessary to decide upon the alternative strategic thrusts, either offensive or defensive, that can be used by the organization to achieve its business goals. Wiseman identifies five alternative thrusts, including differentiation, cost, innovation, growth and alliance, to form a matrix. This will result in an evaluation of current business processes supporting the strategic thrust to be adopted by the organization, and identify new areas of process improvement to be supported by IT.

IT induced Business Reconfiguration

Work by Nolan (1974, revised 1979) provided the first framework to track the stages through which organizations pass, as they apply IT in support of the business. A main assertion of his work was the simple, but obvious, fact that these stages represent an evolution for an organization, and to proceed forward implied having successfully completed the previous stage. Ten years later, following the personal computer revolution, that heralded increased IT innovation and still greater organizational dependence upon IT, Venkatraman (1990) identified new stages for the organization to proceed through. Venkatraman suggests that the focus for organizations in the 1990s is upon the recognition and exploitation of IT, and his model recognizes the importance of business process re-design, the virtual or networked organization and potential for organizations to redefine the scope of their business. Above all, to proceed through these stages implies major organizational transformation, and many organizations have not yet started on this path. In practical terms, this model provides a checklist and challenge for management, to assess whether they are taking the fullest advantage of IT, and poses the question as to whether the necessary organizational changes are in hand to make this possible. Some researchers have taken Venkatraman's model as a basis for defining "strategic applications" as being "those systems that have the potential to make a significant impact on the organization's business strategy by enabling change in the nature and/or conduct of the organization's business."

Integration Summary

Alignment of business and IT strategy for an organization is a complex issue, and the above section represents just some of the thinking behind it. However, it is an important issue to grasp if the fullest benefits of electronic commerce are to be realized, not only contributing to survival in a turbulent business environment, but to establish the foundations for long-term growth through competitive differentiation. The very nature of electronic commerce and its implied close working relationship within a trading community means that many different organizations need to share the same vision of how their business can be re-shaped using IT. For some organizations it maybe less about achieving competitive advantage and more about avoiding competitive disadvantage, since the use of such techniques are rapidly becoming the norm in specific industry sectors.

Electronic Commerce Strategy Development

There are a number of key factors that an organization needs to consider when developing a strategy towards electronic commerce.

Business Driven

Electronic commerce initiatives are business led activities, with an implicit acceptance of process change and often involving the use of high-energy change initiatives, such as Business Process Redesign (BPR). It is important to be able to describe project outcomes in terms that can attract top management's commitment, such as: order to remittance time reduced from 30 days to 12 hours; stocks and work in progress slashed by 50%; customer service improvement up five points on the index, etc. Electronic commerce initiatives cannot succeed on their own, and are usually accompanied by fundamental changes in the way in which the business is run. Management must set the agenda, determine the goals, ensure they are aggressive but realistic, and navigate the organization through the resultant turmoil of change.

Customer Focus

Will the resultant new electronic commerce supported business processes make it easier for the organization to target its potential customers, so they know more about its products and services? While the need exists to provide more and more information to customers, the real urgency is to make it easier for buyers to do business with their selected seller/supplier. Customers can easily be lost, despite satisfaction with the product or service supplied, due to inaccurate or cumbersome administration of the relationship between buyer and seller, such as inaccurate invoicing. Telephone companies that traditionally are bad in providing meaningful usage details to support their invoices, have been exploiting this inadequacy to achieve competitive advantage and improve customer satisfaction. Data communications and networks form the foundation of electronic commerce, and together with messaging technology provide a unique mix to develop innovative customer-focused applications that strengthen buyer and seller relationships.

The Extended Organization

When looking to establish an electronic commerce environment, organizations should seek to be in a position to exert influence over their business/trading partners that make up the extended enterprise. However, to be successful, this needs to be undertaken in a supportive manner so that an open, boundaryless culture is created, where the mutual inter-dependence of all parties is seen as beneficial, rather than a disadvantage. Today, many large/medium sized organizations and their trading partners are clustered in trading communities of common interest, based upon the extended enterprise concept. The next millennium is likely to see dramatic changes in the way in which organizations trade with one another, as these closed communities give way to open electronic trading, involving greater participation from Small to Medium Enterprises (SME).

Remaining Flexible

The old maxim "the only constant thing in life is change" seems more relevant today than at any time in corporate history. The key to future success is not only creating a culture that accepts and relishes change, but also in developing electronic commerce strategies that ensure the organization is not "locked-in" to specific information technologies or software products. One way to remain flexible is to adopt an open systems strategy for the acquisition of software, or when deciding upon corporate IT standards. Failure to retain such future flexibility in being able to rapidly respond to new business requirements will be damaging.

Integration

Most organizations already have a heavy investment in legacy IT applications that cannot immediately be replaced, and often have to exist alongside new business processes for some years. Care should be taken to integrate, as far as possible, legacy applications within new electronic commerce initiatives. This type of activity is particularly resource intensive, and is best organized using cross functional teams with the detailed knowledge of existing processes and empowered by management to make it happen.

Information and Knowledge

While data has a cost, information has a value, providing the incentive to develop an information resource/warehouse culture within the organization. It is important to establish ways in which information can be freely made available to those that can make the optimum use of it, in decision making and improving customer service. Will new electronic commerce initiatives create important new information sources that can be exploited for business benefit? Knowledge is the most enduring asset of any organization, and the scarce and precious knowledge held by employees needs to be incorporated into new applications. With the conflicting demands for improved customer service and yet reduced costs, organizations are deploying more knowledge-based systems to provide customers with the assistance they seek. Internet Web technology is particularly suited to this type of application, helping customers through problem identification and resolution.

Key Supporting IT Strategies

Electronic commerce and business communications play a critical role in the day-to-day operation of many organizations, internally through corporate-wide E-mail/information services, and externally for the exchange of business transactions with trading partners. While business strategy provides the starting point for process improvement, this section examines some of the key trends that need to be factored into the development of IT strategy.

Thick architecture

As described earlier in this chapter, business and IT strategies need to be closely linked if new electronic commerce initiatives are to fulfil their promise. Figure 8.5 illustrates the interplay between the two, and highlights the importance of developing IT strategies throughout the lower four layers, which reduce the choice of conventions, rules and standards in use throughout an organization. When making the choices, there is a strong preference for the use of open standards or those that have a strong market acceptance. The resultant "thick" IT architecture makes it easier to focus on the real use of technology, rather than worrying about interfacing issues.

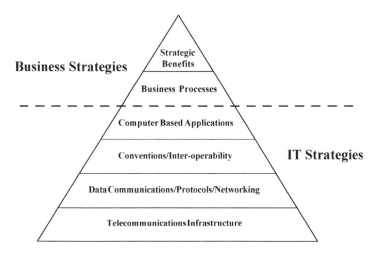

Fig. 8.5 The six layer model.

Application Software Packages

The marked swing away from custom IT developments, with their inherent problems of rising costs and extended time-scales, has resulted in the increased popularity of application software packages, particularly Enterprise Resource Planning (ERP) systems. Such packages include a number of separate modules that, once implemented, form a fully integrated system. In an environment where speed is important, custom development has proved to be too risky for many organizations, whereas the implementation of software packages appears to have a better track record. Use of well proven software packages, based upon "best of breed" business practice, and a growing knowledge base to assist with implementations, is rightly viewed as attracting a lower risk of failure.

Networking

Electronic commerce and business communications is based upon data communications and networks, yet in many organizations the required skill-set to support this vital element in the IT strategy is lacking. On a national and global basis, telecommunications services continue to expand at an impressive rate, bringing further improvements in cost performance. This is critical to the deployment of a new breed of electronic commerce applications that require greater bandwidths than in the past. While there are many backbone network services based upon the ITU-T X.25 standard, it is clear that the business world is favouring the use of Internet technologies, and TCP/IP has emerged as the network protocol of choice.

Electronic Messaging

For many organizations there is no choice in their use of electronic messaging technologies, the business community to which they belong mandates its use, and having such a capability is a condition of doing business. There are primarily two types of electronic messaging technologies in use – those that concern people and those that concern applications. At the desktop the trend appears to be towards a reduction in the variety of E-mail systems in use, with a growing preference to choose a single E-mail package from one of the popular vendors for deployment throughout the organization. However, for most external traffic the trend is to provide gateways that support the Internet's SMTP/MIME standard. These gateways usually also provide support for any incoming X.400 traffic.

EDI is considered to be at the heart of many electronic commerce applications, and organizations need to possess the necessary knowledge of EDI standards, particularly UN/EDIFACT in Europe and ANSI ASC X12 in North America. Since newer developments combine the principles of EDI with Web-based applications, knowledge of document mark-up languages (HTML and XML) is also becoming an important skill-set.

Desktop Strategy

A personal computer on every desktop is increasingly becoming the norm for many organizations, and with it the need to develop a desktop strategy. There are several factors that make this urgent, including: the need to reduce software variety and thereby minimize support costs; deliver end user training to increase productivity; eliminate illegal copies of software; introduce virus protection; provide back-up facilities to safeguard important corporate data, etc. With increased access at the desktop to the Internet, management policies need to be developed, so employees clearly understand what are acceptable corporate practices for its use. This concerns access to undesirable material published on the Web, and non-productive use of resources (cyber-skiving) during business hours. Figure 8.6 illustrates a simplistic view of desktop integration with a growing presence of LAN facilities (printing and file storage), office packages (word processing, presentations, spreadsheets, etc.), communications (E-mail and calendaring) and information access (Lotus Notes, Microsoft Exchange and Internet Web).

Security

This represents one of the key concerns that organizations voice when asked about their plans for electronic commerce, particularly sending E-mail messages and EDI business transactions over the Internet. This is a factor why some organizations have opted in the short-term, to continue their use of EDI VAN services. However, much progress has been made with the introduction of "firewall" technologies to protect corporate Intranets from unwanted access. In addition, many of the standards are now in place to conduct secure messaging over the Internet, and products are becoming available that implement these open, Internet-based standards. Organizations need to assess the security risk involved in their electronic commerce activities and introduce the appropriate security measures to combat them.

Key Supporting IT Strategies Summary

This section has highlighted some of the important IT trends that need to be factored into the development of IT strategy. By their nature, they have a special relevance to the successful roll-out of an electronic commerce programme.

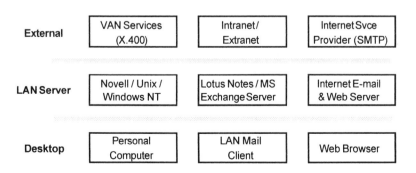

Fig. 8.6 Desktop strategies.

Indeed, throughout this chapter the critical inter-dependence between business and IT strategies has been stressed. For some organizations this requires the development of a new working relationship between the business managers and IT professionals, built upon a greater understanding and empathy from both sides.

Part C

9. *Open Systems*

Introduction

The adoption by organizations of an open systems strategy as an element in their overall corporate IT strategy can bring significant benefits in reduced cost and insulation from expensive conversion projects in the future as IT requirements change in response to new business needs.

The extent of open systems usage across the IT spectrum is far-reaching, and work still needs to be undertaken to establish a complete and stable standards environment, particularly following the increasing popularity of open standards based Internet technologies. For the purpose of this chapter, the term "open systems" not only refers to those information technologies using international standards developed by recognized standards bodies (ITU and ISO), but also to those evolved through the Internet Engineering Task Force Request For Comments (RFC) standardization process.

Many of the larger organizations are tending increasingly to include reference to the requirement for standards conformance when purchasing new products and services. Indeed, governments as a major IT user have gathered together a collection of OSI standards referred to as Government OSI protocols, or GOSIPS, which are used in their procurement process. Awareness amongst small to medium enterprises of open systems *per se* is still relatively low, except where the competitive nature of open standards-based technologies creates a highly competitive marketplace in which IT prices continue to fall.

In addition, the Commission of the European Community (CEC) continues to press hard for the harmonization and liberalization of the European telecommunications marketplace, aimed at encouraging competition which it believes will be of benefit to the consumer. The CEC 1987 Telecommunications Green Paper (followed by Part 2 in 1995) has had a very profound effect on the structure of telecommunication services within Europe. The result in many European countries has been the break-up of the Post Telegraph & Telecommunications (PTT) monopolies into postal and telecommunications services, and to encourage value added network service companies in the private sector to compete with the newly established private telecommunications operators. The CEC has also turned its attention to the non-basic services marketplace, and has issued an Open Network Provision directive that seeks to simplify the conditions of access to the network infrastructure for service providers. The CEC policy that has directed Europe towards the establishment of a lively and competitive telecommunications environment has been firmly based upon open standards, particularly those international standards developed by the ITU and ISO organizations.

For senior management, IT represents an increasingly important asset of the organization both in sustaining the tactical operation of the business and in providing new ways to create competitive advantage. Flexibility and speed are features of an open systems environment that become critical when new applications are required to respond rapidly to new and changing business goals. To successfully introduce open systems within an organization requires strong user support, including the inevitable user champion and a comprehensive IT strategy built upon the business direction of the organization. The IT strategy needs to describe in detail how open systems are to be introduced into the organization, and indeed, how they will contribute to meeting the business requirements. Such an approach underpins the "thick" IT architecture described in Chapter 3, which also forms part of the IT strategy statement.

The last two decades have seen an ever increasing availability of information technology within organizations as well as for private individuals. Undoubtedly, one of the factors contributing to the pace of IT adoption has been wide ranging support for the development of "standards" across the whole of the computing environment. For many reasons, which will be explored in this chapter, the process of establishing standards continues to be an ongoing activity. There are many stakeholders in the standardization process, but two important developments have taken place in recent years: first, a realization that in the case of information technology, national and even regional standards have little relevance, and because of the growth in the global information society, adoption of international standards is critically important; second, there has been a greater insistence by the user community on the procurement of products and services that are open standards based. The procedure, originally started by government procurement agencies centred around Open Systems Interconnection (OSI), has now spread to the private sector, but is not exclusive to OSI-based standards.

Worldwide Problem

IT has continued to face major criticisms with claims from its critics of its relative immaturity as a business function – frequently illustrated by major projects with excessive delays in implementation, and costing considerably more than the original forecast. In some situations, the dynamics of the business environment and marketplace has moved at such a pace that applications are almost obsolete as they go live. Even with a stable business environment, the pace of technology itself has meant that, for some major projects on implementation, better technology solutions exist to fulfil the original business requirement. Finally, with the proliferation of different technologies and their associated application development environments, the maintenance task for the IT function has grown considerably; limiting the resources that can be applied to new applications. Indeed, the ongoing annual costs attributable to the operation, support and enhancements of a system

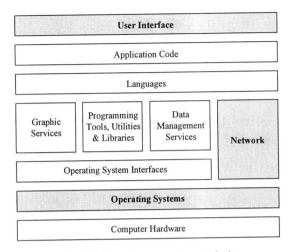

Figure 9.1 Scope for open system standards.

can vary anything between 40–55% of the original development cost. By limiting the variety of information technologies in use within an organization, whether by a preferred supplier strategy or through the use of open standards-based technologies, ongoing costs can be reduced.

In some studies it has been found that application backlogs mean that delays of anything from six to fifteen months are typical before work can start on new applications. Perhaps of more concern to business, in an increasingly competitive business environment, is the lost opportunity cost of achieving the business benefits attributable to major new IT developments/applications.

The conclusion of many IT professionals and users alike is that IT needs to be made a lot easier to use, with a greater consistency on which the technology is based, and yet allowing sufficient scope for competitiveness and innovation from suppliers. Expressed another way, being able to reduce the number of alternatives, and hopefully focus upon the best features and functionality from each, should make technology choice easier. Assuming open access to IT standards and a growing market demand, the number of suppliers offering these open system products and services is likely to increase. This is confirmed by industry trends showing open systems as representing one of the fastest growing sectors of the computer marketplace, having annual growth rates in excess of 25%, much higher than the industry norm. The user community is clearly demanding and implementing open systems.

The term "open systems" is therefore closely allied to standards across the whole computing environment that are not owned by any single business, but rather controlled by a body, promoting their usage and offering ready access to the detailed specifications.

It is not surprising that the adoption of an open systems policy for an organization can be a vitally important element of its IT strategy. Since it has the potential to reduce development times, deliver the business benefits a lot sooner, as well as providing the flexibility to catering for future requirements.

Why Use Standards?

Other factors impacting on attitudes towards standards have arisen as a result of the tremendous impact that telecommunications has had upon the nature of applications now available, which both extend and integrate a company's operation. In Europe, post and telecommunications services have traditionally been run by public administrations, frequently existing as a monopoly as far as the provision of the basic services is concerned. With the establishment of the ubiquitous public switched telephone network, which links telephone subscribers around the world, these administrations soon realized the potential for offering data communication services that would be capable of linking computers together in a similar ubiquitous fashion as the telephone service.

Work started in the mid 1970s to develop a series of recommendations for public data networks based upon the International Organization for Standardization (ISO) Open System Interconnection (ISO) model. In addition to the development of these standards, initiated and supported by the international telecommunications authorities, there was a progressive movement by government to liberalize and re-regulate some of the services operated by the monopolies. This has also had a major impact on attitudes towards telecommunications standards in a business environment demanding greater flows of electronic business communications.

Unfortunately, not everyone views standards in a positive manner, and some preconceptions have been built up. It has been widely believed that the application of standards can frequently result in sub-optimal performance of systems. Clearly, with any specific performance intensive application, where this is absolutely fundamental to its success, this may indeed be the case. In such situations it may well be desirable to take an alternative proprietary approach as opposed to the adoption of standards, but this should be kept to a minimum. To a large extent, the real contribution that open system standards can make to an organization lies more in the longer term, and offers major strategic impact as well as operational benefits.

In the early 1990s the Department of Social Security (DSS) was undergoing radical changes in its organization and management structure as part of the UK Government's "Next Steps" programme. Several executive agencies emerged, designed to introduce a business approach within the DSS. Since that time, IT has become key to the DSS's operations, and is regarded as a vital element in the process of change.

The adoption of an open systems strategy has made an important contribution to the upgrading of the DSS's IT services, and resulted in wide ranging benefits, including:

- considerable improvements in administrative efficiency,
- better quality of service to customers,
- enhanced support to staff,
- cost savings achieved through freedom of choice,
- long-term cost efficiency through reduced requirement for specialist in-house skills.

Other well known organizations in the UK that have advocated the use of open systems and have been able to substantiate the benefits through well documented case studies include the Automobile Association, British Aerospace plc, Glaxo, London Metropolitan Police, National Westminster Bank plc and the Yorkshire Building Society.

It is clear that the introduction of the IBM PC in the early 1980s based upon an operating system environment from Microsoft and the *de facto* standard that this created, has in real terms meant progressive price reductions owing to increased competition. This has given birth to a new industry of IBM PC clones, each capable of supporting and running IBM PC compatible software.

The opportunity to reduce IT costs and achieve greater purchasing flexibility has been a major driving force behind a number of organizations embracing open systems as part of their business strategy. While it is true to say that in some sectors there are wide variations in the application of open systems, there is a continuing trend to reduce the variety of such systems and, at the same time, to enforce conformance by users. This is often seen in the request for tenders that are received by suppliers, which increasingly have a section listing the standards to which the supplier is expected to conform. Clearly, while there is still a significant amount of work to be undertaken on the wide ranging nature of IT standards, including operating systems, networking, document formats, etc., considerable progress has been achieved, resulting in a fair measure of agreement on standards and profiles for the more important IT functions. These developments continue to make a significant contribution to the increasing use of electronic business communications.

Many suppliers have seized the opportunity provided by open systems to use it as a proactive method of product and service differentiation and, as a result, have produced a number of tools that assist in the migration from proprietary systems to open systems. Finally, with the growing dependence of business upon information technology for its day-to-day operation, security continues to be a key and important issue, since breaches of security can have a severe impact, indeed threaten the continuing existence of a company in some industries. In this context there is no doubt that open systems embrace a wide range of security measures, certainly no less than those in the proprietary environment.

What are Standards?

Standards in themselves are not computer programs, languages, products or packages, but often represent the results of extensive work by a large number of people extending over long periods of time. Typically, the standardization model shows us that this process starts with the innovator or the provider of technology working closely under the auspices of a recognized standards authority. Ideally, a point will be reached where the recommendations are embraced by a recognized standards authority in the form of a ratified standard, which can then be expected by users to be embodied into products and services. There is yet another model of open systems standards activity used within the Internet, which will also be discussed later as another important process contributing to standards development activities.

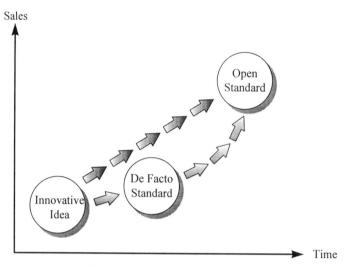

Fig. 9.2 *De facto* and *de jure* standards.

Often there is a differentiation seen between what is known as industry (*de facto*) and public/open standards (*de jure*), and it is not always the case that one transitions directly from one to the other. As an example, System Network Architecture (SNA) from IBM is an accepted *de facto* industry standard (proprietary) which has failed to achieve a public standards status when compared to the Open System Interconnection (OSI) architecture. Equally Ethernet, originally developed by Xerox, has achieved great popularity as the preferred LAN media access method and has evolved to become both an IEEE and ISO standard.

De Jure Standards Makers

There are two important voluntary standards organizations, the ISO (International Organization for Standardization) and the International Electrotechnical Commission (IEC), both of which have a wide brief within their respective areas of interest. However, each of them has a specific interest in the area of IT standards, and in 1987 established a joint technical committee known as JTC1 which combined their interest for the setting of IT standards. A further organization important as far as IT standards is concerned is the International Telecommunications Union (ITU), which is a formal treaty organization run under the auspices of the United Nations. It has complete responsibility as far as telecommunications affairs are concerned, and establishes the international regulatory standards which are administered by governments throughout the world.

One of its committees, the ITU Telecommunications Standardization Sector (ITU-T), formerly known as the International Telegraph and Telephone Consultative Committee (CCITT), is of great importance as far as information technology is concerned, particularly in its development of recommendations for data communications networks and terminal equipment. In itself the ITU-T is not a standards organization as such, but through its study groups it prepares recommendations which are adopted by its members, and forms the basis of inputs to the ISO/IEC standards making progress.

At a European level there are several bodies that contribute to the development of IT standards, such as the European Telecommunications Standards Institute (ETSI) based in France. In addition, the Comite Européen de Normalization (CEN – the European equivalent of ISO) and Comite Européen de Normalization Electrotechnique (CENELEC – the European equivalent to IEC), while tending to deal with non-IT standardization, are active in the telecommunications area. ETSI was created in response to the Green Paper of the CEC, and is an open forum bringing together the most highly qualified experts in Europe to work on common problems in the telecommunications sector. ETIS's task is to set uniform telecommunications standards for Europe which will be adopted by each EEC member state, thus linking national networks, services and ensuring interoperability of equipment.

In addition, at a European level the European Workshop for Open Systems (EWOS) works under the direction of ETSI on open system standardization matters. EWOS holds a distinct place within the European standization process, and is primarily entrusted to draft functional standards proposals, also known as profiles, needed for open systems. Profiles define combinations of OSI base standards in which options, subsets and parameters are specified, in order to obtain a desired functionality. Profiles are an important and necessary step towards interoperability.

The results of the pre-standardization activities of EWOS are laid down in EWOS Documents (ED) which serve as input proposals to the European standardization bodies CEN, CENELEC and ETSI for adoption as European pre-standards (ENVs) or standards (ENs). EWOS is open to all interested parties, and includes amongst its members manufacturers, vendors, software developers, service providers, users, research centres, etc.

To complete the picture, each country has its own standards bodies which take the international or European standards and create national standards as appropriate. Examples of national bodies would be British Standards Institute (BSI), Deutsches Institute fur Normung (DIN) and Association Francaise de Normalization (AFNOR). As stated earlier, these European and national standards organizations are increasingly being seen as less relevant for IT standardization, where the demand is for international standards.

Internet Standards Process

However, another important open systems standardization activity concerns Internet standards, where typically an innovative idea that receives the necessary level of Internet Engineering Task Force (IETF) support will move directly to become an open *de jure* standard. The organizational process that steers the Internet is entirely structured around voluntary membership, and is based upon the Internet Society, which has in excess of 100 member organizations and approximately 4000 individual members in over 105 countries. It appoints a council known as the Internet Architecture Board (IAB) that regularly approves standards and allocates resources such as address space. Another important component in the process is the Internet Engineering Task Force (IETF), which is broken into some 70 Working Groups and co-ordinated by the Internet Engineering Steering Group (IESG). Once an initial proposal has been made, a Working Group (WG) charter and chairperson(s) will be approved by the IESG and IAB. The WG produces and debates Internet drafts, known as Requests For Comments (RFC) by E-mail and meetings that proceed through various stages of experimental, proposed, draft before becoming an Internet standard with a unique RFC number assigned. The Internet has been highly successful, largely through the way in which it has been able to evolve its standards in a pragmatic, practical, global and speedy manner. Indeed, those engaged in the evolution of Internet-based standards tend to view the evolution of international standards by the ITU and ISO as being undertaken at a much more leisurely pace.

What are Open Systems?

Building upon the concepts introduced earlier in this chapter, open systems can be considered as those systems and components which provide true vendor independence for users, achieved by conformance to open standards in all aspects of the computing environment. The reference to vendor independence clearly impacts upon competitiveness and the choice that is available, whilst conformance to standards can protect the user's investment in applications development. Since standards for open systems are freely available to any vendor, this makes multi-sourcing of IT components by the user possible. Finally, the reference to all aspects of the computing environment illustrates the wide scope of open systems, and is an indication of the scale of effort involved in gaining the necessary agreement on standards.

In the open systems environment, all communications protocols, application programming interfaces and other peripheral interfaces are specified and made public with the aim of achieving connectivity across differing hardware platforms, and thereby offering hardware independence, portable software and lower costs. Netscape uses the term "crossware" to describe the process of delivering software which operates across a wide range of hardware platforms without any significant difference in functionality.

With a simple computer application accessed by dumb or intelligent terminals linked directly into a host computer, the main concerns for IT management are the portability of the software onto different computers, often referred to as an "alternative processing platform". This could simply arise due to the existence of computing equipment from different suppliers within the organization, or the desire to change the supplier. Another consideration for IT management might be the need to cater for increased traffic volumes, whereby the application can be transferred to more powerful equipment without changes to the application: ideally the existing computing environment should be scaleable to respond to changing capacity demands. In the next stage, when different computers are connected

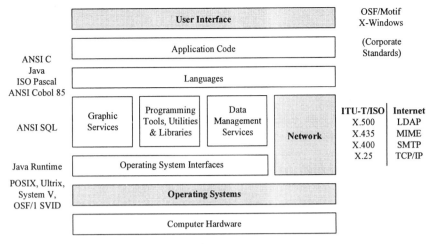

Fig. 9.3 Examples of open systems components.

together, known as "networking", the prime consideration is to ensure that a data communications path can be successfully established between them. The ability to readily establish interconnectivity is an important step, but merely a step in being able to ensure that applications running on the different computers can co-operate with one another, thereby providing true inter-working. As an example, the transfer of a file from one computer to another implies co-operation between both systems.

Earlier, reference was made to the scope of the standard setting process for open systems, which covers all aspects of the computing environment (Fig. 9.3), and consideration will now be given to two specific aspects, namely operating systems and networking. A later chapter examines in more detail standards in electronic commerce using a similar analogy of the computing environment.

Operating Systems

At the centre of open systems implementation is the operating system environment, and in particular UNIX. This operating system was originally developed by AT&T laboratories in the late 1960s using a Digital Equipment Corporation processing platform, and primarily to satisfy an internal requirement to achieve software portability. However, since that time, with its increasing use by academic and research institutions around the world, and from the mid 1980s by the business community, it has become the symbol of the move towards open systems.

UNIX was envisaged as an operating system that would facilitate the connection of different types of computers, and as such was designed from the outset with networking in mind. A network architecture was developed known as TCP/IP (Transmission Control Program/Internet Protocol) which, alongside the OSI X.25 architecture, provides the basis for open systems data communication. In a networking environment consisting of UNIX platforms, communication services such as electronic mail and file transfer are considered as basic features required by the user environment. These additional service elements were created by the early users of the UNIX and TCP/IP; to be further developed by academic and research communities as their networks were progressively interconnected to form the Internet. Suppliers of equipment running the UNIX operating system typically distribute the TCP/IP data communications suite of programs with their software.

Since AT&T only offered UNIX to academic institutions in the 1970s, UNIX and the C programming language were ported to many hardware platforms and enhanced by the research community along the way. An added benefit of the academic world's involvement with UNIX was the opportunity that this provided for a wide number of students to gain knowledge of UNIX and C, which later benefited the UNIX marketplace once UNIX had become more widely available. However, one major disadvantage with UNIX has been the proliferation of different versions, which have emerged primarily because it was written in a high level language and was thus easy to modify. While most versions of UNIX have similar functions, the fact is that no one version has been established as a standard. There are several UNIX clone operating systems that are freely available from the Internet, including NetBSD and Linux, each offering a high level of compatibility with the IEEE POSIX standard (see the next section).

UNIX Standards Makers

In 1987 AT&T, together with Sun Microsystems, announced their intention to co-operate on the release of all future UNIX versions of System V. Other vendors who had derived their own versions primarily from System V saw this as an attempt to take over the future direction of UNIX, and naturally were unhappy with this position. In 1988, a group known as the Open Systems Foundation (OSF) was formed, one of its aims being to create vendor independent versions of UNIX primarily as a response to the move by AT&T and Sun Microsystems (who at a later point formed UNIX International (UI), a further grouping of suppliers).

In addition, it is worth mentioning the role of the IEEE, well known for its work particularly in the area of local area networks where its recommendations now form part of the OSI standards. In the area of UNIX, the IEEE produced a series of standards for a Portable Operating System Interface for UNIX (POSIX), which whilst not specifying the operating system itself, is nonetheless an important contributor to addressing the portability requirement.

Another group that emerged in the 1980s was the X/Open Company, founded in 1984 by a group of vendors, which continues to be a very active forum for open systems through its Common Applications Environment (CAE), and indeed, which does not limit itself purely to UNIX. It has its own board of directors, and includes among its membership representatives from both OSF and UI (until UI was wound up in 1993, when its membership of X/Open ceased). Its membership has expanded to include a large number of commercial and government users, as well as independent software development organizations.

X/Open appears to be a less politically motivated organization than OSF or indeed UI was; and seeks to integrate international and *de facto* standard specifications into its Common Applications Environment. These specifications assist vendors to build open system based products; and vendors whose products conform to these specifications may enter into a trademark license agreement and carry the X/Open brand. This brand is now widely used as an open systems procurement tool by commercial and government organizations worldwide.

The positioning and competition created between UI and OSF in the late 1980s did not help the harmonization efforts of the standards makers to resolve the differences between their respective UNIX implementations, namely UI UNIX SVID V.4 and OSF 1.1, to bring stability to this important and central area of open systems. There has been pressure for both organizations to use the X/Open Portability Guide (XPG) and POSIX as the middle ground for their implementations. As the XPG goes well beyond "portability", X/Open no longer refers to it in these terms, but simply describes it as the XPG, or the X/Open Common Application Environment Specifications.

The period that followed in the early 1990s saw a rapid increase in the open systems interest from the user community, together with a widening of its scope to include such topics as Application Program Interfaces (API), transaction processing and user friendliness. When in 1993 UNIX SVID development moved out of the control of AT&T to Novell Laboratories, seemingly to provide a more independent basis for future development, UI ceased to exist.

Rationalization continued in 1994, when Novell transferred the UNIX brand to X/Open, and in 1996 the Open Group was formed from the merger of X/Open and the OSF. Spec 1170 was the working name for what has become the Single UNIX Specification. The Single UNIX Specification is a comprehensive set of operating system-related API specifications adopted by X/Open as the single specification definition for UNIX systems, conformance to which is required for the use of the UNIX trade mark.

Networking

In the business environment of the late 1990s, no computer system exists in isolation, but needs to communicate with other parts of the organization, and therefore frequently forms part of a corporate backbone network. Among the popular network architectures still in use are *de facto* industry standards dominated by IBM's SNA and DEC's DECNET, both proprietary in nature. However, TCP/IP, which ships with a range of operating systems including Unix and Windows NT, is becoming the network protocol of choice for the business community, used for both local and wide area networking. TCP/IP is a mature network protocol used for many years as the basis for the Internet, and continues to see development in support of its increased use on a global basis. Strangely, while strongly supported by governmental agencies in Europe and by telecommunications operators around the world, the OSI network protocol X.25 seems to be destined to be eclipsed by TCP/IPs or will merely to provide the physical layer alongside Ethernet to deliver TCP/IP.

Clearly, the ability to disseminate information to where it is required in the organization has great value, and permits the introduction of new business processes hitherto not thought possible. Networking is the mechanism that allows this to happen, and brings with it some mysteries that even the most seasoned IT professionals would admit that they do not fully understand. In view of its importance to making electronic commerce and business communications a reality, the next chapter presents a layman's guide to the subject.

New Meaning for Open Systems

The term "open systems" was originally associated with information technologies based upon international standards, developed by recognized standards bodies, notably the ITU and ISO. However, resulting from the ever-increasing popularity of Internet technologies, this situation has now changed. Open Internet based standards developed under the supervision of the Internet Engineering Task Force and their RFC standardization process, are now considered to be included within the term "open systems".

Microsoft's domination of the personal computer desktop environment has established *de facto* industry standards for operating systems and applications software, which are of a proprietary nature and exist outside the "open systems" movement.

10. *Communications Fundamentals*

Introduction

The development of telecommunications technologies as a branch of IT has made it possible to develop exciting new applications needed to support the Information Society. Yet despite this growing dependence upon telecommunications, appreciation of its capabilities as well as the basic principles on which is based appear to be lacking amongst users and even amongst some seasoned IT professionals.

Networking is essentially concerned with two phases: first, the connection; and secondly, the communication or interworking. The telephone provides a good analogy, where a connection is established once a number is dialled and the receiver is picked up. At this point, communication or interworking can occur by users speaking at each end of the telephone line. The purpose of the call is analogous to an application, where an empathy or co-operation is required between both parties if full communications are to be successful.

Different rules or protocols exist that are tailored to different telecommunications requirements, such as networking within a building to communications over large distances, as well as satisfying the need for differing speeds. In this context it is helpful for users to have an appreciation of the rules covering the more popular network architectures of OSI and TCP/IP.

Electronic business communications and the evolving world of electronic commerce is inherently about the use of an information technology known as telecommunications, used alongside more traditional computing techniques. Personal computers provide a wide range of facilities for the user in their ability to create and process information, but frequently this is just one part of a business process involving another person or application often located in some other geographic location. Telecommunications provides the bridge between these two environments and significantly enriches the value of the information exchanged. For many organizations these capabilities offer significant new ways to run their business, indeed in some sectors such as financial services and travel it would be impossible to offer the types of services by any other means. Telecommunications technology has provided the possibility for business scope and goals to be re-defined.

The benefits that telecommunications brings are not only restricted to the larger organization, but in the longer-term will have a major impact to the home consumer providing a range of new services, from home banking, leisure services including videos on demand, computer games, video phones, home shopping, directory services, tele-working, etc. Several initiatives are well underway in North America, Europe and Japan to make possible this movement to what is termed the "information society" which requires a number of elements to come together. One critical element is establishing the infrastructure or information highways that can support much greater telecommunications traffic volumes than at present. This involves the re-cabling of whole countries using fibre optic technology, as well as developing techniques that allow greater traffic volumes to be sent over the existing copper cable still in extensive use between switching centres and the consumer, often referred to as the "local loop". Even with twisted pair copper cable, high speeds can be achieved between 10/100 Mbps (mega bits per second). Agreement is needed upon the basic services that will be offered over this infrastructure providing the containers within which information can be transported, and finally, the information content itself based upon the nature of the application services to be offered. This is a simplistic view and does not address some of the human issues of how some these new services will be accepted. However, for organizations the decision to use electronic business communications is becoming no longer a choice, but mandated by the business community in which they operate as the means of conducting business, in much the same way that the telephone and facsimile has become.

While it is clear that organizations and home consumers are experiencing a growing exposure to telecommunications-based applications and services, this appears to be an area where knowledge is most lacking. This chapter is designed to help the reader gain a basic understanding of telecommunications, not as an expert, but at least to heighten their awareness of the underlying concepts on which this technology is based and provide a basis for sensible discussion with telecommunications specialists.

Computer Communications

For simplicity, in the rest of this chapter the prefix "tele" (derived from the Greek meaning at a distance) will be dropped and "communications" (meaning to transfer or exchange) will be used.

In common with other areas of IT, the greatest problem about understanding computer communications is grasping the basic concepts, which is made more difficult by the jargon that gets introduced. Take heart, since even some computer people avoid communications and networking because they do not fully understand it. In the IT context a network is created once two or more computers are connected together and configured in such a way that communications can take place between them. This could be at one geographic location such as an office where a number of microcomputers are connected together to form a Local Area Network (LAN); or the linking of several host computers within or across country boundaries to form a Wide Area Network (WAN).

The critical point to remember is that communications or networking happens in basically two stages – the connection and the communication. The communication is sometimes called interworking; everything else is just a complication of this basic concept. Unfortunately, the semantics are such that the use of word "communication" tends to imply a specific function, whilst "communications" typically is used describe the whole process, which can be confusing.

Connection is about providing the path to move digits around; communication is about adding meaning to the zeros and the ones being moved about. To be clear, when people refer to "connecting a DEC VAX to an HP9000" they probably do not really mean "connect", but mean that the two computers can interwork? If zeros and ones are moved between them, they are connected, even if neither end understands the other, but this is probably not what is required. Frequently, a good deal of discussion concerns the connection itself, and the rules and conventions that need to be respected by both machines for this to happen, e.g. X.25 rather than the use made of the connection once it is established, such as transferring a file. Therefore, it is perfectly correct to refer to running file transfer over X.25; the important point here is the degree of co-operation between the two computers, since running two different file transfer systems would not achieve the required level of interworking and communications would fail.

Signalling techniques involve:

● transmission of signals from the PC is achieved by electrical voltage pulses (digital);
● this digital information is binary, and therefore has only two possible states, either 0 or 1;
● these states are represented by different voltage levels;
● a combination of pulses (bits – either 0 or 1) represent a character.

The Telephone Analogy

Taking the analogy of the Public Switched Telephone Network (PSTN) to speak to someone in France from the USA simply requires the 'phone to be picked up in the USA and the number dialled. Clearly, lots of standards are in place (switching signals, voltage levels, disconnect signals, etc.) between the world's telephone companies to ensure that the signals dialled and sent out by the 'phone result in a phone ringing somewhere in France. Even more standards ensure that when the person in France picks up the 'phone, the 'phone stops ringing, the ringing tone stops in the ear piece and cost charging starts. So far this whole process is about establishing a connection and, if it worked successfully, voices would be passed between USA and France, and vice versa. This is connection, the ability to move sound around. If this were computers and not people, then zeros and ones would be moving around.

But there could still be a problem if one person is only speaking English and the other is only speaking French – then it is impossible to communicate, although a connection has been established. Communication has failed. It probably would not be much good complaining to the telephone company that the 'phone does not work. This simple analogy of using the telephone network suggests that the process is broken down into a series of tasks, according to a hierarchy, with a check and balance as the connection is established and communication takes place, with a similar process in reverse as eventually the conversation is completed.

Transferring a File

Exactly the same situation applies to computers where a high level of co-operation is necessary to ensure successful connection and communication between them. In the transfer of a file between two computers, some of the typical tasks to be performed would be:

- The originating system must inform the network of the identity of the desired destination system.
- The originating system must determine that the destination system is prepared to receive data.
- The file transfer application on the originating system must determine that the file management on the destination system is prepared to accept and store the file from this particular user.
- If the file formats used on the two systems are incompatible, one of the two systems must perform a format translation.

Since the last two tasks can be readily performed by a single function, it appears that only three functions are required to implement a simple file transfer application. To summarize the reasons for having the three separate functions, first, the file transfer function contains all the logic that is unique to the file transfer application, such as password security, file commands and the files to be transmitted. These files and commands need to be transmitted reliably; a similar reliability

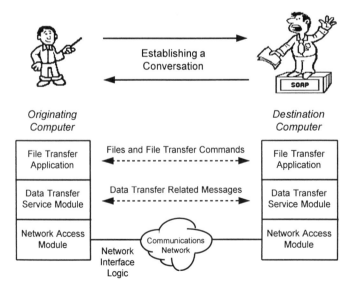

Fig. 10.1 Transferring a file.

requirements arises in a number of different applications, including electronic messaging. Therefore, this reliability requirements can be met by a separate communication service function that can be used by a wide range of different applications.

The communication service function ensures that the two computers are active and ready for data transfer and keeps track of the data being exchanged to assure delivery. Because these tasks are independent of the network used, the process for actually dealing with the network is separated into a network access function. In this way if the network is changed, only the network access function is affected. Back to the earlier example of "running file transfer over X.25." It is of course possible to run the same file transfer application over a range of different network access functions, including TCP/IP (together with a physical layer usually provided by Ethernet or Token Ring).

Network Architectures

From the above, it is apparent that rather than a single function, a structured set of functions arranged in some hierarchy performs the connection and communication process; this structure is frequently referred to as the communications or network architecture. Indeed, as computer vendors realized the potential of communications as a means of selling more equipment, there was a natural tendency to introduce proprietary (belonging to that vendor) network architectures. Some examples of these include IBM's System Network Architecture (SNA) and Digital Equipment's DEC Network Architecture (DECNET).

In general terms communications involves three prime elements, namely networks, computers and applications, which equate to what has been previously described as connection, communication (or interworking) and co-operation, respectively. Co-operation is a new term characterizing a higher level of understanding needed between applications, which in most instances can be considered to be outside the network architecture. In consequence, it is not surprising that within this hierarchy, communications is broken into two relatively independent functions or layers with a third layer concerned with the application itself. With some generic applications such as file transfer, electronic messaging and

Communications	*IT Function*	*Service Performed*
Co-operation ➡	Application ➡	Interoperability
Communication ➡	Computers ➡	Interworking
Connection ➡	Network ➡	Interconnectivity

Fig. 10.2 Networks, computers and applications.

directory services, it is possible include a large part of these functions within the network architecture, more specifically in what is termed the "application layer". This relieves the applications programmer of work, and means that it is only necessary for them to understand the generic interface over which data will be exchanged and focus in detail upon the end user application.

The differing network architectures referred to earlier add further divisions to these three basic layers.

Communications and Standards

Clearly, two computers from the same vendor are unlikely to respect the same structured set of functions, often referred to as interfaces and protocols, needed for communications to take place between them. Attempts to connect a computer from a different vendor supporting a different network architecture are unlikely to succeed without some additional work to map or gateway between the two environments. This can be considered as beneficial to the larger vendor, since it locks the customer into the vendors technology. During the 1980s there was an increasing resistance to this type of situation, resulting in the open systems movement, strongly supported by governments and the user community. As an example, the fortunes of IBM which was largely based upon proprietary IBM technology, has received a battering, resulting in some fundamental changes in IBM's technology strategy. While open systems applies across the whole computing environment (as described in the previous chapter), this section primarily relates to open systems within a telecommunications context. Ideally, irrespective of the vendor, computers should be able to communicate with one another if they support the same open network architecture. In practice, there are two network architectures that are considered as open, each with different origins described more fully in the earlier chapter on open systems – that based upon the Open Systems Interconnection (OSI) model (Fig. 10.3), and the other, TCP/IP, originally developed for the US Department of Defence and used within the Internet.

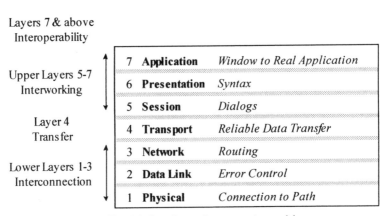

Fig. 10.3 Open System Interconnection model.

OSI Network Architecture

The OSI model, originally defined by ITU-T and adopted by the ISO (International Organization for Standardization), sets out a seven layer structure to handle communications basically expanding upon the three layers described above of connection, interworking and applications.

The bottom four layers of the OSI model are concerned with the movement of the zeros and ones (the connection), and the top three layers are concerned with what zeros and ones to move or what to do with them (the interworking). The names of the seven layers are:

- Layer 7 – Application – provides the interface or window into the application.
- Layer 6 – Presentation – formats (using a syntax) and converts data.
- Layer 5 – Session – establishes and terminates dialogs/sessions.
- Layer 4 – Transport – manages the reliable end-to-end movement of data.
- Layer 3 – Network – concerns the routing of data to the correct destination.
- Layer 2 – Datalink – transmits and controls data to and from each node.
- Layer 1 – Physical – connects nodes electronically forming a path.

While each of the layers is important for the functioning of a network, the layers of most interest in understanding the process are the application layer, physical layer and the middle transport layer, which is concerned with maintaining the reliability of the connection.

OSI standards within this seven layer model are fully defined, although there is still some remaining work to be completed that affects the higher layers. Importantly at each layer there are a variety of different standards for different needs. For example at the top, standards for file transfer would not be of much use for connecting terminals, whilst at the bottom, standards for LANs would not be suitable for WANs.

This realization can be make the implementation task seem unnecessarily difficult, since at the different layers there are various choices to be made. Taking a simple analogy of a son or daughter returning to their flat after a weekend with their parents. Upon safe arrival they ring home letting the phone ring four times before hanging up. The parents know that this means safe arrival of their son or daughter. So in this instance there is a high level application standard running over a connection established via the telephone network. However it is rather restrictive, since if the son or daughter wanted to also indicate that a gas bill had arrived, a different application standard would be required.

Because there are many standards at each layer, some governments have selected a subset or profile, primarily to assist in procurement and implementation. These are known as Government OSI Profiles or GOSIPs. It may be helpful to think of an OSI profile as a vertical slice through the seven layer OSI model grouping together a set of choices.

Internet TCP/IP Network Architecture

In the late 1960s the US Department of Defence (US DoD) issued a set of military standards for computer communications protocols based upon experiments with

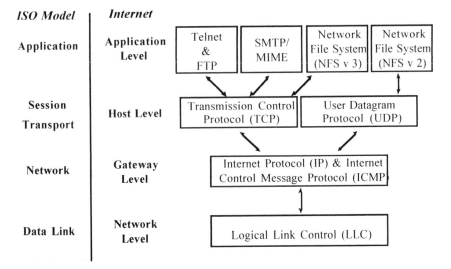

Fig. 10.4 Internet TCP/IP architecture.

its packet switched network ARPANET. While there are five standards making up the US DoD specifications, they are collectively known by two of them, namely Transmission Control Protocol and Internet Protocol (TCP/IP). TCP/IP divides up the layers differently to OSI and consists of four layers, with TCP being used instead of the OSI transport layer; and IP mapping onto the upper part of the OSI network layer. TCP/IP does not include any unique protocols for network access, and indeed uses a protocol appropriate for the particular network, e.g. Ethernet or X.25. TCP/IP is delivered as the standard network architecture for computers running the Unix operating system. Whilst TCP/IP has been the network architecture of choice for the academic and research communities, its popularity continues to grow within the business community, particularly as it is very suitable for use in LANs. Apart from its usage within the Internet, it has also received a significant amount of publicity from its adoption by Microsoft who bundle it with their highly successful Windows 95/97 and New Technology (NT) operating systems.

The Internet Protocol (IP) is the Internet's most basic protocol. It is a datagram orientated protocol that treats each packet independently, such that each packet must contain the complete address information. IP makes no attempt to verify if packets reach their destination, nor does it checksum the contents of the packet, just the IP header. When IP was initially specified, it was impossible to predict the tremendous success of the Internet, which is causing issues with diminishing network addresses and overflowing of routing tables. A working party has been looking at this problem since 1992, and there are now recommendations for an IP new generation (IPng), although some work has been done to extend the life of IP version 4.

TCP/IP is not an ISO standard, but subject to maintenance and development via the Internet RFC process as described in the previous chapter. The same basic principles outlined earlier for network architectures equally applies to TCP/IP.

Types of Connection

The characteristics of the connection have an effect on what interworking can be achieved over it. Standards for computer connections have been around longer than for communication, so it is much better understood.

Terminal Connections

Originally, most connections were simply terminal to host computer, and the connection was relatively easy to achieve, by connecting a cable between the terminal and host computer.

In this scenario, as terminal usage grows, so the number of cable connections grows at the same rate. Aside from the heavy cost premium associated with the additional cabling, in most cases, the capacity of the existing cable is able to support more than one terminal. The obvious approach is to connect a concentrator or cluster controller at both ends of the cable, which allows multiple users to run their terminal sessions concurrently down the same cable or line. The ability to handle multiple sessions down the same cable is known as "multiplexing": the cable effectively gets divided into a series of virtual cables or channels, each capable of handling a proportion of the traffic.

Modem Connection

At some point the distance between the terminal concentrator and the host computer concentrator or communications controller becomes too great, resulting in loss of signal. At this stage, modems may be introduced at each end of the cable and connected to the concentrator devices. If it is just impractical to physically extend the existing cable, then it is possible to use another cabling system, such as the telephone network, to provide the physical connection to which the modems are attached. This provides the scope for connecting terminals that are large distances away from the host computer to which they are to be connected. This later type of connection is termed "dial-up", and can apply to single terminals or concentrators, connecting to a host computer via modems over the telephone network (Fig. 10.5).

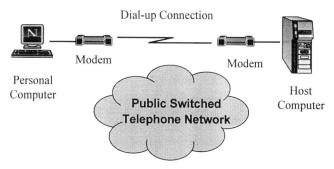

Fig. 10.5 PC dial-up connection.

Digital Switching Technology

Generally, digital switching technology stops at the local exchange, where devices convert transmissions between digital and analogue to reach the customer over the local loop. With the progressive re-cabling (using fibre optic technology) of telephone networks and the use of digital switching technology at their heart, line quality has significantly improved as well as providing much greater line capacity; a function of speed and number of conversations. This means that modems for data communications can be used at much higher speeds, typically from 9600 bits per second (bps) to 33,400 bps. By incorporating data compression techniques such modems under ideal conditions can achieve effective bit rates in the order of four times the analogue baud rate.

Quoting line speeds can be confusing as they are not always quoted in bits per second, but sometimes as baud. While there is a subtle difference between the two terms, in most cases, bits per second is intended, and depending upon the coding scheme used, a set number of bits correspond to a single character (usually 7 or 8 bits). Examples of coding schemes include:

- The PC uses a code to represent the alpha and numeric characters that it sends, the most widely being used are ANSI ASCII and EBCDIC.
- ANSI ASCII (American Standard Code for Information Interchange) is an 7 bit code that has 128 valid characters. An eighth bit is used for parity checking. Extended ASCII is an 8 bit code that caters for special international characters.
- EBCDIC (Extended Binary Coded Decimal Interchange Code) is IBM's standard 8 bit code with 256 valid characters and where error checking is provided by special algorithms.

Popular Modem Standards

Whilst line quality of the telephone network has greatly improved, there is still the possibility of unwanted noise being introduced onto the line, possibly at the local connection, resulting in transmission errors occurring. In consequence, error detection and correction techniques are very important to robust data communications. In a voice conversation there is simply a request to repeat the sentence, and much the same process is used in data communications to cause the corrupted data to be re-sent when an error is detected. The emerging standard for combining data compression and error detection/correction is V.42bis, and is normally incorporated within the modem itself.

The following is a summary of some popular modem standards: ignore any words that have not been explained up to this point and focus upon the broad concepts:

- V.32 is an ITU-T (formerly CCITT see earlier chapter on Open Systems) standard for asynchronous and synchronous 4800 and 9600 bps full-duplex modems. It is a modulation standard. The difference between V.32 and other standards is similar to the AM and FM standards used in radio broadcasting. Not only are they at different frequencies, but they also use different modulation techniques.
- V.32bis is a ITU-T standard for asynchronous and synchronous 4800, 7200, 9600, 12,000, and 14,400 bps full-duplex modems. V.32bis supports rate negoti-

ation, which allows modems to change speeds to the highest rate common between the two connecting modems.

- V.34bis is a new ITU-T standard. It doubles the throughput of V.32bis and takes maximum advantage of today's high quality voice-grade telephone lines reaching speeds of 28,800 bps and 33,400 bps (with maximum throughput under ideal conditions of 115.2K bps and 133.6K bps, respectively).
- V.42 is a ITU-T standard for modem error checking. It prevents a noisy line from causing data loss. With V.42, data is "packetized" and sent between modems to ensure that it is transmitted accurately.
- V.42bis is a ITU-T standard for modem data compression. It can achieve up to a 4-to-1 compression ratio and implies the V.42 error checking protocol.
- MNP (Microcom Network Protocol) is an error-correction de facto standard. In fact, the V.42 standard includes MNP as an alternate method of error correction, in case the other modem is not V.42 compliant. Consequently V.42 modems can reliably connect with MNP modems. There are 10 different classes of MNP. MNP Class 4 provides error control, while MNP Class 5 provides data compression.

While this section is concerned with the connection itself, the trend towards higher speeds is largely due to the changing nature of applications running over the link and growing population of IBM PCs (and IBM PC clones) and Apple Macintosh computers. These applications are no longer moving simple text messages, but handling a wide range of different message types, including word processing, spreadsheets, presentations using graphics, image, voice, and even moving image (video). Information in these forms is not only being sent using E-mail as the transport vehicle, but accessed in database and bulletin board systems such as America On-Line. Speed becomes a critical service element when accessing bulletin boards (or indeed Web servers on the Internet), either in browsing the information content or transferring files from the central repository. With the increasing use of computing in the home and the growth in laptop/hand-held computers, dial-up connections continue to be an important means of computer access. For the business traveller, access to a telephone point in their hotel and their computer configured with a suitable modem and software means uninterrupted business communications while away from the office. Growing use of wireless communications using a portable phone connected to the PC even removes this dependency.

Permanent Connections

From within the office environment, where conditions are more static, it is possible to look to other alternatives for connection that deliver higher speeds and offer a superior quality link than can be provided over the telephone network, as well as being more cost effective. In addition, high speed modem technology can still be expensive, particularly when large numbers of users are being connected from a single location.

One popular approach is to obtain a voice grade leased line from a telephone company (now known as a Private Telecommunications Operator) that "by-

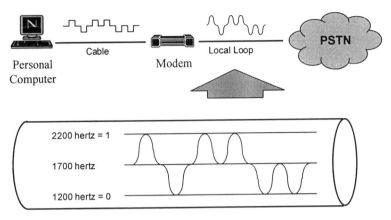

Fig. 10.6 Analogue to digital.

passes" the switching systems providing a permanently available connection. Since this is still an analogue circuit, modems are required, but no dialling takes place. Leased lines are of course ideal for point to point connections, but do not provide any flexibility if a connection to a new locations is required; a further leased line would need to be obtained. Payment for a leased line is usually by a fixed monthly charge (varying based upon the capacity of the line: quantity of traffic that it can handle) for whatever the usage. Depending upon traffic volume patterns, it may be a more cost effective option than a dial-up connection.

As described above leased lines are like dial-up connections transmitting data in an analogue form, creating sound where the function of the modem is to convert the digital data from the computer in zeros and ones into sound and back again (Fig. 10.6). However, in practice most leased lines provided by the PTO for data communications will be digital grade circuits and not require the use of modem technology.

With the increasing digitization of the telephone trunk network, with analogue access only existing at its periphery, there appears to be some unwanted switching between digital and analogue signals across the connection path, considering that signals emerge from a computer in digital form. Responding to this requirement, during the 1980s the former telephone companies introduced full digital point to point data communications services known as Packet Switched Public Data Networks (PSPDN) running at much higher speeds. These digital networks were based upon X.25, the OSI network layer protocol, that now forms the basis of a ubiquitous global network established by telecommunications operators interconnecting their country digital networks, in a similar manner to the Public Switched Telephone Network (PSTN). X.25 is often described as a packet protocol, since the data is progressively wrapped in envelopes to form a packet of data with a header (used by the corresponding layers in the network architecture).

Asynchronous versus Synchronous

The final thing to understand about connection is the method used by terminals

Asynchronous Communications Protocol

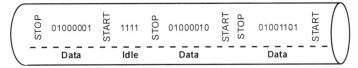

Synchronous Communications Protocol

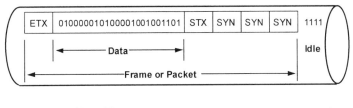

Direction of Data Transmission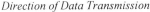

Fig. 10.7 Asynchronous and synchronous communications.

and hosts to separate the ones and zeros into their individual characters, namely asynchronous (character by character) or synchronous (block by block) transmission (Fig. 10.7). Asynchronous transmission is typically considered to be a low-speed, character by character, human to host communication protocol. To differentiate between the characters and synchronize transmission, i.e. indicate where one character ends and the next character begins, the communications software adds a start bit and stop bit to each end of the individual 8 bit character. This is how the receiving device can differentiate between the bits and correctly interpret the individual characters. Synchronization (timing) of the asynchronous transmission takes place for every character sent or received; the start/stop bit tells the receiving terminal that a new character is on its way or has just been sent. Synchronous transmission is used for high speed, computer to computer communications. Blocks of characters, called packets or frames, are transmitted between the sending and receiving devices. With synchronous transmission, the sending and receiving devices are re-synchronized for each block of data, and therefore no start and stop bits are required. This enables continuous streams of data to be sent efficiently in large blocks, since the amount of control information accompanying the data is less than in asynchronous transmission.

Types of Network

Integrated Services Digital Network (ISDN)

To achieve operational economies as well as broaden the range of services that could be offered based upon digital services, a further standard has emerged to integrate voice and data over the same service which is known as the Integrated Services Digital Network (ISDN).

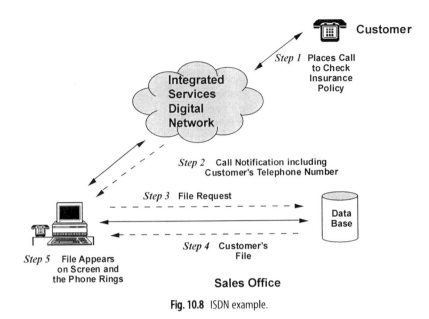

Fig. 10.8 ISDN example.

This implies that only digital devices are connected to the ISDN network requiring a digital telephone that converts sound into digital signals within the handset. Not only can such a network handle voice and data, but also image, moving image and facsimile, either separately or concurrently, over the existing copper cables that extend into the home. The basic option of ISDN provides the user with access to two virtual connection paths capable of handling 64K bps and running any combination of two digital services concurrently, together with a 16K control channel normally used by ISDN for control signals (Fig. 10.8). With the appropriate network infrastructure (e.g. fibre optic circuits and high performance switching), ISDN offers a primary rate interface capable of running multiple concurrently digital services.

Establishing a connection between a terminal and a host computer is well understood. With the ever increasing power of the personal computer, high quality voice-grade circuits and advances in software error detection/data compression techniques, dramatic progress has been made in pushing up modem based network access speeds. So much so that a V.34bis modem becomes highly dependent upon the power of the personal computer (PC) to deliver the required data rate to achieve the modem's full potential.

The pace of change in modem technology coupled with a highly competitive marketplace forcing prices down has started to pose a real threat to alternative high performance networking technologies such as ISDN. In the case of ISDN being solely a digital technology, no provision exists for a similar function to the rate negotiation that exists between two modems. However, with an ISDN primary rate interface and suitable end devices, "bonding" or "grouping" of the 64Kbps B channels can occur to significantly increase the bandwidth available to the user.

Global Networks

With the advent of micro- and mini-computers, as well as the ability to establish higher speed connections, networking has moved far beyond the simple terminal to host computer networks described originally. Large global networks now serve many business sectors, including the banking community operated by SWIFT, airline booking systems for all the worlds' airlines, SITA, the Internet serving the academic, research and business communities, etc., but all are based upon the concepts and principles as described in this chapter. Many of these networks are in effect the interconnection of smaller networks that exist over a wide geographic location (WANs), or local to a specific building complex (LANs).

Local Area Networks (LAN)

With the advent of the microcomputer in the early 1980s, it was not surprising to see a growth in technology known as local area networking, which allowed microcomputers to be interconnected for the purpose of sharing resources such as disk devices, printers and communications. LANs now form an important part of the IT strategy for both large and small organizations, and created a whole new software industry of application products geared towards team working (known as "groupware"). At the connection level, the most popular LAN standards are Ethernet ISO 8802.3 and Token Ring ISO 8802.5, which cover the bottom two layers of the OSI model.

All personal computers and other devices connected to a LAN have an address (a long and unique number); to send a message, the sending personal computer breaks the message into "packets", puts the destination's address on the packet, adds a sequence number and its own address, and puts the packet on the network. All devices connected to the LAN receives the packet and having decoded the destination's address, ignores the packet if it is for someone else. In the case of an Ethernet LAN, rules define what happens if two devices try and send a packet at the same time: basically they both stop, and try again a short time later. This all means that ISO 8802.3 LANs are not inherently secure – everyone receives everything, and is trusted to ignore the packet addressed to other devices.

LAN bridges can help solve this security problem (as well as that of distance) by learning the addresses of each device that exists on the LAN and filtering out those packets which do not need to travel to other parts of the network; this also helps improve performance by reducing unnecessary traffic.

Wide Area Networks (WAN)

In the case of Wide Area Networks (WAN) based upon X.25, intelligence is obviously needed in devices attached to the network, in order to break the messages to be sent into packets and to re-assemble received packets into complete messages. For devices that do not have this ability, for example personal computers that are not equipped with X.25 connectivity, boxes can be provided to handle the packet assembly and disassembly. For an X.25 network this is called a PAD (Packet Assembler and Disassembler).

Interworking

The previous section covered the types of connection that are possible between computers, while this section deals with communication or interworking that may take place over a link once a connection is established. These interworking functions still largely relate to standard features, utilities or generic applications incorporated within the operating environment of both computers. It is possible that a custom developed application (such as order entry) existing on one computer may use some of these services to move data to another application (such as stock availability) on another computer. Typical services might include the services outlined below.

File Transfer

Movement of a file from one computer to another, which undertakes any code conversion that is necessary to make the file usable on the receiving machine. The OSI standard is File Transfer, Access and Management (FTAM), whilst File Transfer Protocol (FTP) is the equivalent within the TCP/IP architecture. Both FTAM and FTP have been implemented on a wide range of equipment from different hardware vendors.

Terminal Emulation

Probably the most obvious requirement is to establish connection to a host computer which may be anything from a large mainframe computer to a personal computer, with minicomputers running UNIX somewhere in the middle. When running terminal emulation software on a personal computer, once the connection is established, the host computer thinks it is talking to one of its own terminals such as a Digital VT100/200, TTY terminal or IBM 3270 series. The Digital VT100/200 terminal is designed for asynchronous operation, whilst the IBM 3270 series operate in a synchronous mode.

File Sharing

This provides the capability for a file or files created and stored on one computer to be accessed by multiple users either being directly connected to the computer or being connected via a network. Naturally, the owner of a file can set certain attributes associated with that file that mean it can only be read and not deleted, etc. This capability is used extensively in the TCP/IP environment – more specifically, on the Internet – and came from Sun Microsystems, who developed the Network File System (NFS) protocol, which has become the *de facto* standard for a file server under UNIX. However, there is no similar equivalent under OSI, although X/Open have developed a standard called Remote File Sharing (RFS) which uses the OSI Transport Layer. At the LAN level, there are a wide range of proprietary file server standards, including Novell, IBM and Apple.

Remote Login

When connected to a host computer as a local user, or indeed having established a connection to a host computer using terminal emulation as described above, Telnet (part of the TCP/IP suite) allows the user to connect to a remote computer over a network connection and appear as a local terminal with all the facilities normally made available to its local terminal users.

Electronic Messaging

Electronic mail (E-mail) and Electronic Data Interchange (EDI) have fast become established as critical applications running over business networks supporting the day to day running of many companies. There are many considerations impacting electronic messaging that are discussed throughout this book, including the co-existence of the two *de jure* open E-mail standards of X.400 (ISO/IEC) and SMTP/MIME (Internet). However, in the context of interconnection both OSI/X.25 and TCP/IP based networks are capable of supporting these E-mail standards. In addition, it is important to note their co-existence with *de facto* LAN based client/server PC desktop standards from Microsoft and Lotus, which combine rich functionality of the client software with the ability to talk to native X.400 and SMTP/MIME communities.

Interoperability

The previous sections have reviewed the importance of connection and communication (also known as interconnection and interworking, respectively) between computing environments and the different forms they can take. However, it should be clear that this does not in itself guarantee successful communications between two network based computers unless full interoperability between applications exist.

As an example, it is possible to successfully transfer a word processing file from one computer to another and yet the recipient is unable to work with the file. This is likely to be due to the fact that each user is running a different word processing package or different versions of the same package, such that interoperability does not exist between the two different applications. While this illustration points to a generic problem, there are specific developments taking place concerning document standards that are discussed in a later chapter, aimed at addressing the exchange of compound documents including word processing files.

Microwave and Satellite Communication

In addition to terrestrial communications media such as copper and fibre optic technology, use is also made of microwave and satellite communications in telecommunications networks. Microwave systems involve directional radio broadcast transmissions at super high frequencies, and requires that the sending and receiving antenna are in a line of sight between one another. The typical antenna is a parabolic dish attached to a tall tower or building within sight of the next microwave relay station. Microwave is particular cost effective when the terrain is not suitable for alternative terrestrial guided media, and can be used to transport the full range of media including voice, data and image. When obtaining a leased line from the telephone company it is possible that the path between the two terminations maybe served by a combination of media, including terrestrial circuits and microwave links.

It was Arthur C Clarke who published an article in 1945 that showed a satellite in a circular equatorial orbit at the correct altitude could provide a communications relay station. However, it was not until 1964 that the International telecommunications satellite organization (Intelsat) was formed, and the following year that Intelsat 1 was launched providing 240 telephone channels or 1 TV channel. Much progress has been made since that time, and satellites today are capable of handing over 350,000 telephone channels. In addition, they connect into terrestrial communications networks in much the same way that microwave systems do, and extend telecommunications to areas of the world that lack the basic infrastructure, such as Eastern Europe and parts of Africa; indeed, a communications satellite can be considered as a microwave relay system in the sky. Services are established using a satellite in a geostationary orbit, together with a central hub ground station. Since the sender and receiver locations use Very Small Aperture earth Terminals (VSATs), they can be deployed relatively easily. VSAT technology is therefore extremely useful when disasters such as fires, earthquakes, severed cables, etc. wipe out traditional terrestrial voice and data communications services.

High Performance Networking

With the changing nature of electronic commerce and business communications, there is a growing trend to make much greater use of multimedia, with the result that applications have become more interesting and user friendly. A typical Powerpoint presentation has grown from a 250K bytes to 6M bytes in a very short period of time, and as moving image (video) is incorporated, so quantum leaps in files sizes will occur. As soon as greater bandwidth becomes available, so it seems to be consumed!

Fast Packet Switching

The traditional packet switching technologies such as X.25 assumed a physical environment in which errors could be introduced, and therefore placed much greater emphasis upon error detection as data moved from node to node. Whilst this achieved a highly reliable error free environment, considerable overheads were incurred in the checking process as packets passed from node to node across a network. The new high performance networking technologies, such as frame relay, assume a physical environment in which far fewer errors will occur, and in consequence, error detection need only take place upon entry and exit points of the network rather than at the nodes (switches). This means the protocol overheads are reduced and much higher data transfer rates can be achieved. In addition, while circuit switching tends to allocate a specific bandwidth for the duration of the session irrespective of how much it is used, fast packet switching is designed for bursts of transmission where the user gets unlimited access to the whole bandwidth for short periods of time, and it is therefore ideal for unpredictable traffic profiles. In some senses, it is like travelling on a busy motorway with a speed limit of 70 mph, where the average speed is as low as 10 mph with bursts of 30 mph, but other periods staying stationary. In these circumstances, frame relay is much more considerate to the driver, and guarantees if the speed limit is 70 mph, that with varying bursts of speed as required, 70 miles will in fact be achieved within the hour.

An organization constructing its own high performance network will have at its heart a number of fast packet switches connected together using leased lines to form a backbone network. A fast packet switching protocol will be used between the switches, while the interface for connection to the switches will be the frame relay network access protocol (really an interface definition), which is only suitable for data communications. Network routers running in a LAN environment will support the frame relay interface and can be connected directly to such a backbone network.

Asynchronous Transfer Mode

Another important high performance technology is known as Asynchronous Transfer Mode (ATM) and is yet another packet based protocol, i.e. data is transferred in containers known as packets of small sizes, usually of fixed length. ATM

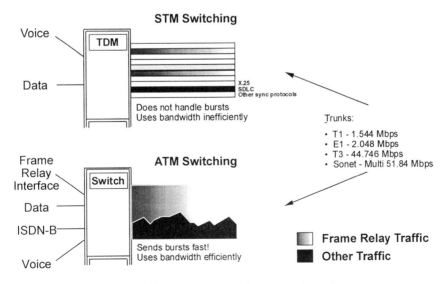

Fig. 10.9 Synchronous and asynchronous transfer mode.

is a cell-relay standard that not only supports, data and image, but also voice communications. Frame relay and ATM are not mutually exclusive, and indeed, will work together, the former being a standard interface to existing equipment and the latter providing and even more efficient movement of data across a wide area backbone network.

Summary

This chapter has explored some of the basic principles impacting computer communications that make electronic commerce and business communications a reality. The critical point to remember is that communications or networking happens in basically two stages, the connection and the communication. Everything else is just a complication of this basic concept. It is not an exhaustive description of the subject, as there are many excellent books available, but rather is intended to provide the functional user with a greater appreciation of the subject as it applies to electronic commerce and business communications.

Since computer communications is very much an evolving technology environment where a number of different technologies are rapidly coming together (telephony, data communications, television and multi-media) there is a tendency to view the subject in an unnecessarily complicated manner. The secret is understand the basic principles and to think through the simple analogies presented in this chapter; and above all, to not be afraid to ask questions if certain points are still unclear.

11. *Desktop Computing*

Introduction

As new technologies come to market, and new working practices ingrain themselves into our everyday lives, the way we work and the environment we work in continue to evolve. From an aesthetic viewpoint, one can clearly see the movement away from the typing pools surrounded by offices, to more open areas, fostering the exchange of ideas and encouraging communication.

The tools at our disposal have changed accordingly, in line with the environment they operate within. Visions of the early desktop conjure up huge machines, with little computing power in relation to the ever smaller boxes in today's offices. Furthermore, the introduction of the Local Area Network (LAN) and the ever emerging influence of the Internet environment facilitated many new ways of working – some of which we are only beginning to exploit to their full potential.

In this chapter we examine the evolution of the desktop from several key aspects:

- The desktop's interaction with the environment that it operates in – internal and external networks.
- The desktop hardware and its evolution.
- The software that drives it.

Moore's Law & Hardware Evolution

Doctor Moore was an insightful man – the man who co-founded Intel Corporation, today one of Wall Street's favourite companies, prophesized back in 1965 that the number of transistors that can be fitted on to a chip would double roughly every 18 months. Several decades later, Moore's Law, as it became known, still holds more or less true. The technological advancements that we have seen continue to amaze and dazzle. In the mid 1960s and late 1970s, capital and especially advanced information technology was considered the scarce and expensive resource. Workers were viewed as replaceable, and IT tools were the expensive cost. Today, billions of bytes of information flow at the touch of buttons 24 hours a day around the globe, tended by highly educated and competent individuals – technology hardware has now acquired the status of a commodity, and the emphasis is on satisfying the need of knowledge workers by providing tools that are not only powerful, but intuitive to use as well.

We have seen the emergence of a desktop machine, in recent years, capable of performing calculations and feats only possible by the archetypal monolithic mini or mainframe machines. Intel corporation, the organization responsible for the phenomenally successful 80x86 and Pentium family of processor chips, continue to work on their next generation of processor chips, leveraging new advances in silicon and other technologies. To put the power of the Pentium chip into perspective, its abilities compare to the processing power of a large mainframe machine, typically in use 20 years ago.

Organizations have the infrastructure already in place to facilitate co-ordination and communication possibilities never imagined in the competitive marketplace of the last decade. The competitive factor is no longer the technology, but the availability and effective use of a skilled and competent workforce to fully utilize the tools that are available to them. A key requirement has always been the ability to "humanize" the technology, effectively making it simpler to use for the average, non-technical user.

The changing aspects of the workplace, and how we do work, have put increasing emphasis on being able to take our work with us. Traditionally, this was only feasible in a limited sense, but advanced miniaturization of complex technologies gave birth to the portable machine – as each new technology comes to market, we are treated to ever smaller, ever more powerful machines. The shift caught the imagination of users, and the focus moved to more functionality in ever smaller boxes. This demand pull is still evident, even though the market emerges with ever smaller units capable of processing power that match any respectable desktop machine.

This trend is not entirely a new phenomenon. The idea of the modern notebook goes back many years, perhaps more than one would originally imagine.[1] In the early 1970s, Alan Kay, working at the Xerox Palo Alto Research Centre (PARC), prophesized a notebook-sized computer capable of recognizing handwriting and able to communicate with other systems through radio frequency. At the time, PCs were not widespread, and his comments seemed somewhat off the mark. His vision is today a reality in the form of advanced palmtop units, which grow richer in functionality in every release.

Costs of portable PCs have dropped considerably as their popularity continues to increase, but it is not only sizes that have shrunk, with each new model costing less and offering more. The sizes of these machines continue to decrease, and consequently the fastest growing segment of the personal computer market is the sale of portable machines, with forecasts predicting that sales of portable PCs will equal the sales of desktop PCs by the end of the decade. Corporations have embraced this trend for portable computing in the form of a more permanent set up in the office, or home, via a docking station solution coupled with a full size screen, which the portable units plugs into. The user is effectively "plugged-into" the internal corporate network, as well as access to external networks such as the Internet, easily and without hassle.

Reduced Instruction Set Computer (RISC)

RISC technology has been around for some years, but has not made inroads into the mass market. This is despite the fact that RISC chips outperform Complex Instruction Set Computer (CISC) chips, which currently dominate the PC marketplace (used extensively by organizations such as Intel Corporation). In addition to the increased power, the chips are smaller and cooler, an important factor in today's preference for more portable machines.

Traditionally, RISC based machines were used for specialized applications, such as scientific based calculations requiring large amounts of processing ability. This lack of mass market penetration is beginning to change, albeit slowly. We are only beginning to see the increased power of RISC technology being directed at the personal computer marketplace, through research and marketing efforts by major players such as IBM, Apple, Motorola and Hewlett Packard, to name just a few.

Apple Computer, IBM and Motorola joined forces to attempt to exploit the technical superiority of RISC architecture, and to also attempt to compete with the dominant position Intel has achieved in the marketplace. This trio developed the PowerPC microprocessor. The first systems built using this chip were marketed by IBM back in 1993, in their RS series of workstations. It was in March 1994 that Apple brought the PowerPC to the desktop, marketed under its Power Macintosh family.

Despite some initial divergence from the intended common platform that PowerPC was designed for, Apple and IBM finally agreed on the specifications of a common PowerPC Reference Platform (PReP). IBM and Apple are not the only players pushing the RISC chip, although they are arguably the ones that have been marketing to the desktop market most aggressively.

Apple has been moderately successful with its Power Macintosh family of products, but this still only represents a small fraction of the desktop market that Intel controls. The major impediment to gaining market share has never been the technical superiority of the chip architecture, but rather the lack of compatibility with the Intel series of chips which dominate the desktop market. The superior performance of the RISC chips, over Intel's offering, can clearly be highlighted when examining industry standard benchmarks; SPECint (integer calculations) and SPECfp (floating point calculations) – see Figure 11.1.

RISC technology has breached the desktop, and is clearly technologically the correct choice, but the reality is that market dominance is dependent on

	Clock (MHz)	SPECint	SPECfp
SUN Microsystems Ultrasparc	167	250	300
MIPS Technology MIPS R10000	200	300	550
IBM/Apple PowerPC 620	200	220	350
Hewlett Packard PA-RISC 8000	200	350	500
DEC Alpha 21164	266-300	290-330	440-500
Intel Pentium P6	150	150	125

Fig. 11.1 RISC vs. CISC performance (source: Gartner Group, November 1994).

application and operating system support. Furthermore, understandably software developers prefer to produce for the platform that is going to reach the greatest market. In recent years that has been the desktop operating on the Intel and Windows based environment.

Success will be derived by producing a RISC based PReP compliant chip that offers Intel chip compatibility. Development of this is already underway with IBM investing research funds into a chip that will emulate the Intel chips. Hewlett Packard has teamed up with Intel, attempting to build the next generation of RISC technology with this compatibility.

The Role of The Network

In the early 1980s, the advent of the personal computer provided the user with a means of solving problems locally, without the hassle of having to deal with a centralized MIS department. This was facilitated with tools such as Visicalc and Lotus 123. Importantly, people could buy these tools at a departmental level, with discretion of which hardware and software left to the local level.

As the number of these PCs grew, there was a logical need to share expensive resources (such as laser printers – driven by high quality printing requirements), and the sharing of files. It was sensible to link these machines together using a Local Area Network (LAN) and the mid 1980s saw a huge growth in the number of LANs implemented. The early installations again suffered the fate of the initial PCs bought. Discretion for these installations were left at the local departmental level, and large organizations soon found themselves dealing with many different topologies, utilising different software solutions.

The networking industry was beginning to blossom, especially with the introduction of Wide Area Networks (WAN), as LANs were co-ordinated and linked together. Manufacturers, developers and far sighted organizations were quick to see the potential of linking machines and sharing information as well as expensive resources. More recently, organizations are realising the potential in utilizing this infrastructure for more potentially rich applications, such as workflow functions and more collaborative groupworking. Users themselves are also demanding more network based facilities, in order to easily access and share information located on servers and corporate databases – this need has an added dimension when considering resources located in geographically dispersed locations.

While the corporate world was going through its own small revolution, the prominence of the Internet was growing at ever phenomenal rates. By the early 1990s, some far reaching organizations were beginning to experiment and utilize Internet technology. By the middle of the decade, arguably the roles had reversed, and the majority of organizations were utilising Internet technologies to some extent. It was becoming more commonplace to see an Internet E-mail address adorned on many business cards, and organizations now had a new headache – communications outside of the internal network.

The need to network has become a necessity in organizations today, whether this is via physical or remote links, internally or externally. The marketplace has acknowledged this requirement and many machines now ship complete with

Internet ready networking capabilities, and associated software to allow the communication and interaction between individuals. Indeed, operating systems themselves are being oriented towards networked applications, with facilities to share personal storage domains and facilitating application sharing, and most releases boast "plug and play" capabilities so that computers can link and be linked with minimal effort. This is not only affecting the way we work, but also the way we play – most machines directed to the consumer market are functionally rich in hardware specifications, Internet ready and boast high capacity modem facilities.

In the corporate world, the way departments and consequently whole organizations work and communicate has been radically changed – information is considered the lifeblood of an organization. In the contemporary organizational environment, extending the biological analogy, the network (whether LAN or Internet-based) can be viewed as the veins carrying that information. Consequently, the amount of resource afforded to network technology and the importance of availability has increased dramatically. This is reflected in the prominence of vendors like Netscape and Novell, who are major players in these markets.

On the hardware side, larger and larger bandwidths are being provided within the corporate environment, as new technologies such as image and voice are being integrated across networks. The widespread use of fibre optic cable allows the bandwidth hungry multi-media applications that are appearing on the desktop. The network itself is also taking on a new form; the concept of a LAN is being re-defined as a growing army of mobile workers, armed with notebooks, demand to join the network of computers from various locations around the world. These themes are further explored in the chapter on Mobile Computing (Chapter 16).

Internet Impact – The Pandora's Box

As we approach the turn of the century, the sheer impact of the Internet on everyday life – at work and at home – is simply breathtaking. Today, from the desktop linked into the Internet, or company Intranet, individuals are treated to a whole array of real time information. Searching this vast domain becomes ever easier with new browser technologies, and ever more powerful search engines that can be highly customized.

This has posed some interesting questions on the desktop, and its associated hardware. The role of the computer continues to change and the advent of the Network Computer (NC) offers new possibilities. These network computing devices promise much, and yet open up a Pandora's Box of jargon such as thin and fat clients, applelets, Java beans, virtual machines, and so on. We can usefully categorize the NC as a station that executes tasks, known as applets, that are typically downloaded from a network. Being functionally simple, they can operate across a variety of networks and platforms – typically, they do not house any floppy disks or CD-ROMs.

Today, several specifications exist although the technology has not caught enough imagination to gain critical mass. All the major players are behind the Network Computer concept, with differing specifications.

Software Evolution

It has not only been hardware that has seen some fundamental changes in the past years. The supporting software libraries to help us work have mushroomed and we found ourselves facing difficult choices as the numbers grew; many organizations experienced a period of decentralization, controlled and more often uncontrolled, where users were empowered to make choices according to their requirements. The widespread use of corporate networks and their growth clearly brought home the need for a homogenous set of tools, and a process of consolidation took place; the introduction of a "suite" of software illustrated the trend.

Furthermore, software technologies fuelling the growth of the Internet continued to be propelled by Gopher and browser technologies. Netscape, best known for its Netscape Browser software, was catapulted into the mainstream when the company launched its product – instantly valuing the organization at millions of dollars.

This section of the chapter examines the evolution of the desktop Operating System (OS), the introduction of the Graphical User Interface (GUI) and its continual evolution, the role of Internet software technologies, as well as look at popular software packages and the impact they have made in the organization.

The Emergence of MS-DOS

With the emergence of the IBM personal computer in the early 1980s, developed by a team of technical wizards, IBM gained prominence in the desktop market thanks to an aggressive marketing campaign. These machines were slow and heavy and would boast a couple of hundred kilobytes of memory, a megabyte or two of storage and operated at speeds that would send most to sleep today – many of us may have used, or at least seen these machines gathering dust in a forgotten room within our organizations.

The Disk Operating System (DOS) was licensed in 1981 to operate on machines that utilized the Intel 8088 processor, featured in the early PCs, and was designed to utilize the available technologies of that day. The machines have evolved, and in latter times, we have chips such as the Pentium, which operates hundreds of times faster than the 8088, yet one still see the use of DOS which can only perform one task at a time. Even subsequent evolution of the Microsoft Operating System (OS) required DOS. This alone is a testament to Microsoft's marketing muscle, to have such antiquated technology still providing millions of dollars of revenue. Consequently, for almost a decade, users were subjected to interacting with the machine via a keyboard designed to slow the individual, and an operating system, MS-DOS, riddled with unfriendly jargon and associated commands.

The emergence of the Graphical User Interface (GUI) and the mouse pointer device, whose progenitors can be identified as Xerox Corporation (who failed to exploit the technology) and Apple (who arguably did exploit the technology, but not to its full potential), has the potential to address this orthodoxy, and has succeeded in becoming the new popular standard. Microsoft Corporation, the original developers of DOS (for IBM), has succeeded in making their Windows GUI, arguably the *de facto* standard on the PC platform. It is almost impossible, or at least very difficult, to even purchase a new PC machine without having Windows software pre-loaded.

Users are beginning to see the end of DOS, in favour of a more intuitive and user-friendly interface between the individual and the machine, although the software will be in use for some time, with such a huge installed base. This trend is underway but progress has been slow when one compares the evolution of the underlying system's software with that of its hardware.

Bridging the Cognitive Gap

The challenge faced by all organizations, whether in the private, public or other sectors, is effective utilization of the immense computing power that the average user has at their disposal. Organizations have invested billions of dollars in advanced technology, yet white collar productivity statistics have either been stagnant, or never even getting close to double figures. This paradox has been somewhat arduous to explain, and a lot more challenging in eliminating. The reasons are numerous, but perhaps the most important is the misguided belief that throwing technology at the problem was the panacea – traditionally, technology has been difficult to use and understand, especially when the supporting processes were not in place.

Machines need to be made to fit into the human environment rather than attempting to force humans to conform to theirs; zealots of technology can sometimes underestimate the impact of this. Few can forget their first feelings of helplessness when switching on one of the early personal computers, only to be faced with a blank screen and blinking cursor. Those that had not mastered the arcane language of DOS, consisting of complex command lines, could not progress further. If that was not challenge enough, each application required its own competencies and language, creating the need for specialists in each area. Hardly the best way of realising promised productivity gains from technology.

Thankfully, not all innovators subordinated the human in favour of the machine. The work at the Xerox Palo Alto Research Centre (PARC) has been innovative and refreshing. Apple Computer Inc. had built its empire on the back of its user-friendly interface, inspired by the work at Xerox PARC; the machine was engineered to support the needs of the interface, completely eliminating the mysterious blinking prompt in favour of more intuitive icons and pull down menus. Microsoft has followed suit with its Windows range of operating software. For many, the Apple Macintosh interface was always seen as being more intuitive than the Windows product, although the distinction becomes increasingly blurred as new releases of Windows come to market. For instance, within the Macintosh environment there is no need to deal with confusing .BAT and .SYS files; Windows has only exacerbated the problems for users who just barely understood these files under DOS! The GUI should be making these underlying command transparent and therefore easier for the user, rather than more complicated.

The challenge of the GUI is to bridge the gap between our goals and thoughts, and the means of attaining these goals via the use of our computers. When we have achieved this, we may finally begin to see a reduction in the paper we use; when we write or communicate via paper, there is no need to think about how to enter the data, and therefore lose concentration of the problem in hand. An effective user interface can address this, and other stumbling blocks such as having to read lengthy manuals before using a piece of software. Who has the inclination, or the time, to learn what the machine can achieve and cannot. *Learning by doing*, as an old Chinese proverb describes it, *is the truly effective way of learning*. Intuitive interfaces and utilising metaphors encourage the user to experiment and hence learn. Ensuring a consistency between applications significantly reduces learning times for new software and encourages confidence in users.

Work by US researchers have validated these hypotheses by projects conducted in 1989 and 1990,[1] which compared GUI users and Character User Interface (CUI) users. An excerpt is provided below.

- GUI users accomplished 58% more work than CUI users in the same time period.
- GUI users expressed less frustration, rated at 2.7 out of 10, compared to 5.3 out of 10 for CUI users.
- GUI users were better able to explore and learn the capabilities of their applications, by 23% more than CUI users.

In conjunction with increased usage of GUI approaches, the trend is being augmented by speech recognition software and pen technologies. The umbilical link connecting us to the computer is perhaps about to be changed, when examining recent trends. Not before time: the QWERTY keyboard was designed for the original mechanical typewriters, and the layout was governed by the overriding need to slow the typist down, so that the mechanical keys would not get jammed. This antiquated design has endured for decades, and even with the advent of the mouse pointer, pioneered by the work of Douglas Engelbart at the Stanford Research Institute in the 1960s, the keyboard is still the primary form of input. There have been new keyboard designs that have followed a more intuitive layout, but these have not been successful in the market place.

On the desktop, Operating Systems (OS) promise to make our link with the computer more invisible and less arduous. As more applications support these emerging technologies, such as pen computing and voice recognized inputs, implications for the way we work are unclear. As the technologies mature and become more stable, our link with the tools we work with will hopefully become easier to use and more akin to the paper and pencil, where we do not have to think about how to enter data.

As new releases of software come to market, the use of new interface technologies are transparent – this is clearly the way forward, and the latest versions of the Operating Software available to use attest to this trend; the challenge lies the making the user interface as transparent and as intuitive as possible.

Network Operating Systems

Earlier in this chapter, the prominence and growth of network infrastructures, whether internal networks typical of most corporate organizations, or Internet influenced topologies, were discussed. The software driving this trend has evolved almost as fast as the underlying hardware – especially in the area of Internet applications. Here we examine the historical evolution of the networking software, as well as taking a look at future trends that are emerging in the marketplace.

David and Goliath

In the 1990s, Microsoft has attained monolithic status within the personal computer market place. The company, that was founded in 1975 by Bill Gates and Paul Allen, built its foundations on its first product – a version of BASIC developed for the MITS Altair, an early PC. The company received its first big break when their product was chosen to supply an operating system for IBM's first PC. Since then, it has grown to become the world's largest software vendor – Bill Gates has metamorphosed from David into Goliath.

Microsoft's release of its last major Windows Operating System enjoyed, perhaps, one of the most spectacular marketing campaigns ever seen for a software product. The sheer marketing muscle of the organization is one of the success factors of the Windows product gaining such prominence over other offerings, such as Apple Computer's product. Since its launch in the early 1990s, the product has been continually updated and evolved to maintain its leadership position – the product line is outlined in Fig. 11.2.

On the desktop PC platform, Microsoft's products unquestionably have the lead and the future OS can be represented (not necessarily led) by the organization's forthcoming projects. The trend for the OS of the next millennium is heavily reliant on embracing the integration of intelligent devices into existing infrastructures, as well as ensuring enhanced Internet capabilities.

Since the early releases of Windows, the product has been criticized for not being user friendly enough, and critics pointed to the advanced interface of the Apple Macintosh as the benchmark. Nevertheless the product, through Microsoft's effective strategy and marketing, entrenched itself on the majority of every desktop PC

Version	Characteristics
Windows	First Windows product – launched in 1985
Windows v3.1	16-bit GUI – the defacto standard on the PC platform
Windows For Workgroups (v3.11)	Windows v3.1 superset, intended for LAN use and resource sharing
Windows NT	32-bit operating system, primarily designed for high end workstations – launched May 1993
Windows NT Advanced Server	LAN operating system component of Windows NT – launched May 1993
Windows '95	Desktop system with 32-bit processing capabilities and new GUI – launched August 1995
Windows CE (Compact Edition)	Windows software environment for hand-held mobile devices
Windows '98	Next evolution of Windows Operating System
Cairo	Next evolution of Windows NT with object oriented programming capabilities

Fig. 11.2 Windows product line.

sold and used. Windows '95 addressed many of these concerns, and gained a reputation not enjoyed by any other software product in history (see the Case Study below).

On the server end of the market, domination has been somewhat more difficult with Novell gaining a significant market share. Windows NT is a true 32 bit operating system, and hence is capable of running more than one program, or task, at the same time achieving true multi-tasking capabilities. As opposed to Windows '95 which uses Intel's CISC technology, NT has the capability of running on RISC based systems and on systems that utilize more than one processor chip. The overhead for this type of functionality comes at a price though, with the system requiring significant amounts of RAM to run the OS. Windows NT represented the first Microsoft product that did not rely on DOS to function, as opposed to v3.1 and Windows '95, hence possessing an advanced and robust architecture making it more reliable and stable. This puts it in the league with other strong "true" operating systems such as IBM's OS/2 and Unix solutions.

Windows NT is being evolved into what Microsoft has termed the 'Cairo project', and it is this product that represents the real direction that operating systems may take in the next decade. The focus is on storing data as objects, descriptions of where to find the data rather than in files. It is this orientation on objects that represents Cairo's greatest strength. This modular approach to an operating system, with 'independent co-operating parts' supports the trend of open systems which theoretically poses an interesting situation for vendors such as Microsoft – third party developers could easily produce elements for the OS, and hence perhaps reduce their hold.

CASE STUDY – WINDOWS

The day of August 24, 1995 saw an event that the computer industry had been anticipating with bated breath: the world-wide launch of Windows '95, the next generation of Windows GUI OS. This launch perhaps represented the most publicized and hyped event in computing history – evidence of the huge cost and marketing effort behind it. Indeed the famous song by the Rolling Stones used in the advertisement campaign alone cost a reputed $8 million, one element of a $100 million advertisement initiative involving Windows and Office '95.

So why all the fuss? Partly because Microsoft's marketing machine had successfully delivered a very effective result, but also the promise that Windows '95 would end all the idiosyncrasies and shortcomings that Windows 3.1 users had learnt to live with. Coupled with this was the promise of a new user interface (supporting filenames in excess of eight characters), improved plug and play capabilities and increased support for remote computing and multimedia.

Despite the majority viewpoint, Windows '95 was not a new operating system that liberated the user from DOS, as many had imagined, but a major hybrid upgrade that represented a significant change to v3.1. Windows '95 was a multithreading, pre-emptive multi-tasking 32 bit system – this basically allowed the system to process in background with robust memory protection, allowing improved processor performance and easier use. In addition built in networking facilities and plug-and-play functionality improved connectivity, whilst reducing complexity. This meant less hassle for the user when setting up new applications or hardware.

Remote networking was also addressed through the introduction of a new framework, centered on a universal mailbox and the "Briefcase" concepts. The latter allows the synchronization of files as well as records and fields (using OLE 2.0) between a variety of computers. Communication was also improved with the software supporting many approaches, easing hardware connectivity. Even infra-red technology was catered for. The universal mailbox represented Microsoft's future direction in the desktop integration arena, with directory services supporting E-mail addresses, fax and telephone numbers, etc.

Windows '95 was a major improvement to preceding versions, and begun to offer some of the benefits of "true" 32 bit operating systems such as OS/2, although many of the benefits were only available when using native applications (supporting the new features); hence the release of the new Office suite in conjunction with Windows.

The Other Players

The Microsoft route to the future is just one vendors vision, and the other players in the field are also developing their paths to the next generation of OS. All share large areas of overlap, and with all products the key to success will be achieving critical mass in terms of support from third party vendors. One only needs to look back at IBM's OS/2 product, which is technically superior to Microsoft's, yet it is the latter that enjoys wide market success.

The playing field can be divided into three main contenders at the time of writing:

- Apple, IBM and Motorola – the group is based around the PowerPC technology, and IBM moving OS/2 into a modular OS based on various micro-kernels. The group anticipate the consolidation of UNIX, OS/2 and Taligent (an object oriented programming system being developed with Apple and Hewlett Packard where facilities are implemented as objects).
- Intel, Microsoft and DEC – utilizing the Intel range of chips, and basing the future OS on the Windows infrastructure.
- HP, Novell, Next and Sun – the group could consolidate their RISC technologies under NextStep. Novell itself has been working extensively on its Netware modules and already possesses a large market share of the server OS market.

When examining server operating system forecasts, many advocate the dramatic rise of the Microsoft solution (Windows NT) gaining market share at the expense of others. In the market of midrange machines, Ovum[2] estimates the Windows NT product to represent approximately 30% of the installed base by year 2000. Figure 11.3 outlines an additional forecast by Forrester Research.[3]

Within the general trend, the vendors are moving towards an environment much desired by users: a true enterprise wide distributed computing environment that would make transparent the different platforms. Desktop operating systems are evolving into powerful systems that can support object-oriented programming. The focus is very much on the development of an OS consisting of a micro-kernel representing the OS, with modular building blocks that can be developed by any third party, providing the user with a truly open and versatile OS environment.

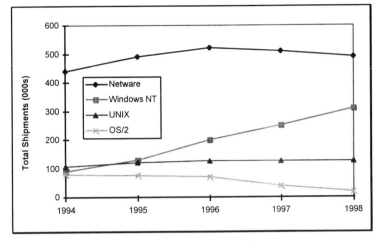

Fig. 11.3 Forecast of operating system shipments.

Software Suites

The trend of decentralization reduced the role of the data processing and IT departments. Functional departments were afforded autonomy in controlling the way they worked and consequently the tools that they required to do their work. The emphasis had moved from proprietary written software solutions to the use of standardized "off the shelf" software packages. Each user, or groups of users purchased the solution that best met their needs. This usually meant buying the most advanced word processor, spreadsheet or graphics package.

Inevitably, as corporate data and information was disseminated, problems of sharing data between entities and departments became evident. Where information could be shared, retaining the integrity of data was an increasingly difficult task to manage – the underlying models and applications were all different. This situation has led to organizations being encouraged to adhere to one a set of common applications throughout the company. The need has influenced the advent of a range, or suite, of software packages from one supplier.

With the huge take-up of the Internet and increasing uses of Internet based technologies, suites are also being enhanced to provide these additional functionalities. Examples are Lotus including a Java-applet version of SmartSuite; Microsoft adding Internet features to their new Office Suite (Small Business Edition and Professional), including its Internet Explorer product.

The suite approach has arguably taken off not only for the integration aspect, but perhaps more importantly for the firm, the huge cost savings that could be made – essentially it was a good deal. Furthermore, large users could negotiate substantial discounts making the savings even more considerable. For instance, an office suite costing in the region of several hundreds of dollars, at retail list price, can be reduced down to around a third of that cost when bought in bulk quantity. Ironically, we see a return to centralization with suite solutions being imposed throughout organizations.

Advantages

The advantages of going down the "suite" path are numerous, and outlined below.

The Cost – As already discussed, the cost savings can be considerable, and this is one of the primary driving forces behind the growth in buying software in this package.

Increased Integration – Organizations are benefiting from the increased integration possibilities that suites can provide. Manufacturers are also expanding their market share on the back of promoting additional tools and technologies that facilitate easy sharing of data between applications. Inserting a graph into a word processed document is easily performed, with relevant button bars appearing within the word-processing application. Additional integration features include task managing software such as Microsoft's Office Manager (MOM) and the ironically named Desktop Application Director (DAD) from WordPerfect and Borland. Applications also support additional macro facilities that allow corporate users to customize functions from multiple programs to synthesize new products to meet their needs. The suite has been marketed as more than just a collection of programs collated in a convenient box.

Consistency – With each application possessing similar menus and button bar icons, the user can adapt and learn new applications much faster. Training costs can also be reduced by employing suite software.

Control – Large organizations have a difficult time in controlling upgrade costs, and associated problems that occur when different elements of the organization are using different versions of the same software. Corporate desktop initiatives are also much easier to implement and associated savings can be discerned when requiring support from just one vendor.

Disadvantages

It is difficult to envisage how buyers can go wrong with taking the suite approach. After all the suite concept was the biggest hit in the early to mid 1990s, with the largest market share netting almost $1 billion for Microsoft alone. The trend had continued, with suite packages of software representing $2.5 billion in revenues in 1995.[4] Despite the advantages, there are some distinct disadvantages associated with taking this strategic viewpoint to software acquisition.

Best of breed – A collection of software packages from one vendor are seldom all market leaders within their fields. Purchase the Lotus suite, for example, and you get the industry acclaimed 123 spreadsheet package, but are also given the less popular AmiPro word-processing package. There is a trade-off, especially when users are familiar with a specific package. Enforcing a change can cause resistance, whether covertly or overtly. In some cases, the costs of the social pain greatly outweighs the financial gain.

The 80:20 Rule – Suites are an excellent example of the 80:20 rule, where 80% of the users are really only using about 20% of the functionality in each suite – for the majority of the users, these added features are simply not required and subsequently not used.

Networking the Suite – You cannot break up a suite – running the word-process-ing software on one machine, and the spreadsheet on another is not permitted. If one element of the suite is being used, then the licenses for the other ele-ments are also being effectively utilized. This can cause some difficult admin-istration problems within a networked environment, and in some cases it is more sensible and cost effective to purchase individual licenses. The latter point is an important one, and can be one of the most important decisions an organization can make, when evaluating the suite approach to individual packages. Consider an organization with 1000 PCs, with 50% of users using word processing, and the rest using a spreadsheet package – only 500 copies of each application are needed. If this situation involved suite licensing, then the 500 using word-processing would effectively be utilising the entire suite license, hence requiring the full 1000 licenses.

A cost analysis needs to be performed to establish working patterns, and software usage peaks. Situations can be complicated by many users opening a series of soft-ware applications, in a minimized manner at start-up: they may well not use that application at all, but that suite license is effectively unavailable to another user.

Evolution of the Suite

The origin of the suite concept centred around bundling discrete products from one manufacturer in a competitive package, encompassing the key software prod-ucts required by an average user – word processing, spreadsheet and graphics software. Further subsets included "Professional" suites, that included database and project management software options. Essentially, as time has gone by, each product has become more integrated with the other, reflecting the requirements and working habits of users.

Today, suites still are essentially several discrete products, but the trend of a more integrated offering is already visible in Microsoft's Office and Lotus Notes Components products. By the next millennium, we should see software packages capable of versatile document creation, whether spreadsheet or word processing, in one simple and functionally rich package.

Notes

1. P. V. Jones, "A GUI Puts a Friendly Face on Computing", *Business Quarterly*, Spring 1993, pp. 110–113.
2. *Ovum, Markets for Operating Systems*, August 1996.
3. Forrester Reseach Inc, *Server O/S shootout*, Vol 11 Number 12, October 1994.
4. Gartner Group – "Are Suite Dreams Made of This?", S. Levin, Research Note: March 8 1995.

12. *Group Working*

Introduction

Working patterns have always been characterized by the need to communicate and share information. Business has always been a group activity, requiring several people with differing competencies to work together. Since computer technology impacted business life some decades ago, the need to communicate over greater geography and within shorter time scales has taken on more prominence.

The infrastructure to allow groups to work together is already available through the networking of standalone machines. In the past, the justification of linking personal computers centred on the sharing of expensive resources. LANs are now facilitating the use of technology in sharing information and helping individuals work more effectively with each other. The focus has become more strategic.

The late 1970s saw the emergence of the term "Groupware". Over the years, this has represented many different things and as the concept became more fashionable in the mid 1980s, the plethora of products purporting to be "groupware" mushroomed, and correspondingly other terms that are similar to, or used synonymously with, groupware followed suit. Examples are collaborative computing, multi-user applications, workflow computing and Computer Supported Collaborative Working (CSCW).

There is confusion as to which terms applies to which product – throughout this book, the term "groupware" is generally used, although the different aspects relating to each term is discussed further. What exactly is groupware? Many definitions exist and the term means different things to different people. A good working definition is:

> *"a collection of software programs designed to support people working in groups"*

We can attempt to usefully separate this collection of programs into some distinct categories, listed below:

- Groupware environments.
- Workflow software/computing.
- Conferencing and consensus-building software.
- Scheduling/Diary software.

Examples of software would include desktop conferencing, E-mail, bulletin boards, meeting support systems, group calendars and voice enabled applications. Many software solutions offer one or more of these elements – examples of these are discussed later.

The Evolution and Growth of Groupware

Arguably the most basic and earliest forms of groupware were simple E-mail facilities. Indeed a less glamorous definition of groupware may be "E-mail with bells and whistles". At the core of any groupware product is the ability to ease communication – this invariably translates into some form of E-mail.

The 1970s saw the growth of computer mediated communication. At this time, groupware was defined along the lines of "group processes and the software to support them". The use of the term "processes" is an important one to highlight up front. The purchase of a groupware package then, and now, did not immediately lead to focused and functioning teams. There has to be emphasis and examination of processes and how they need to change.

Groupware evolved further in the 1980s when attempts were made at office automation to support workers – the theme was to help people work together. The term became popular in the mid to late 1980s, where productivity successes were being cited and lessons from successful implementations were learnt. The software was becoming more sophisticated and refined.

The groupware concept fitted in nicely with the business thinking of the early 1990s, when many organizations were expending great efforts to re-design processes, and aligning technology to these newly created work patterns. These products were being used as the building blocks for disseminating information, co-ordinating people and activities. As power is devolved further down the organization, teams require information that was historically held at the apex of the traditional pyramidal organizational structure. Groupware infrastructures were increasingly being used at the beginning of the decade, to disseminate this information to all, or subsets of employees.

The collection of groupware software addresses four main tasks performed in offices:

● Finding and collecting information.
● Using this information.
● Communicating and interacting with others.
● Attending/initiating meetings.

Some proponents of groupware also saw the technology as a means of reversing the "Productivity Paradox". This phenomenon highlights the huge investment made by organizations in technology, but deriving only marginal improvements in productivity. By aligning technology to the way people work and the dynamics of human interplay, true benefits in productivity could be realized. Arguably, we already have enough technology on our desks to support everything we want to do.

These factors, amongst others, have contributed to the growth of the groupware market. The consultancy firm Ovum estimated the market in 1994 to be worth $2.5 billion. All projected estimates concur that the market will experience healthy growth in the next ten years.

We can begin to see several groupware products being increasingly adopted into organizational environments. These programs are discussed within the various categories in this chapter.

Groupware Environments

Products that provide the basic infrastructure to build a technological group working environment, would fall into this category. Typically, the actual pieces of the puzzle would be either developed by the organization purchasing the environment, outsourced to a developer or purchased "off-the-shelf".

This type of product is perhaps one of the most popular for large organizations, as it provides the flexibility to build features that address the needs of the business. This product would be categorized by possessing an E-mail engine, several databases, bulletin boards and calendaring features. The emphasis is on enabling collaboration between people, regardless of their physical location or the time zone they work in.

An excellent example of this type of product would be the Notes product by Lotus Corporation (see the case study below), which further evolved and was renamed to Lotus Domino in early 1997. Microsoft has concentrated into further developing its Exchange product, which although launched into the market after Lotus Notes, was gaining market share at the time of writing. As with Notes, MS Exchange is also being upgraded to support the various Internet based standards such as HTML, and improving the cross collaboration between its other Internet based products, such as Microsoft Explorer.

CASE STUDY - LOTUS NOTES

Lotus corporation were perhaps one of the most successful in producing and marketing a groupware product, which is now used by some of the world's largest companies. Launched in 1989, it is utilized in diverse organizations such as Price Waterhouse, General Motors, Texaco and Chase Manhattan Bank. In 1995, approximately 1.4 million users were using Notes.

Notes allows electronic documents to be shared by authorized personnel, via databases and bulletin boards. Communication is aided by an electronic mail functionality. Keeping information up to date does not necessarily require a central remote system, or hard wiring to a network. Geographically separated users can access databases with the latest information thanks to a process called *replication*. Relevant information is copied to all connected servers at user determined periods (every few minutes if need be).

Notes is a development environment rather than an application. Applications that use the underlying technology have to be developed, and as such existing systems can be a useful part of the new solution. Lotus have catered for all the major hardware/OS platforms, including personal computers (OS/2, Windows, DOS), Macintoshes and UNIX workstations.

Making optimal use of a product like Notes requires some significant investment. Using the estimates provided by Lotus, for every $1 spent on the Notes software, and additional $3 to $5 needs to be spent on consultants, trainers and additional software.

Notes also possesses links to on-line services and the Internet, via Internotes Web Publisher – allowing the creation of Web server Notes databases. Many other manufacturers have also joined up with Lotus and its Notes product – IBM is shipping Notes Express, a restricted version of the full software, with its OS/2 Warp package. Apple is providing it with selected Macintosh computers.

With IBM's purchase of Lotus in early 1997, the Notes product was further evolved and IBM, through its Lotus subsidiary, is attempting to address Microsoft's strong-hold. At the heart of the strategy is the utilization of the foundation of Notes installations – the Notes server was renamed to Domino, with a focus on utilizing key Internet compliant applications and systems. This includes the incorporation of Java technologies, as well as IIOP and CORBA adoptions.

With a huge installed base, Lotus Notes/Domino is addressing the increasing requirement for Internet based applications, although the adoption of intranets not based on this technology are increasing.

The Advent of the Intranet

The role of products such as Lotus Notes/Domino and Microsoft Exchange have blurred in recent years, as organizations have increasingly begun to embrace Internet based technologies in a more aggressive manner. The advent of the Intranet – essentially an internal information system, configured to integrate various Internet based technologies – has begun to challenge the use of products such as those offered by IBM and Microsoft. Intranets are not new, with the early configurations consisting of various UNIX stations utilizing TCP/IP protocols. What is more recent is the widespread adoption of this type of groupware technology, and the wider scope outside of sharing files and rudimentary E-mail facilities.

This rush to embrace the concept of the Intranet has also led to major manufacturers ensuring that their offerings also support these technologies. Examples are Lotus with their Domino product and Microsoft with the Exchange product, adopting Internet based functionalities – the implications for the increasing blurring of these approaches are unclear, although the Intranet application is still a relatively simple approach, as opposed to offering some of the advanced database functionalities afforded by groupware products such as Domino and Exchange.

Workflow Software/Computing

Mention workflow software or computing, and most people will immediately think of some type of imaging system, or associated software. This is hardly surprising, as these systems brought the term to the mainstream. Workflow has changed and evolved though, and many different levels of functionalities exist – this is where the confusion begins to manifest. What is workflow?

When considering any work process, groups of people and information are involved – the information flows with the flow of the work, being enhanced or added to at each stage. Whatever the job, people must have access to the relevant information, at the relevant time.

Workflow computing is the act of providing the data at each step of the work process, and workflow software automates the transfer of information to support this flow. The essential principle is to examine business issues and to translate them into a solution that can be improved using technology.

It is workflow's group orientation that sometimes leads to confusion with 'groupware' products. A simple example is the workflow of a document, say in an insurance company. In order to process a claim, the relevant document may be routed between several groups of people. A typical flow could be:

1. Claim case opened by administrator.
2. Adjuster adds comments after viewing.
3. Manager signs and validates claim.
4. Accountant prepares payment of claim.
5. Payment generated and sent to claimant.

Although simplistic, the example illustrates the several departments that the document has flowed through. It is applications like these that early forms of workflow improved significantly – helping to tie departments more closely together, and to reduce "in-tray" delays. It is also these types of paper-intensive industries that allowed imaging companies to do extremely well with workflow solutions.

Once the workflow has been established, software can automatically route information or documentation to the relevant area/person, suspend and archive information, hence cutting delays, inefficiencies and costs. The benefit to the customer is also significant, as the organization is able to complete the cycle in a much shorter time frame.

Workflow possesses some key functionalities:

- Routing – probably the most critical aspect of any workflow application is the ability to route information or documents.
- Audit Trail – it is important to be able to track and report who has added or modified.
- Integration – the ability of the software to work and interact with existing applications.

Links with Business Process Re-engineering (BPR)

Workflow dovetails nicely with BPR initiatives. As processes are changed, workflow allows technology to increase productivity by automating the transfer of information involved in that process.

Just as there are several different levels of applying BPR techniques, workflow supports BPR in different ways. At the most basic level, workflow helps to identify what does, and does not work well in the way a business operates. Productivity gains can be achieved by utilizing technology to help automate these processes. This is a basic to intermediate level of workflow application. An example of this would be the installation of document image processing to move and image documents within an organization.

At the other extreme, workflows can be completely rebuilt, and processes are not simply optimized, but completely changed. New infrastructures and technologies are established to support this new way of working. As processes are changed to meet new challenges, many organizations are demanding applications that can allow inter-departmental collaboration – whether this is just simply exchanging documents electronically, or more sophisticated needs. This is where a new and growing breed of workflow applications are being utilized. One survey identified 54% of the Fortune 1000 companies to be using workflow and re-engineering in tandem.[1]

Just as processes cannot be cast in stone, workflow has grown to possess a more supple form, where applications can be changed easily. This feature has unsurprisingly been implemented on flexible client/server architectures. The infrastructure is usually interconnected LANs, supporting powerful desktop PCs.

Typically, it is internal processes that are benefiting from workflow the most today. This includes financial, administrative processes and the customer service function. Much of this is due to workflow's in-ability to deal with ad-hoc requirements well – this is discussed further later.

Evolution of Workflow

Today, workflow means much more. Workflow is no longer just associated with distinct products, but is distinguished by a set of features and capabilities that are being built into a variety of applications, even at the desktop. For instance, Microsoft's Word possesses basic workflow features.

The introduction of new features is making the application of workflow techniques more widespread. Traditionally, the technology made huge improvements in back-office applications, where the routing of information and needs of the user were within manageable boundaries.

Today workflow needs to break out of fixed routing, as it was in earlier imaging systems. The emphasis is not so much on the flow, but on the management of work. Work management applications are now beginning to address the requirements of knowledge workers whose tools are paper, fax, telephony and the desktop, i.e. usually a suite of applications, including electronic mail. These needs, by virtue of their *ad hoc* nature, makes automation a more complex issue.

Two ways that workflow is meeting these requirements, are via:

- Electronic Forms; and
- Intelligent Agents.

The Intelligent Agent

Workflow is evolving to meet needs that are *ad hoc* in their nature. One manifestation of this on the desktop is the advent of the intelligent agent.

The intelligent agent is automated workflow, which the user can define. The results are much more proactive, rather than reactive – as opposed to receiving information and then acting on it, the intelligent agent can "search" for the information required, and/or perform some transformation to the data before routing it on. The agent is performing a myriad of tasks, and is closely linked to the idea of the "integrated desktop" of the future. Within workmangement, a good example of this in operation may be the following.

Orders are received electronically via EDI – each order is processed via the processing manager. An intelligent agent functioning on a workstation desktop may perform the following tasks:

- Credit status of customer is verified.
- Check if present order is within credit limit.
- Can order be fulfilled.
- Process order.
- Adjust inventory accordingly.
- Send out confirmation.

Each event may trigger an action that is routed to other areas within the organization. The "intelligence" can be as complex as the user wants it to be. At another level, intelligent agents may be used to collect information. For instance, a Marketing Manager who requires up to date information on certain products may set up an agent to collect any clippings on these products – this information is routed automatically to the desktop.

This capability of intelligent routing differentiates it from groupware (although increasingly groupware products are incorporating workflow technologies).

The Information River

Workflow is growing up – simple elements of workflow are appearing in almost every desktop application. The introduction of workflow can range, from a core business application, typically dealing with back/front-office administrative work processes, to desktop applications. The former is expensive and usually host-driven, whereas the latter is relatively cheap and easily implemented.

With the trend of workflow taking on a "management of work" approach, the challenge for users is to integrate this new technology into new processes. This is already evident, with re-engineering initiatives relying on workflow technology. Workflow techniques are also being integrated into suite software packages – a good example being Wordperfect's offering.

As the technology matures, one can see the relatively rigid simple workflow computing of yesteryear, taking on a more fluid and flexible appearance – conceptually emerging as an "information river". As data and information flows through the organization, workflow technology will route, enhance and deliver it to its ultimate destination. Users will be able to tap into this resource, directly or via personal intelligent agents. The river will be functionally rich, embracing not only text, but voice and video.

Conference and Consensus Building Software

Conferencing software promizes many benefits for groupworking – especially for meetings with staff over geographical areas. Related to this area is the growing field of video conferencing technologies, which are discussed later in this chapter.

Software that has been around for some time, but has not yet hit the mainstream, centres around facilitating discussions and meetings using computer technology. Often also referred to as Group Decision Support Software (GDSS), the underlying theme is to provide an environment that constructively helps the decision making process, whilst reducing or attempting to nullify some of the negative aspects of group working. Consensus building software attempts to create a level playing field among people who have some input into the decision making process.

Typically, the set-up involves a series of participant terminals, which can be located in one room, or various locations. Each participant in the discussion contributes, often anonymously – the argument is that because prejudices cannot be applied to the idea promoted, comments are more honest and decisions are reached in a shorter time than without the software.

Scheduling/Diary Software

Anyone who has attempted to schedule a meeting with several busy professionals immediately recognizes the value of being able to automate this tedious and iterative process. This is where group scheduling software comes into play – interest in this type of software has been muted until lately. Its popularity has grown with the increased use of E-mail and groupware products.

Group scheduling software basically scans on-line personal diaries for mutually free time, notifies participants of proposed meetings and automatically updates calendars if each participant is able to attend. In conjunction with this, the software may also allocate an appropriate conference room.

Users of the IBM Professional Office Systems (PROFFS) will recognize this feature immediately – they have been benefiting from it for some time now. Typically, the new breed of calendaring and scheduling software possesses, at minimum, the following attributes:

- Electronic calendars.
- Meeting scheduling capabilities.
- Personal "to do list" function.

The key players in the market have positioned themselves in the market. Microsoft with Schedule+, Lotus with Organizer and Wordperfect is advocating its Office product, which provides an integrated messaging, scheduling and workflow capability. In addition there are many smaller providers, each offering product capabilities that meet the above core attributes, as well as other value added features. Key to their success is the ability to integrate into other environments.

Challenges with Scheduling Software

The benefits of scheduling and calendaring software are apparent, but implementation does not always improve productivity. This apparent paradox is easily understood if the underlying assumptions of the technology are not realized.

For instance, saving time and work when scheduling meeting necessitates everyone else involved doing some more work. For the system to work, each person needs to maintain an up-to date diary. This is fine for those that are accustomed to maintaining an electronic schedule, but for those that are not, a new way of working is implied. This change in working style is resisted at times, due to the short term inconvenience.

As a secretary may tell you, although a "slot" in a manager's schedule may be open, they are not actually free during this period. Again, without the secretary, an application cannot determine this, and usually requires a re-scheduling process once that slot has been tentatively booked. New terminology and practice is required to allocate periods of time – many see this as an activity that is not only difficult, but too much hassle. This often results in the act of "blocking out" periods of time, when in reality the manager may be available.

Many of the calendaring and scheduling products on the market today utilize an underlying E-mail facility to function. The store and forward nature of E-mail post offices can cause frustrations with the system, due to the delays experienced when different servers are being updated. This situation is exacerbated with busy schedules and rooms that are in high demand.

Scheduling software is a powerful tool. Many implementations are supporting an entry into a broader workflow approach, where the tool is being used as a delegating and directing mechanism. The software is growing up at a fast pace, and increasingly being incorporated as one piece of a broader puzzle – Microsoft's Windows for Workgroups comes complete with a scheduling tool; Wordperfect incorporate their software in their Office suite of programs.

Justifying and Implementing Groupware

Groupware is considered a "good thing", but it can be difficult to near impossible to justify its implementation using standard financial engineering tools. Groupware's greatest benefits are often intangible and therefore difficult to quantify using widely used and accepted measures. Often it is the indirect benefits that the technology brings that outweigh the original perceived benefits.

There has, nevertheless, been some indication of benefit. Lotus Corporation conducted a study in 1992,[2] involving 32 companies using its Notes product for a year or more, on networks with 200+ nodes. Highlights included a minimum Return on Investment (ROI) of 15%, and an average three year ROI of almost 200% – typical payback was four months. These figures were doubled when hardware was not included.

A critical point though, is the training, consulting and maintenance costs that environments such as Notes necessitate. Using the figure supplied by Lotus, for every dollar spent on software, up to five are spent on consulting services. Even having taken these costs into consideration, companies using groupware have gained from significant productivity gains.

Deployment of groupware depends heavily upon addressing technical and social conditions of the organization. Groupware changes the dynamics and decision making processes of an organization. Handled badly, the implementation can be dizastrous. Issues that need to be handled include:

- Conflict – new processes need to be built, and hence new skills. Not everyone believes in investing in these skills.
- Deskilling and Job Loss – there is a very real fear that jobs will be either deskilled or simply replaced by the technology.
- Ownership – information needs to be clearly identified as being owned by the individual or the team.
- Reward systems – these need to be aligned to the new group working environment being implemented.

There are numerous other social impediments to implementing groupware successfully (for a fuller discussion, see Ainger et al.).[3]

Groupware – Here to Stay

Group scheduling, workflow and the groupware environment is here to stay. As with all aspects of groupware, organizations are tentatively exploring this new technology as it matures – the organizational changes in the way we work cannot be fully predicted or hurried. The need to adapt to this new way of working is going to differentiate those that can derive competitive advantage and those that resist and struggle with the change.

Organizational change needs to be anticipated. The technology will replace and deskill some workers and communication and authority structures will change. This decentralized control should not be dim the prospect of introducing the technology. Groupware fits in well with the new emerging organizational structures that are increasingly being implemented.

Videoconferencing

The marrying of technologies has always been a popular dream, and certainly the convergence of television and computing has been one of the most promising. Videoconferencing has been around for some time, and it has only been the beginning of this decade that advances in electronics are allowing the widespread use of the technology.

The roots of videoconferencing can be traced back perhaps as long ago as 1927, when Herbert Hoover used a video booth in Washington DC to communicate with a Bells Labs videophone in New York. More recently, in 1964, AT&T introduced its PicturePhone – since then, the quest to videoconference has taken on almost a religious fervour. Evangelists include the telecommunications companies world-wide. This is not surprising when one considers the sheer amount of data being transmitted when using the technology – moving this amount of data means large profits for these firms.

For instance, a colour moving image confined to a 320 by 240 pixel quadrant generates 4.8 Mbytes of data a second. One minute of uncompressed colour video uses 287 Mbytes of storage. It is not surprising that one of the keys to unlocking the widespread use of videoconferencing has been effective compression techniques.

Growth of Videoconferencing

In the early 1980s, a fully equipped videoconference room with all the "extras" may have cost up to $500,000 – this also required private communication links that could amount to $50,000 a month. Videoconferencing was certainly not cheap. This has changed in recent times though, with leaps in compression and computer technologies. In the mid 1990s, quality systems could be purchased for $20,000 utilizing switched dial up public networks that cost around $10 an hour. The cost justification has become simpler.

Market estimates agree that the technology will really take off in the latter end of the decade. Indeed, in 1993 estimates indicated that almost half the Fortune 1000 companies had purchased videoconferencing systems.[4]

The technology has been dominated by a few organizations; PictureTel, Compression Labs and VTEL. Standardization between these companies is still an issue – although they are publicly agreed that interoperability is key to the success of these systems, each continues to market proprietary technology. The situation is reminiscent of the fax machine, whose growth did not really mushroom until one type could communicate reliably with other types. Since applications tend to mostly be inter-company use, end users have not been particularly concerned with this.

This lack of adherence to a standard to not due to the lack of the existence of one, but more a criticism of the low video and audio quality that the standard bodies have defined. In 1990, the CCITT standards body defined the H.261 (or Px64) international standard for codec interoperability, and compression – codecs convert analogue video signals to digital signals for transmission. This has been superseded by the H.320 standard, the international specifications for audioconferencing and videoconferencing.

Videoconferencing on the Desktop

The trend of the desktop becoming more multifunctional and flexible is evident – video conferencing has been available for a desktop machine for many years, but it has been the dramatic drop in the price of powerful processors that have made it a viable business solution.

A desktop videoconferencing system typically requires a Pentium based computer as a base, and consists of a camera, microphone, speakers and video circuitry and software required for compression and decompression. Price varies according to the video quality, and continues to drop as use permeates every day business use. Approximately 20,000 desktop units were shipped in 1994.

Pushing the desktop market are players like Intel, as well as the telecommunications companies – the hook is the need for fast processors required to work with videoconferencing technologies. Typically, this translates well for Intel's powerful processors, such as the new family of Pentium chips. Intel itself has launched and aggressively marketed it's videoconferencing system, the ProShare 2000.

Desktop products are growing at a phenomenal rate, especially as units now cost less than $1000. There is some mis-alignment with integrating the units with other desktop applications though. Two primary choices exist:

- Using a circuit switched system – this typically translates into an analogue or an ISDN connection; or
- Integration into the LAN environment.

Circuit switched solutions are the most popular, and as ISDN coverage world-wide increases, the option becomes increasingly practical. The latter is more attractive, but less prevalent at this time. The huge bandwidths that video requires can have a dramatic impact on LAN performance, whose typical infrastructure today cannot meet with the demands. This will probably be addressed in two or three years time, when ATM technologies boost LAN network capacities, from the average 10–20 Mbits, by a factor of ten or more.

Videoconference – Glorified Videophone?

Videoconferencing, whether on the desktop or not, is more than videophone. Although the two technologies share the key components of image and voice, videoconferencing tools have a critical third dimension – that of the ability to collaborate on-line. This is via shared desktop applications, or the use of a whiteboard.

Essentially, at its most basic, a whiteboard provides the freedom to communicate written or graphical communication between parties, and usually manifests itself in the form of a tablet. Products on the market are more functionally rich, and co-operate with desktop applications, such as Word and Excel.

It is this key functionality that provides the added value. Whiteboards and data-conferencing products have been on the market, and utilized widely for some time. Data-conferencing products allow screen-sharing of applications, allowing both users to edit documents. These products will usually operate with a modem making them very accessible and flexible.

For many organizations, the added bonus of video is not justified even at today's relative low prices. Other reasons for not using video, for instance, is the availability of a suitable telecommunications infrastructure, i.e. South America still lacks a robust digital service. Much depends upon the application.

Applications of Videoconferencing

So what applications are videoconference systems being used for? They tend to vary, but by far the most popular is meetings, internally, locally and geographically dispersed. With business taking a more global stance, and the time taken for an executive to clear a calendar for an international meeting (up to six weeks, including an average of three days for the meeting), the use of the technology can afford some real advantages.

Currently, the majority of the meetings are point-to-point, but users are discovering real advantage in multi-site meetings, despite the relatively high cost, due to the switching technology.

One area in which organizations have perceived great benefit is in saved travel expense. Companies have spent immense sums on necessary business travel, and this has increased in latter times due to the increasing globalization of organization and business needs. The potential savings that can be made by video conferencing are therefore attractive not only from a financial perspective, but also from a resource point of view – this can include factors such as:

- Time savings derived from less travel.
- Less jet lag.
- Increased productivity.

There is little quantifiable evidence to indicate that the take-up of videoconferencing technology has indeed produced significant travel savings. In fact, many cite other productivity savings as greater, but due to the difficulty in putting a figure on this, travel is used as a good cost justification. Yankee Group[5] surveyed 100 telecommunication and information system professionals about videoconferencing replacing travel. 16% found the technology had replaced travel "a lot", one third indicated little impact on their companies' travel, and 51% noticed it replacing travel a little.

Many are reluctant to use videoconferencing technology for key meetings, especially first time meetings. The nuances that are picked up when face to face do not translate well, especially due to the slight time lag and the fact that people can easily move away from the camera at key points – not so easy when one is physically present. After all, would you want to play poker over a video-conference link? Other important aspects are echo cancellation, fidelity and lip synchronization. Many users of videoconferencing have found that it is the quality of the audio, over the video, that makes for a successful conferencing session.

High value applications are numerous though, and include scenarios such as:

- Distance learning.
- Managing geographically dispersed projects.
- Entertainment and broadcasting.
- Internal meetings.

The Value of Videoconferencing

Many organizations are finding the only way to practically assess the value of videoconferencing, whether at the desktop or not, is to pilot the technology. With costs dropping every quarter as its use propagates throughout business and practice become more widespread, the technology becomes more attractive.

There are a wide range of products now on the market – the key is in selecting the right solution for the needs of your organization, and how it should be implemented – whether this is via desktop use, using circuit switched technology or a larger installation.

Notes

1. Susan A Cohen, Re-engineering Workflow, Volume 11, Number 5, Forrester Research, August 1996.
2. David Coleman, "Justifying Groupware", *Network World*, January 10 1994, p. 27.
3. Ainger, Kaura and Ennals, *Successful Human Centred Systems in Business*, 1995.
4. Joan M. Feldman, "Bane of Business Travel", *Air Transport World*, September 1993, p. 44.
5. *Videoconferencing: The Future of Group and Desktop Systems*, Yankee Group, 1993.

13. Security

The Elusive Search for Security

Around 2000 BC the Egyptians developed what was perhaps the first key operated lock mechanism. This device consisted of a solid beam, carved from hardwood and hollowed from the end to create a slot. When locked, this beam was prevented from moving by the means of pegs in a staple, that were attached to the hollowed beam. Unlocking the lock required a key, typically a foot in length or more. This ancient design evolved into its modern day equivalent known as the tumbler lock, still using fundamentally the same technology. The only major difference is simply the size.

The centuries have gone by, with essentially the same technology adequately serving the same purpose – offering an acceptable level of security for those that required it. In the last few decades, though, we have seen the need and demand for a new type of lock and key – one that cannot be physically discerned or touched, yet secures virtual connections and possessions that have significantly greater value than those protected by the old technology. The advent of the digital information age requires sophisticated and complex digital locks.

Introduction

This chapter explores the emerging security measures that are available to organizations wishing to make their electronic dealings more robust and secure. The increasing use of diverse applications, such as EDI which embraces virtually all sectors, means that by the nature of the information exchanged, secure and impenetrable systems are of critical importance.

What, then, is the appropriate response from commerce, government agencies and standards bodies? Certainly, the increasing fusion of different technologies has attracted much debate on the subject, as corporate and civil liberties are compromised and violated. Potential abuse through the use of computers and global networks is increasing daily, and new innovations in technology bring to bear novel new ways of abusing the system.

The debates have centred on a triad of thinking. Social scientists have advocated attempting to educate and reduce the imbalance between those that have a good grasp of the technology, and those that do not. A more ethical framework is re-enforced at different levels of education and a new culture is required. The lawyers see a need for the updating, and creation of new legislation, in order to address idiosyncrasies that are prevalent in the system which do not adequately cover new technology and work practices. The latter concerns have perhaps lagged more than they should. By far the greatest discourse has been from the technologists who see the way forward as the introduction of better systems and network security technologies. All three approaches have an equal amount to contribute, and what is needed is further efforts to synthesize these thoughts.

Organizations face a paradox: the challenge is to implement and use "friendly" systems, yet the user-friendliness and ease of access are two major factors that create a greater potential for misuse. As complex algorithms become more sophisticated, allowing greater levels of security, users are subjected to increased processing time frames. We can never achieve total security, and will always find ourselves playing catch-up with those who can compromise the system. Even when we do have widespread access to futurist biometric security technologies, such as retina, fingerprint and voice recognition, methods to bypass and foil the systems will blossom. Technologies to break the systems receive the same efforts as those trying to protect – the rewards of compromising a system can be substantial.

Successful operation in this environment is then derived from understanding the tools available, and to get close to total security, or at least closer than your competitor. An optimization process is usually considered, where a balance between security and ease of use is achieved. The process and end result depends upon an assessment of the security risks faced by the organization. This implicitly implies the need for a strategy, usually requiring commitment from top management, coupled with extensive IT audits to uncover improper use of the security tools available. All too often, it is not the underlying technology that compromises the system, but ill-trained personnel or errors in the installation and set-up process. Security of the system is only as secure as its weakest link.

Computer Fraud

The image that computer security often conjures up, due largely to the popular press, is one associated with the teenage hacker, trespassing in critical and confidential system domains via the public telephone network, leaving cryptic messages and sometimes causing damage. Whether this electronic trespassing is by those who are seeking an intellectual challenge, or those intent on more fraudulent purposes, it is a real and worrying threat, especially with global networking traffic ever increasing. This modern worry has attracted much media attention and alerted organizations, often of significant size with matching security systems, to the vulnerability of their set-ups.

Perhaps less publicized, are the alternate threats that originate from more mundane sources than the hacker – often these are more serious and result in a larger monetary loss. Computer based fraud is thought to cost up to $4 billion worldwide. More likely this number is underestimated as most organizations are too embarrassed to admit to it. The key to protecting computer networks from unauthorized access lies in the effective utilization of modern data security technologies, such as encryption, authentication and effective firewalls, discussed in detail in this chapter. Not only does this protect against malicious intent, but also offers individuals data privacy that protects their electronic communication.

Computer fraud is high profile and gains much attention, and consequently, traditional thinking, and a first response by many when asked about security results in security being defined or discussed in terms of secrecy and confidentiality. This is only one aspect of a triad of security aspects that are relevant to electronic commerce, with the other two being perhaps even more important in many respects. It is critical that information that needs to be accessed, can be accessed at the relevant time and that accuracy is maintained. The availability of data ensures that information is accessible within set time frames, without extensive security algorithms making retrieval times unacceptable. Integrity of the data and information used to make decisions attracts many security implications – emphasis centres on threats of the data being inadvertently altered, or changed without authorization. The old adage of "garbage in, garbage out" is apt in this case. These three aspects of security, *Confidentiality*, *Integrity* and *Availability*, have become to be known as the CIA model. The framework is a useful one for those thinking about security aspects within their organizations. All three aspects of the model are covered within the scope of this book, but this chapter focuses on the confidentiality aspects of the CIA model.

Passwords

Newer encryption techniques are a vast improvement on the traditional password system, yet the associated cost and implementation issues of implementing cryptographical methods are slowing their take up, not to mention the impact that they have on high speed networks. Password security is simple, cheap and a very effective defence against computer crime, if used effectively – 80% of all passwords are contained in 100 known names or words, making the choice of password important. All too often, uncomplicated guidelines to password choice are ignored, making the technology less effective. The repercussions of not adhering to security guidelines are all too clear in retrospect when vulnerable data is violated, especially within systems where passwords can be re-used, or users are not forced to change passwords every time period.

The increasing use of the Internet for computer crimes is a well known occurrence: the Federal Bureau of Investigations (FBI) claim that in 80% of the FBI's computer crime investigations, the Internet was used to gain illegal access to systems. This has prompted emergency teams (such as the Computer Emergency Response Team on the Internet) to send alerts over the global network warning millions of users about illegal network monitoring – the act of installing "sniffer" software to monitor network port activities, and to collect log-in information, most often passwords.[1]

The case of the "Internet Worm", released by Robert T. Morris Jr. in November 1988 is illustrative.[2] A program that replicated itself in order to infect connected computers (known as a Worm) was written and let loose into the Internet community by this student at Cornell University. The worm possessed a list of over 400 passwords to bypass connected systems, and also utilized a complex algorithm to break unknown passwords. The small program infected 6000 computer systems in a short period of time, replicating at an astonishing speed, and hence not only causing havoc with systems being violated, but also extensive processing congestion on the systems that were infected.

Although passwords can be viewed as a dated technology, if used sensibly they represent a very effective and cheap security solution. Unfortunately, it is the laxity of the users that usually result in passwords being compromised. Often, users will not change their passwords unless they are forced to. In an environment that allows re-usable passwords, and where general security is low profile, the potential risks are enormous. A survey[3] on the use of passwords that was carried out, outlined results utilized to substantiate the hypothesis that password usage did not follow simple known guidelines, such the use of abstract words containing several characters (typically more than six). The results are outlined in Fig. 13.1. Almost three quarters of the passwords used contained six letters or less.

As Warman states,[4] assuming one check takes 1 millisecond, a system with a similar password distribution could have all of its passwords compromised within 89 hours.

Prevention of unauthorized access can be enhanced through the use of a challenge and response system, used in conjunction with the password system. This approach, which is relatively cheap and gaining wider acceptance and deployment, consists of an electronic device, similar to a calculator which is used to obtain a code in response to a logon input. As codes are different each time, typically changing every several seconds, hackers cannot use the same code to enter the system.

Securing Electronic Commerce

Electronic commerce promises many efficiencies, and potential competitive advantage as underlying technologies are utilized in electronic trade. Highly

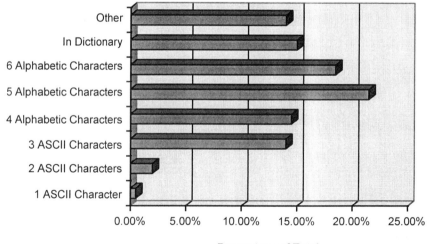

Fig. 13.1 Password distribution.

contingent on the success of this way of conducting business is the widespread availability of accepted measures that ensure sufficient privacy, auditability and security. Key to the emerging electronic commerce community is the use of electronic mail, and for many years technologies have been enhanced and improved to ensure increasing levels of security, centred on the use of cryptography. These can be usefully categorized into three general approaches for the provision of security within electronic mail environments:[5]

- *Document Oriented* – This approach transforms an original message into a formatted message prior to submission. Control information about security parameters, such as type of encryption coding, etc., are encapsulated into a overall document (an example being Internet PEM, discussed later).
- *Message Oriented* – In this case, all security parameters are incorporated into the original message content. Examples include the SDNS (Secure Data Network Systems) Message Security Protocol (MSP).
- *Envelope Oriented* – Utilized in the X.400 (1988) security extensions, and also known as the P1 protocol, the approach makes use of a token (a signed logical data structure) put into an envelope also containing the message.

The adoption of electronic commerce has been increasing since the 1980s, and by the turn of the century the importance of conducting business in this manner will be paramount – in conjunction, its widespread use depends heavily upon having the relevant security mechanisms and technologies in place. Ironically, much of the technology has been available for some time, but widespread adoption has been slow (for instance the S/MIME standard, discussed later, is a good example). The tremendous growth of the Internet in business communications has fuelled this adoption, and the trend continues. This widespread adoption is helping to propel this paradigm shift, making global electronic commerce increasingly more mainstream.

In the following sections, we explore some of the technologies and terms associated with security technologies, their adoption in enterprise-wide systems and the Internet, as well as examining technologies being developed for future applications. The processes possess a wide range of terminology and jargon, which are discussed and clarified.

What is Cryptography?

Cryptography is the art of writing, or solving ciphers – disguised ways of writing or representing symbols. It has been increasingly utilized to protect communications, especially on networks in the past decade, and the process of encrypting data has gained credence as a secure and robust mechanism. Encryption is the process of altering data (termed plaintext) into unintelligible data (termed ciphertext). This transformed requires the use of keys to encrypt and decrypt the data, discussed in the next section. This process of hiding data behind a sequence of code words, alone is not the answer to thorough security, and is usually one element of a range of cryptographical techniques to protect networks.

Cryptography has been around for decades, and attracts large amounts of military funding, not only in the creation of new ciphers, but in cryptanalysis – the art of breaking them.

The Use of Keys

Everyone is familiar with the use of keys – two people wanting access to the same house, protected by a lock, would require the same key. Similarly, users can transmit data through physical and virtual networks around the globe, but to ensure that their communications are not tampered with, or integrity violated, some form of protection is required. In Fig. 13.2, the sender is using encryption to "disguise" the data sent, by the use of an algorithm – mathematical algorithms are used to scramble the message and a message string is produced and appended to the original message. The recipient would then use the same algorithm to decode the string. The coding and decoding processes are controlled by a *key*.

Simple encryption of text (referred to as ciphertext) cannot be decrypted unless the receiver has access to an identical key. In situations where Key A and Key B are identical, the process is termed a *symmetric* (secret key) cipher. This process is outlined in Fig. 13.2, where the encryption algorithms are usually public (discussed later) and the symmetric keys are private.

This is not the exclusive case, though, and situations are possible where a pair of distinct, yet mathematically related, keys are utilized for cryptographic purposes – this process is known as an *asymmetric* (public key) cipher. One key is only known to its owner (the private key) which is used for decryption, while the other is publicly known, referred to as the public key, used for encryption. In Fig. 13.3, Key A or Key B could be either public or private keys, and data encrypted using a private key can be decrypted using the public key, and vice versa.

In general, symmetric ciphers, or secret-key encryption, tend to be more popular due to the excellent levels of performance they can provide, when compared to asymmetric ciphers, or public key encryption. For instance, DES, a symmetric cipher, is about 100 times faster in software than RSA, an asymmetric cipher (DES and RSA are discussed in the next section). Consequently asymmetric ciphers are not often used to encipher data directly, but are instead used alongside with symmetric ciphers.

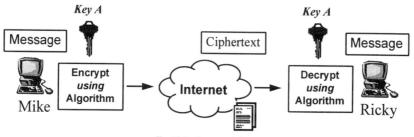

Fig. 13.2 Symmetric keys.

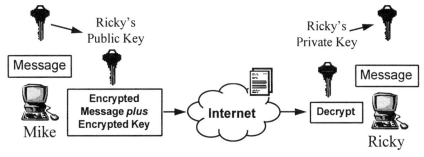

Fig. 13.3 Asymmetric keys.

Asymmetric ciphers (like RSA) can be used in conjunction with a symmetric ciphers (like DES) – once a secure communication channel is established by two parties, a key to use for symmetric ciphers (e.g. DES) can be exchanged to decrypt all subsequent messages. The transmission of a secret key across a network is risky, and therefore an asymmetric cipher (e.g. RSA) is used to ensure that the exchange of keys is not compromised. This provides high performance coupled with increased security in the exchange of keys.

Public key cryptography was invented in 1976 by Diffie and Hellman[6] – the system provided two keys, one public and one private. All information communications utilized the public key, without the private key ever being shared.

Algorithms

Many different cryptographic algorithms are in use today, but by far the two most popular and established are DES and RSA. It is claimed that these two methods are virtually unbreakable, and the proponents state that it would take supercomputers years to decode encrypted messages using these security methods. Newer algorithms are also appearing, IDEA being a well known example.

Data Encryption Standard (DES)

The first, known as Data Encryption Standard (DES), was adopted by the National Bureau of Standards in 1977 as an official standard, and in the early 1980s, adopted as a financial industry standard. The standard was developed by IBM and 17 man years were spent attempting to break the system, in order to verify the technique's robustness. DES has been studied widely, and is perhaps the most well known and established system in the world.

As well as single user encryption, to safe-guard personal files for instance, DES supports symmetric cipher encryption, or secret key encryption – both sender and receiver must share the same key. As it was designed initially to operate on hardware, it is very fast – typically a thousand times faster than RSA, and up to a hundred times when implemented via software. Despite its wide take up, the standard's largest short coming is that it does not possess the capabilities to support public key encryption techniques. Despite this, DES is still used widely and has never been broken, despite efforts over it long history, although with advanced supercomputing resources becoming increasingly available, the continued use of DES into the next century is questionable. This view is shared by many in the industry, and in 1997, the US Department of Commerce launched a project to identify a new stronger algorithm to replace DES. There is also a variant of DES, known as Triple DES, available. Essentially, this approach utilizes two independent keys, providing a significantly enhanced level of technology.

Rivest–Shamir–Adleman (RSA)

The second is the Rivest-Shamir-Adleman (RSA) method, which uses prime numbers and the use of keys – special numbers used to encode and decipher messages. The technique was developed in the late 1970s at MIT with public funding by three individuals who have given their names to the algorithm: Ronald Rivest, Adi Shamir and Leonard Adleman.

This method possesses the capability of utilising a known and distributed public key, overcoming the problems associated with many other encryption methods (including DES). Private communication therefore does not require the secure exchange of encryption and decryption keys between sender and receiver prior to secure communication. RSA should not be viewed as an alternative to DES, but rather an enhancement – the technique is widely used in the exchange of private keys. This provides added safety, without the performance issues that would be experienced if the whole message was encrypted using RSA. Furthermore, RSA provides the added feature of a digital signature capability. It is the latter functionality that is fuelling much of the growth of the technology, rather than encryption. This is in part due to the strict export policies the US government advocates.

RSA is widely licensed and incorporated into many company products, such as: Apple's Open Collaboration Environment (OCE), Lotus Notes and Microsoft Mail amongst others. The technology has also been incorporated into a number of formal standards and accepted by industry standard groups:

- RSA is utilized within many Internet based security protocols, such as the Privacy Enhanced Mail (PEM) initiative.
- The Society for World-wide Interbank Financial Telecommunication (SWIFT) standard uses RSA.
- RSA is an element of the CCITT X.509 security standard for messaging.
- RSA algorithms are accepted by the International Standards Organization (ISO) 9796 guide-lines on security.
- Industry groups, such as Public-Key Cryptography Standards (PKCS) whose members include Apple, DEC, Lotus, Microsoft and SUN, endorse RSA functions.

RSA has more recently taken additional steps to ensure its algorithm becomes one of the *de facto* standards, by disclosing the details of its RC2 algorithm – this was one element of having its S/MIME technology accepted as the industry's preferred standard for E-mail encryption. RC2 was already in use in a number of major applications, such as Lotus Notes, Microsoft Windows and Netscape Communicator products, to name a few.

International Data Encryption Algorithm (IDEA)

First published in 1991, this symmetric key algorithm has gained attention and favour with users. The key length of IDEA is over twice that of DES and patented in both in and outside of the US, although due to its relative infancy, it has not been as widely tested as the DES standard.

IDEA became popular when it was incorporated in the widely used Pretty Good Privacy (PGP) electronic mail security programme, which was distributed freely on the world wide web (discussed later). As a result, it is probably one of the most widely used encryption algorithm for electronic mail in the 1990s.

Authentication and Integrity Checks

Usually associated with encryption is the authentication of messages, used by the recipient to ensure that the message has not been tampered with during transit. Confidentiality may not be an underlying requirement, but the receiver of the incoming message needs to be assured that the message was not modified in any way, prior to receiving it.

Authentication verifies that the message has indeed originated from the sender unmolested – the two parties can be sure of each other's identity by the use of a protocol.

To ensure that the contents of a message have not been tampered with, an additional code is appended to the message which is a function of the message – this integrity check value is then regenerated by the recipient of the message. If the two values agree, the data has not been modified. A more robust mechanism is to utilize a secret key in the process of generating the integrity check value – one such mechanism, widely employed by the financial industry, is known as the Message Authentication Code (MAC).

If the protocol is supported by a public key scheme (as is the case when using RSA) it is important to ensure that users of other public keys do indeed own them. This is supported in the X series of standards (X.509) and is achieved through the use of certificates and authorities (see later).

Digital Signatures and Repudiation

Digital signatures provide an additional value over and above message authentication. The recipient of a signed message has *proof* that the message was from the sender. The electronic signature is therefore message dependent as well as signer dependent. The distinction is an important added value, especially in applications such as electronic funds transfer, as the signature cannot be attached to any message and cannot be forged by any recipients.

The signature is formed by computing a value (known as the hash function) representing a complex function of the data transmitted, effectively making a digital "fingerprint" of the data (known as the message digest). This signature is then

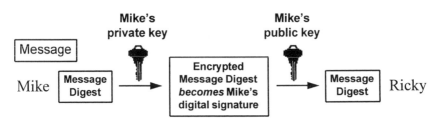

Fig. 13.4 Digital signatures and repudiation.

encrypted using a private key, as outlined in Fig. 13.4. The received signature is subsequently validated using an algorithm (such as RSA) as an element of a multi-step process:

- The receiver computes the hash function using his or her own algorithm.
- The function is then transformed using a public or private key and compared to the computed function.
- The results are compared – an identical match would signify a valid signature.

A certificate(s) may also accompany a digital signature, providing proof of the identity and public key of the signer – this is discussed in more detail later. Digital signatures utilize the strengths of public key encryption. As both sender and receiver can verify that the document did indeed originate from the person who "signed" it, digital signatures cannot be repudiated. The term describes the act of a user denying receiving or originating a message. This feature allows digitally signed documents to be legally binding, and is referred to as *non-repudiation.*

Finding the Key – A Question of Management

By the very nature of public key cryptography, one must be able to publicly let others know of their own key, and have access to a mechanism to locate and verify others' keys. Without this the system does not work. The management of keys is provided through Certification Authorities (CA), facilitated via the use of Certificates and maintained by Certificate Revocation Lists (CRL).

Certificates, Certification Authorities and Revocation Lists

A certificate is simply a digital data structure that is used for the purpose of mapping public keys to certain attributes, for example a name or entity. Certificates are issued by Certification Authorities, and verify that the person in question does in fact own the key in question. This certificate is signed by the authority's own private key, as outlined in Fig. 13.5.

For instance, there has to be some mechanism for other users to be able to identify the true owner of a public key – the digital certificate performs this function, much like a general item of identification such as a passport, or driving license. The certificate itself is signed by a third party certifying its legitimacy –

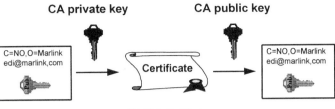

Fig. 13.5 Certificates.

the role of the Certification Authority (CA). The role of the CA can be likened to a notary, or credit bureau.

Certificates hold a variety of information, such as a distinguished name, public keys, validity periods of the certificate (i.e. expiration date), serial numbers and so on. A distinguished name is a globally unique name, formed in a hierarchical structure, used with certificates to provide a name for identifying an individual (or entity) – for instance individuals, organizations, devices and so on. An example of a distinguished name may be:

Country = UK
  State = London
    Organization = ACME Co
      Organization Unit = R&D
        Common Name = Rukesh Kaura

In this case, the entity is an individual, located in the R&D department of ACME Co, based in the UK. Certificates attest to the legitimacy of a public key. Importantly, certificates are also used to ensure the authenticity of digital signatures, with secure authentication involving the enclosure of the certificate(s) with the message sent. For anyone to be able to check on the validity of a certificate, or to get access to the public element of a key, the certificate needs to be stored in a publicly accessible database. Most implementations advocate the use of structures outlined in the CCITT X.509 directory standard, allowing an accepted format for the reading and writing of certificates. The standard, original developed by ISO and the ITU in 1988, has more recently been updated (to Version 3) and is being widely adopted in the emerging Internet standards, such as S/MIME, appearing in applications such as Netscape Navigator and the Visa and Mastercard SET standards. The newer version removed the requirements to use X.400 style addressing, allowing domain name system style addressing, as used on the Internet (i.e. name@domain).

A Certification Authority (CA) provides a reference point to vouch for the binding between a user's distinguished name and public keys within an organization – an authority trusted by users to create and assign certificates. The CA will publicize its public key, which must be trustworthy and accepted for users to gain confidence. Each CA is free to set its own identification criteria prior to issuing certificates. Typically, this may mean a driving license, to more stringent identification methods, such as fingerprints. Each CA should publicize their own criteria, which in turn dictates the level of confidence each user has in that authority.

A number of organizations already provide CA services, and several on the

Internet itself. This includes organizations such as GTE (CyberTrust), Verisign, ICE-Tel, Xcert and the US Postal Service, to name just a few.

Often, a CA may provide a certificate from a higher level CA, vouching for the legitimacy of its key – for instance, this may be a university that has obtained a certificate from a Value Added Network (VAN) provider, such as GEIS. This structure provides hierarchies of CAs. This hierarchy is also well illustrated by the Internet domain, through the use of Policy Certification Authorities (PCA). The CA system was actually developed by the Internet Society, as an element of its Privacy Enhanced Mail (PEM) environment where PCAs are utilized. The role of PCAs are to issue public-key certificates to CAs and certify CAs. Guidelines are drawn up by PCAs, under the supervision and guidance of the Internet society, to be implemented and used by CAs. In general, PCAs carry responsibility for its sub-domains, and are accountable to their higher domain. In the case of the Internet, this would be the Internet Policy Registration Authority (IPRA).

What would happen if you lost your key, or suspected a key to have been violated in some manner? These administrative type questions are handled through the use of Certificate Revocation Lists (CRL). CRLs are simply lists of keys that should not be accepted. They are necessary for the identification of certificates that are no longer valid for various reasons (i.e. the validity dates have expired, distinguished names have changed, the key has been lost, or the private element of the key has been compromised). CRLs are maintained by the CA, which is responsible for administrative tasks for certificates issued by that CA. Checks against CRLs are usually performed automatically by software, typically a User Agent, which may house several CRLs from different CAs.

Some Legal Consequences

The increasing use of digital signatures and certificates has highlighted many "grey" areas where the legal implications of the technology are concerned. Certification Authorities are not yet widely insurable and subject to operational guidelines, although Rules of Practice have been produced. This is changing, albeit slowly – Verisign was one of the first CAs to provide up to $100,000 for protection against economic loss, with others following suit.

In general, government agencies around the globe are beginning to have to face these new technologies, and pass mandates to cover issues concerning digital signatures used in conducting business transactions. Some US States have passed acts involving the use of digital signatures, although the mass introduction in the developed countries is still slow.

The CAPSTONE Project

Following the Computer Security Act of 1987, the US Government's initiative to establish standards for public cryptography, known as Capstone, was launched under the auspices of the National Institute of Standards and Technology (NIST) and National Security Agency (NSA).

NIST, formerly the National Bureau of Standards, issues standards – the Computer Security Act of 1987 authorized NIST to develop standards for ensuring security of unclassified material in government systems. It was NIST that promoted DES as the official standard in 1977. The NSA's mandate is to protect the country's secrets, intercepting and decoding communications since its inception in 1952. The NSA holds some of the most advanced cryptographical technologies, and has huge financial and computer resources.

The Capstone initiative called for the establishment of four major standards for:

- A bulk data encryption algorithm.
- A hash function.
- A digital signature algorithm.
- A key exchange protocol.

Since the launch of Capstone, three of the four standards have been brought to market – these are to become government standards, with agencies enforcing their use with organizations that deal with them. The data encryption algorithm was developed and named Skipjack, coded on hardware known as the Clipper Chip. The hash function that was defined was named the Secure Hash Standard (SHS). The digital signature is now known as the Digital Signature Standard (DSS) and the exchange protocol is being developed.

Of the four standards, only SHS has been officially adopted as a government standard, with Clipper and DSS attracting much controversy that has delayed their official acceptance to date.

The "Clipper" Chip

The US government has been aware for the need for an effective encryption method that can be widely deployed within the US, being an element of the US administration's telecommunications initiative. The result has been the birth of the Clipper Chip, a microcircuit that provides privacy through encryption developed by the National Security Agency. Clipper is also sometimes referred to as Skipjack, named after its underlying algorithm due to potential trademark conflicts with the name "Clipper".

The driving force behind the development of Clipper has undoubtedly been the frustrated efforts of national security agencies having to combat encrypting technologies that were not under government control. The widescale use of Clipper, through the endorsement of the government, allows access to information encrypted with Clipper by federal agencies, facilitated through specified government agencies having access to one of the keys provided with each chip, in what is termed as a *key escrow* system. The keys would be kept by one or more third parties, known as escrow agencies.

The chip itself contains a 64 bit algorithm, called "Skipjack", which uses 80 bit keys (as opposed to 56 for DES) and has 32 rounds for scrambling (compared with 16 for DES). It is also fast at 20 Mbit/s, adequate for handling voice, data, fax and video – AT&T has already launched a telephone that supports the Clipper chip. The chip has been developed so that the algorithm cannot be read from the hardware – in other words, it cannot be reverse engineered. This does mean that software implementations of the technology are not possible. At an estimated $20 for each chip, the additional cost of utilising the technology is relatively low.

This would suggest a powerful and strong encryption device, but many beg to differ. One of the key issues and concerns about the technology is that being a proprietary solution, its methods of working and potential weaknesses are unknown. All encryption systems are eventually breakable, so this is a monumental concern to would be users. Comprehensive testing of the system is suspect, many advocate – after all it took almost 15 man years to produce even a hairline fissure in the robustness of DES, contributing to the underlying confidence in the technology. Clipper does not share this. Furthermore, there are concerns that there may be un-documented "trapdoors", deliberately included to allow government agencies back door access.

The International Chamber of Commerce and the European Union has declared that it will not accept a system that is kept secret by the US government, especially a system for which the keys are potentially held by government agencies (to date, it has not been stated that the escrow agencies will not be federal agencies). This is far from surprising, as foreign customers certainly would not want US government officials listening in on their communications. Add to this the fact that the US Government is considering making the use of the technology law, meaning users in the States would have to ensure that recipients of messages around the globe would also have to use the chip, has made certain groups of users very disgruntled with the approach. If users do not get access to the type of security they are seeking, serious use of the emerging "digital highways" will be impeded. It would seem that the US is following the steps of the French government in outlawing the private use of cryptology.

Certainly there are already many other technologies, many of which are freely available on the Internet, that have proved to be more successful and effective than Clipper. Philip Zimmerman's Pretty Good Privacy (PGP) is one example, discussed later.

The Digital Signature Standard

It was in the early 1990s that the National Institute of Standards and Technology (NIST) was instructed to advocate a single digital signature algorithm as an US standard, between several contenders. The result was the Digital Signature Standard (DSS), which provides a standard authentication technology using the Digital Signature Algorithm (DSA), available without any licensing or royalty fees.

The introduction of DSS causes some issues with the security marketplace, primarily as most organizations already widely use RSA for their algorithms, but NIST has developed its own digital signatures (SHS – Secure Hash Standard). This causes some potential inconvenience for hardware and software vendors, as RSA is increasingly becoming the *de facto* standard in the industry. In addition to this, there are some real concerns about the secure aspects of the technology, with NIST revising its original 512-bit key size, up to 1024-bits after much public criticism. DSS also suffers from the same comments as Clipper, being a new technology that has not benefited from historical usage and the subsequent building of user confidence in the system.

Secure Hash Standard (SHS)

This hash function, proposed by NIST and the NSA, has been accepted as an official government standard, and was designed to be used in conjunction with the Digital Signature Standard (DSS). A hash function is used to generate a string, known as the message digest, that is representative of the original message (a longer string of text). For performance reasons, the message digest is used for digital signatures, as they can be computed in a shorter time using the shorter string.

SHS can, from a variable input size, generate a 160-bit hash function. This is a little slower than popular industry wide used hash functions, such as MD4 and MD5 (which stand for Message Digest 4 and 5, respectively).

Securing the Internet

Since its humble beginnings in 1969 as an experimental US Defense Department network called Arpanet, the Internet has grown. This growth continues at an amazing pace, transforming it into a global metropolis, and like all large cities it is having to face the ugly face of crime. This has led to the need for, and introduction of, several Internet-based security standards – somewhat of a turnaround, as the Internet was never intended to be a secure network, rather one that advocated the free spirit of open communication of its various governmental and academic research communities. As the use of electronic commerce increases on the Internet, privacy issues have also become increasingly paramount.

Many organizations have not fully considered the impact of adequately securing their electronic commerce communications – encryption is certainly not as expensive as it once was, and is now provided as a standard functionality with a range of applications. This is fine with traffic internal to the organization, as the software automatically encrypts/decrypts messages without the user being tacitly aware of the fact, but it causes problems when users are attempting to communicate with other vendor's products – the techniques are usually proprietary. The standards issue is once again key, and the problem is being alleviated with public key encryption being more widely available and employed.

The X.400 series of standards contained extensive security features (in 1988 and 1992 versions), but suffered from a major short-coming. Being closely linked to the X.400 message protocols meant that they could not be used over the Internet mail system, although aspects of the protocols have been updated and are now gaining prominence – an example being S/MIME, discussed below.

We examine some of the standards being widely adopted to re-address the lack of security on the Internet, which in turn is helping to further fuel the growth in the use of the world-wide web for commerce.

Internet Privacy Enhanced Mail

The primary focus of the initiative for Privacy Enhanced Mail (PEM), started in 1985, was to provide a level of security for E-mail users in the enormous Internet community. Although PEM is oriented towards the Internet mail environment, the technology can be usefully employed is a wider range of environments. There already exists an X.400 body part to carry PEM encoded messages, providing a channel for the use of PEM messages through gateways connecting X.400 and SMTP domains. Essentially, the technology supports authentication, message integrity and confidentiality via encryption, using RSA's algorithms for public keys and DES for the encryption of the actual messages.

PEM provides a variety of services, including an optional confidentiality service, which if elected protects messages whilst stored in a user's mailbox, whether this a desktop machine, or remote mailboxes maintained on Message Transfer Agents (MTAs). Additionally, it provides message integrity checking and originator authentication.

Most E-mail systems do not support facilities to verify messages that have been forwarded – the message may well be different to the one sent by the originator. This has serious implications for electronic commerce, especially when E-mail is used for transmission of purchase orders and delivery confirmations, for instance. PEM provides for non-repudiation, i.e. it allows the verification of messages forwarded to other parties. Not only is the message content then verified, but also the identity of the originator.

Cryptography is supported in the PEM environment allowing flexibility to use either secret- or private-key algorithms, although public-key cryptography is advocated due to its ability to support very large user communities.

PEM was an interim step before the availability and proliferation in business of OSI messaging and directory services, but with the take up of X.400 and X.500 being relatively slow in the market, it had gained attention for only a short time. PEM was an important evolution of the Internet as a viable business service, and although work was under way to link PEM with MIME (providing secure multimedia E-mail capability, as PEM cannot handle binary data), the approach has stagnated somewhat and is not utilized widely.

Secure MIME (S/MIME)

Secure Multipurpose Internet Messaging Extension (S/MIME) is an extension of the existing MIME standards, already in wide use in the industry, that was developed in parallel to the MOSS specifications by a private group led by RSA Data Security.

To ensure wide compatibility, S/MIME was developed using the Public Key Cryptography Standards (PKCS), created in 1991 by a consortium of major computer vendors, and in particular one specification denoted PKCS #7. Utilizing these *de facto* standards ensured multi-vendor interoperability, which has been a major factor in the wide adoption of S/MIME in a large number of applications, despite the fact that the underlying MIME technology is relatively inefficient. In addition, by ensuring PKCS compatibility, S/MIME is interoperable with PEM.

S/MIME uses the X.509 certificate standard, utilising the new Version 3 format, introduced in 1996, which supports the "name@domain" convention, used within the Internet. Essentially, S/MIME relies on RSA's public key cryptography to underpin the digital signature and envelope – the latter being used to ensure privacy. The message itself is not encrypted using RSA's algorithms, but rather the

DES cipher, with the key encrypted using RSA's public key. The encrypted message and encrypted key are then inserted into a digital envelope and sent together.

In a move to make S/MIME the industry standard for E-mail encryption, RSA had applied to the Internet Engineering Task Force (IETF) – who had previously worked on the development of Multipurpose Internet Mail Extensions Object Security Services (MOSS) – to establish S/MIME as a security standard for electronic messaging. Already utilized by many major players in the industry, S/MIME is likely to play an increasingly more influential part in E-mail security.

Pretty Good Privacy (PGP)

Philip Zimmerman gained worldwide notoriety in the Internet community when he developed an encryption program called "Pretty Good Privacy" (PGP), based on the RSA encryption algorithm, which was freely distributed on worldwide networks.[7] Zimmerman was being investigated by federal authorities as they attempted to crack down on the distribution of such technologies, claiming that they are utilized by criminals. Zimmerman himself is being investigated for exporting full-strength encryption, which is an illegal act in the US. Strong encryption is classified as munitions, an outdated remnant of World War II – ironic in a country where guns are so freely available.

PGP is available for a number of different platforms, including DEC VAX VMS, UNIX, Microsoft Windows and also DOS. Advocates of the technology praise its near flawless capabilities, and it is rumoured that federal government experts have been unable to crack PGP. Today, there is a commercial version for use in the US, and an international version for non-commercial use outside of the US.

Technically, PGP is similar to MOSS and S/MIME, as well as PEM, supporting digital signature and encryption functionalities, although PGP does define it own public key management system with corresponding certificates. For this reason, it has not been widely adopted in electronic commerce, but does enjoy a huge installed base of casual E-mail users. PGP has also been used with MIME .

Securing the Web

The World Wide Web (WWW) continue to impress and dazzle us with its startling growth statistics, akin to a virus growing and propagating around the globe. With this tremendous commerce opportunity comes a gargantuan challenge to those wishing to exploit the potential – an over-riding concern about security from those interacting in this digital universe. In response to immense demand, security protocols continue to be developed and deployed in this fast developing arena. In the following sections, we examine some of those that are prevalent in the mid 1990s.

Secure Sockets Layer (SSL)

Brought to market by Netscape Communications, the SSL protocol has reached

Fig. 13.6 Secure HTTP session.

widespread acceptance and is in wide use on the WWW today. SSL is essentially used to provide a level of communication protection on the Internet, for applications such as Hypertext Transfer Protocol (HTTP), File Transfer Protocol (FTP) and Telnet. It is most widely recognized, and used, to secure HTTP communications on web pages, and Network News Transfer Protocol (NNTP), however. Security services provided include authentication, integrity checks and encryption. The use of a SSL session can be noted by a URL commencing with "https://", as shown in Fig. 13.6.

Secured HTTP (S-HTTP)

The purpose of Secured Hypertext Transfer Protocol (S-HTTP) is somewhat similar to SSL, in terms of the security objectives, but presents a slightly different solution to the problem – the difference being the level at which the protocol operates at, with S-HTTP operating at the Application Layer, marking individual documents as private, or signed.

As with SSL, the security services provided by S-HTTP encompass authentication, integrity checks and encryption. In addition, S-HTTP also offers the support for digital signatures. S-HTTP was designed by Enterprise Integration Technologies, and supports a wide array of hash-functions, as well digital signature systems. The protocol is relatively flexible, in terms of the key management formats – PEM, PKCS, RSA as well as others. The use of a SSL session can be noted by a URL commencing with "shttp://".

Securing Credit Card Transactions

One particular aspect of securing electronic commerce on the Internet concerns the secure processing of credit card transactions over the network. Several initiatives have been brought to market, with the key approaches being:

- *Secure Electronic Payment Protocol (SEPP)* – designed by Mastercard, together with IBM, Netscape Communications, GTE and Cybercash.
- *Secure Transaction Technology (STT)* – a protocol specified by Visa International and Microsoft chiefly, in conjunction with some other companies.
- *Secure Electronic Transactions (SET)* – Mastercard, Visa International and Microsoft have agreed to cooperate in providing secure credit card transactions over the Internet. Supports X.509 certificates.

The Firewall

Castles of yesteryear were majestic fortifications, allowing a community to thrive whilst offering an acceptable level of protection through a variety of ways – archers, high walls, boiling pitch, and the first level of defence – the moat. This perimeter defence was certainly not impenetrable, but did inconvenience those attempting to enter will malicious intent, as well providing a means of preventing those who wanted to leave. In latter day security, the moat can be likened to a firewall – a means of protecting a private network from the outside world. To extend the analogy, the entry/exit point of the firewall is akin to the drawbridge, and therefore allows for a single point for tracing and audit purposes. Two basic forms exist (although specific implementations vary widely): the wall that exists to block network traffic coming in; and the one that explicitly permits traffic in.

The adoption of firewalls has increased dramatically in the 1990s, especially as connections to external communities and business partners grow. An excellent example is that of the Internet, with organizations keen to use the infrastructure, but are wary of what security issues this can cause. One of the first lines of defence is the use of a firewall, with implementations varying in design and complexity – in each case, the relevant choice is dependent upon the nature of the information being protected, and its respective value to the organization. As with all security measures, much is dependent on a cost-benefit-analysis of having the data violated or compromised. Some of the more popular topologies are outlined below.

Screening Router

A screening router, filtering traffic to nodes within the private network. The extent of the risk with this set-up can easily be controlled, with services being defined as acceptable or not. Although not the most secure solution, routers are popular due to their high level of flexibility and relatively low cost.

Gateway

A gateway (sometimes referred to as the Bastion Host), segregating the outside network and private network, is perhaps the most appealing topology, as not only is this easy and quick to implement, but also requires very little hardware. No traffic is directly transferred between networks, rendering the private network effectively "invisible" to the outside world. The gateway provides a high level of control over dialogue between networks.

Screened Host Gateway

By far the most popular firewall implementation consists of a screening router and a Bastion Host, with the latter residing on the private network. The screening router directs traffic directly to the Bastion Host.

Firewalls are often used for protecting E-mail services, and are an effective precaution when used in conjunction with other security measures. One cannot fully rely on the wall itself as adequate protection, as it is not effective for all applications, with a good example being computer viruses. Another example would be users opening private accounts with external providers, therefore bypassing the firewall in place.

Firewalls are an adequate solution to today's scenario, but as commerce increases, they may not be an effective and practical means to obtain adequate security. One can see the trend of organizations conducting increasingly different types of commerce with other business partners – to have to continually redefine the security parameters of your firewall to facilitate this is cumbersome and expensive. Firewalls can be seen to evolve into more virtual entities, dynamically expanding to include other domains as necessary, by the means of using encryption and strong authentication technologies between the partners. By using key management with outside organizations, commerce with other organizations would be facilitated without having to pass through gateways or routers.

Security of the Future

Several trends in the technology available to us, and the way in which we interact with it, are precipitating new aspects of concern for those responsible for security. For instance, computers are no longer bulky boxes that sit on desktops, but have evolved into a slimline unit, usually no larger than a small A4 book, that can be inserted into a desktop docking unit. These portable machines can be taken anywhere, and hence the information stored on the machine compromised anywhere.

The trend towards open and distributed systems is evident, and increasingly systems are linking various facilities offered by different organizations. These systems pose many security issues, and are often "hacked" into to obtain proprietary information. Good examples are the travel booking systems, like GALILEO and SABRE. The case of the Virgin/British Airways "dirty tricks" scandal in the UK, in which British Airways monitored Virgin booking activity on their information system clearly illustrates the potential for misuse of these distributed systems.

Solutions are being provided, though. With notebooks, security devices are becoming available, which will fit into the industry standard PCMCIA slots providing hardware and software encryption solutions for hard disk units, typically using the DES algorithm or Clipper Chip technology. These "Smart" cards usually have their own battery and are robust enough not to be easily damaged, providing an efficient and easily portable resolution to security issues.

As security technology continues to develop, new innovative solutions are being introduced. One of the most promising and perhaps exciting, is in the field of Biometrics, akin to the techno tools seen regularly in science fiction films.

Biometric Security

The nature of security methods are changing and advancing as the needs of organizations become increasingly more complex, and the technology offered evolves further. The field of biometric security uses human characteristics or behavioural idiosyncrasies to distinguish individuals, and has only been used in high security implementations to date, such as the military and government installations.

Imagine not needing to remember easily forgotten PIN numbers, abstract codes or often changed passwords to gain access to our bank accounts, computers or voice mailboxes. Instead, access may be achieved via retinal scans, finger prints, hand geometry patterns and voiceprints – somewhat more difficult to forget. A new symbiosis of technologies may be used, such as fingerprint analysis and the use of smart cards. In fact this vision is already reality. As error rates become lower, and diffusion becomes more widespread, we may see the distinction of the "old" technologies such as passwords within the next decade. This is certainly not going to be a panacea, as criminal experts will also find more diverse ways of fooling the system. One thing is for sure – breaking the system will certainly become significantly more difficult. Some of the biometric techniques that have been bought to market are outlined below:

Fingerprint Analysis

A high resolution image is captured of the fingerprint, and converted into a mathematical representation. This is then compared to a stored representation, with differing thresholds that can be set by the administrator of the system. This technology boasts high levels of accuracy, and is perhaps one of the least intrusive in terms of user acceptability. In fact fingerprint data can already be held on a 79-character conventional magnetic stripe card, making applications such as ATM transactions feasible.

Retina Scan Analysis

Distinguishing features can be discerned by scanning the blood vessels on the eye's retina using infra-red light. This is perhaps one of the most accurate of the biometric technologies, but also one of the least accepted by users, due to their health and safety concerns (even if unfounded).

Voice Analysis

Voice verification systems are trained by repeating a password, or name, which is used as an access code. Of the three most popular biometric systems, voice recognition has the lowest level of accuracy. Despite this, due to the fact that the necessary hardware (a telephone) is already installed in a huge subscriber base, attention and investment in this technology continues.

There is little doubt that some form of biometric technology will touch our lives sooner rather than later. The question is when? The two major issues faced by the techniques, that of cost and accuracy, and falling for the former and increasing for latter. The finance community continues to pay close attention to the technologies being developed, especially as costs associated with fraud and theft continue to increase. For many applications, the cost to benefit ratios continue to become increasingly attractive.

Notes

1. *ComputerWorld,* 7 February 1994.
2. E. Spafford. "The Internet Worm: Crisis and Aftermath", *Communications of the ACM,* Volume 32 Number 6, June 1989,pp. 678–688.
3. R. Morris and K. Thompson, "Password Security: A Case History", *Communications of the ACM,* Volume 22 Number 11, 1979.
4. A. Warman, *Computer Security Within Organisations,* 1993.
5. S. Wu, "MHS Security – A concise survey", *Computer Networks & ISDN Systems,* Volume 25, 1992, pp. 490–495.
6. W. Diffie and M.E. Hellman, "New Directions in Cryptography", *IEEE Transactions on Information Theory,* Volume IT-22, 1976, pp. 644–654.
7. *Wall Street Journal,* 28 April 1994.
8. M. Elkins, "MIME Security With Pretty Good Privacy (PGP)", RFC 2015, September 1996.

14. Standards in Electronic Commerce (1)

Introduction

This chapter examines in detail the underlying open system standards on which electronic commerce and business communications is based. By definition it introduces jargon, since this is the way of the standards makers, but hopefully the accompanying explanations will allow the reader to navigate through the text without too much distraction. While the base Electronic Mail (E-mail) and Electronic Data Interchange (EDI) standards are mature, they continue to evolve in the light of experience and fresh requirements.

A further factor influencing the evolution of messaging standards has been the pace of technological progress offering dramatically improved cost performance and an increasing investment by the global telecommunications operators in the base infrastructure. This vision has been articulated by governments around the world in particular the US Administration and the European Commission with a growing realization that standards are critical to the long-term viability of the global information exchange in support of a healthy global economy.

The birth of electronic business communications during the 1980s was largely based around proprietary standards supported by the major equipment vendors, and it was not until the mid 1980s that much attention was given by corporate users to open standards. Much of the initial interest was created by the larger organizations that found difficulties in linking the E-mail communities that had sprung up within their organizations.

Other organizations pursuing the inter-company electronic exchange of business transactions with their trading partners soon felt a need to agree a convention for the format of the message, which initially led to industry specific EDI standards in Automotive, Retail, Trade & Transportation, etc. However, more about the evolution of EDI and its relationship with E-mail standards later in this chapter.

Finally, electronic commerce has broadened the scope of electronic messaging beyond its traditional boundaries of simple message exchange, to more complex interactive applications involving information processing. The growth of Internet Web servers is testimony to this evolution and with it will come future demands for further standardization work to be performed.

Electronic Mail (E-mail)

For the moment the focus is upon E-mail with an examination of the two primary

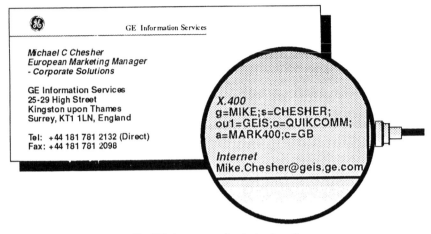

Fig. 14.1 Inter-enterprise electronic mail.

open messaging standards that now dominate global messaging. Since both these standards tend to concern themselves with the exchange of E-mail traffic between local mail systems, a broad range of presentation possibilities exists for the local mail system. Indeed, there is quite a wide choice of local mail systems available, some adding other desktop functions such as calendaring to the same E-mail client software, accessed by the PC user to send and receive E-mails. However, the "lingua franca" for bridging these different local mail systems, particularly for inter-enterprise E-mail (Fig. 14.1), is the Internet standard known as the Simple Message Transfer Protocol (SMTP) and the ITU-T X.400 series of recommendations for Inter Personal Mail.

Past generations of E-mail systems were totally proprietary in nature, requiring gateways to map between the local mail system and the external E-mail transport services provided by SMTP and X.400. This caused a number of problems due to differing addressing schemes, functionality mismatches and lack of consistency in delivery notifications, to name but a few issues. Today, most local mail systems at their external interface offer native implementations of their messaging products in support of the SMTP and X.400 standards.

Both SMTP and X.400 are application layer protocols and therefore independent of the underlying network protocol. Therefore, X.400 based messages can be run over TCP/IP (part of the Internet network architecture), and indeed, this is standardized in RFC 1006. Similarly, SMTP messages could be run over the X.400 normal networking infrastructure, namely X.25 (part of the OSI network architecture), but in practice rarely does (except where X.25 provides the physical layer for TCP/IP). In the case of the Internet there are a number of E-mail services all interconnected via gateways which are used by participating organizations in addition to SMTP and X.400, these include MAIL11, BSMTP and UUCP.

X.400 – Inter Personal Messaging

So what is X.400? In the same way that it is possible for the telephone networks around the world to interconnect, unknown to the telephone subscriber using completely different equipment, a similar situation now exists in the world of electronic messaging. Irrespective of the computer equipment in use, if each supplier adheres to the open standards for networking and electronic messaging, then E-mail messages can be freely exchanged. The ITU-T group (formerly known as CCITT) X.400 series of recommendations simply sets out the rules/conventions for the ways in which inter personal messaging can be successfully achieved by different but co-operating systems. It can be considered as a superset of the many proprietary E-mail implementations which existed in the past, and describes precisely the conventions to be used by implementers, including addressing (identification of originator and recipient), header construction (copies, subject, etc.) and service elements supported (delivery notification, priority delivery, etc.).

X.400 is not strictly a standard but a series of recommendations. However, the International Standards Organization (ISO) has accepted the X.400 model for its own standard ISO 10021 for a Message Oriented Text Interchange System (MOTIS), which is aligned to the 1988 and subsequent X.400 series of recommendations. For simplicity in this text X.400 will be referred to as a standard.

Unfortunately, X.400 introduces a series of new terms which can be confusing for the person attempting to navigate and understand this new environment for the first time. As an example, the standard refers to inter-personal messaging as opposed to electronic mail, but the terms are synonymous.

In practice a user will prepare an E-mail message using their local mail system of choice (Microsoft Exchange, Lotus Notes, Pegasus Mail, etc.). The local mail system will detect whether the intended recipient is another E-mail user on the same system or is to be reached via X.400 (or SMTP), and pass it to a server or gateway for delivery.

The Postal Analogy and X.400

During the 1970s with a growing use of the analogue Public Switched Telephone Network (PSTN) to interconnect computers using modems, the ITU-T saw the opportunity to develop a new digital service specifically for computers. This resulted in the development of the X.25 (network protocol stack) standard, used in Packet Switched Public Data Networks (PSPDN) throughout the world today. It was natural for the ITU-T in the early 1980s to identify the need for a simple global application such as E-mail, that could be transported over the PSPDN and provide a means of growing traffic volumes. This vision resulted in the development of the X.400 standard.

During this same period other companies wishing to offer network based services were severely restricted by legislation in the nature of the services that they were able to offer. Towards the end of the 1980s this situation changed dramatically with growing support from European governments and EEC to promote competition in the telecommunications sector. This resulted in most European countries re-regulating telecommunications services, making it possible for new players to enter the marketplace as well as a liberalising the services that could be offered.

To explain the operation of E-mail systems, the analogy of the postal service is often used. For X.400 this is particularly appropriate, since many of bodies represented on the ITU-T sub-committee, that developed the X.400 standard, originally had the monopoly for both postal and telecommunications services in their member countries.

Using the postal service analogy, the post office is seen as the centre which receives and distributes mail, often to other post offices prior to final delivery to the recipient's mailbox through their front door. The post-box is simply the place through which envelopes or electronic messages pass – it is not meant to be a storage area, and ideally envelopes or electronic messages should be submitted to the post office as soon as they pass into the post-box. However, while not a storage area, the post-box can provide useful audit information, such as the time the envelope passed through it. The mailbox, on the other hand, is a storage area, which receives the envelope or electronic message, to be opened and read by the recipient at their convenience. Date and time stamps recorded throughout this process form the basis of auditability, and in the electronic world provides the means by which delivery and non-delivery notifications are sent.

X.400 Terminology

In X.400 jargon it is the User Agent (UA) function that prepares the message contents (including message header and message body), and usually forms part of the local mail system. The body of the message can be broken up into a series of body parts each containing a different media type such as text, voice, facsimile, graphic, image, etc. So for example, an E-mail message relating to a business proposal could contain a word processed text message, spreadsheet and illustration each in separate body parts. This assumes that the intended recipient has the appropriate software support for the media contained within the multiple body parts, but more about the issues of multimedia documents later.

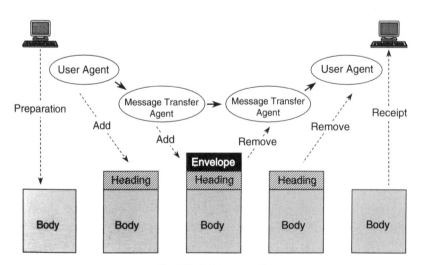

Fig. 14.2 X.400 message flow.

The message contents are then submitted by the UA to the X.400 electronic post office (known in X.400 jargon as the Message Transfer Agent – MTA), using the appropriate X.400 (P3) protocol. This submission by the UA involves placing the message contents in an electronic envelope together with the appropriate addressing information. The computer running the X.400 electronic post office accepts the message, and routes it according to the addressing information on the envelope, to the destination X.400 electronic post office. This destination X.400 MTA removes the surplus heading information (envelope) and presents the message to the recipient UA application. The UA is the point of interaction with the local mail system, which places the message in the intended recipient's mailbox to be viewed when required. Since X.400 merely specifies the rules/conventions, even in a native X.400 implementation, it is possible for developers to introduce their own creativity into the design of the E-mail client software used by the local mail system to send and receive messages.

The protocols used by X.400 (syntax used to communicate between X.400 entities) are all prefixed with the letter "P", so in the above example, P3 is the protocol used by the message transfer layer for the exchange of messages between the X.400 electronic post office (MTA) and message submission/delivery application (UA). X.400 (1988) also introduced the concept of the message store (MS), that can be used for intermediate storage, when user agents are not permanently connected to the X.400 electronic post office (MTA). Access to the message store is via a protocol that can interrogate and selective retrieve E-mail messages called P7, which is very similar to the Interactive Message Access Protocol (IMAP) used in the Internet SMTP model.

When considering the origins of X.400, namely the ITU with its global responsibilities for postal and telecommunication services, it is not surprising that accompanying the X.400 E-mail standard is an infrastructure model, that defines the organizational framework for the administration of X.400 on a global basis. This organizational framework is based upon two distinct types of X.400 electronic post offices (MTAs). First, the X.400 electronic post office that exists in the public domain to provide a delivery service for E-mail messages at a charge, in much the same way that a stamp is placed on a letter and passed to the postal service for delivery. The other type of X.400 electronic post office operates within a company to satisfy its internal business communications needs. The corporate X.400 electronic post office will normally be interconnected to a public X.400 electronic post office, for the delivery of E-mail messages addressed to recipients in other communities, reachable via the public X.400 backbone. A large number of interconnected public X.400 electronic post offices exist around the world, known as Administrative Management Domains (ADMD). ADMDs form the basis of a global messaging backbone to which corporate X.400 electronic post offices, known as Private Management Domains (PRMD), are connected.

Internet Standards

The Internet is the subject of numerous books, and continues to attract a great deal of publicity and worldwide interest. At one level it represents a similar environment to X.400 for global electronic messaging, but its traffic patterns are much greater and, in addition, it offers a far wider range of other services, some of which are not currently included in the X.400 environment. Its origins are from the US military, spreading into the academic and research communities with government funding. As colleges and universities around the world set-up their own computing environments, the Transmission Control Program/Internet Protocol (TCP/IP) architecture became a popular choice. It was not long before campus networks based upon TCP/IP suite were being interconnected, hence the birth of the Internet.

It is important to realize that the Internet is not a single network, and as such there is no single authority for the Internet as a whole. In respect of standards, the Internet Society (ISOC) represents a voluntary organization co-ordinating policy issues and promoting global co-operation of the Internet and its technologies. This is achieved via several key working groups. First, there is the Internet Architecture Board (IAB), which has the final declaration on what constitutes Internet standards. Recommendations come to the IAB from the Internet Engineering Task Force (IETF) which consists of approximately 70 working groups that conducts a significant amount of their work via E-mail, but meet around three times per year. All documents issued by the working parties are classified as Request for Comments (RFCs), and standards go through experimental, proposed, and draft status before being approved as Internet standards.

SMTP/MIME – Electronic Mail

Figure 14.3 illustrates the message model discussed earlier in this chapter for X.400, and shows how the Internet's Simple Mail Transfer Protocol (SMTP) standards map against it. Not surprisingly, there is a great deal of similarity

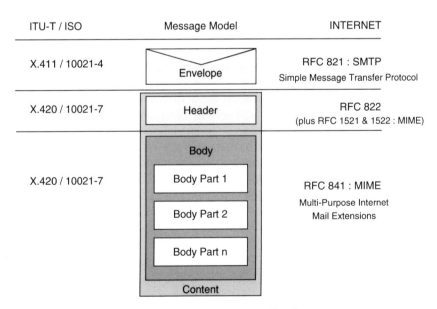

Fig. 14.3 X.400 versus Internet E-mail.

between the two sets of standards particularly with the inclusion of RFC 841 Multi-Purpose Internet Mail Extensions (MIME) which enhance RFC 822 message content to offer many of the features provided by the X.400 multiple body part. Indeed, SMTP is generally accepted as having a simpler addressing scheme than X.400, and together with MIME overcomes a number of the issues with the original RFC 821 & 822 standards. Apart from the multiple body parts, the other main benefits introduced by MIME are 8 bit binary encoding, non-ASCII character set support and indirect file transfer capability. This latter feature is used extensively with the distribution of RFCs, where one body part contains a brief abstract and another body part contains an FTP command pointing to the server on which the complete RFC is stored. When opening the message, well designed E-mail client software will prompt the user whether to establish an FTP session to retrieve the file.

The purpose of SMTP is to manage the transfer of E-mail messages between two local mail systems. It does not accept E-mail from local senders or distribute E-mail to the intended recipients – this is the function of the local mail system. Since SMTP only interacts with the local mail system, it does not see E-mails that flow between local senders and recipients, only those E-mails that are to be sent to another local mail system. This process is handled by the use of input/output queues. The client process is concerned with sending of E-mail to another local mail system and, the server process is concerned with receiving E-mails from another local mail system. The local mail system uses the input/output queues to place E-mails for sending and extract the E-mails received.

POP and IMAP – Message Access Protocols

There are several possible approaches to the creation of a distributed E-mail infrastructure and from an open standards perspective, the X.400 P7 protocol and Internet message access protocols (POP and IMAP) are the best known.

The Post Office Protocol (POP3 defined in RFC 1725) is the oldest and the best known, designed to support "off-line" E-mail processing. In this scenario, E-mails are delivered using SMTP to a mail server (a mail drop), and the personal computer (PC) user periodically connects to the server to download their E-mails to the PC using POP. Once this is completed the mail server deletes the E-mails. In its off-line mode, POP really provides a store and forward "on demand" service to move E-mails from the mail drop to the user's PC, where they can be read when convenient using local E-mail client software.

Therefore, POP is good in an off-line mode for accessing a remote message store (a mail drop), but there are two other modes of operation required by users, namely "on-line" and "disconnected". In the on-line mode, messages are left on the mail server and manipulated remotely using the E-mail client software. The scenario for the disconnected mode, implies that the E-mail client software connects to the mail server, retrieves selected E-mails and then disconnects, only to re-connect later and re-synchronize with the mail server. This phase of re-synchronization with the mail server is important, to ensure that message status (Seen, Deleted and Answered) is updated once changes have been made to any of the retrieved E-mails by the local client software.

The Internet Message Access Protocol (IMAP4 defined in RFC 1730) supports all three modes of operation, namely off-line, on-line and disconnected, while POP only supports the off-line mode. IMAP permits users to optimize the communications path between the mail server and E-mail client software, and is based on the principle that the mail server is the primary mail repository. E-mails are always retained on the mail server, until the user issues a command to delete them.

IMAP provides several facilities that can be used to dramatically reduce the data transmitted between the E-mail client and the mail server. First, there is the facility to determining the E-mail message structure without downloading the entire message. This allows the E-mail client to display information about any MIME message attachments without transferring them. This means that if a two line text message is received with a MIME attachment containing a 10 MB video clip, using the E-mail client, the user can choose to transfer only the two lines of text until they specifically request the attachment. If connected via dialup line from a remote location, such as a hotel room, this can be a tremendous saving of time. A further important feature of IMAP is the ability to use server-based searching and selection as another way of minimizing data transfer, and should not be underestimated.

The Internet uses Simple Mail Transfer Protocol (SMTP) to send messages, because SMTP is indeed simple and there is no particular advantage to duplicating this functionality in the POP or IMAP message access protocols. Likewise, accessing and updating personal configuration information is relegated to a separate companion protocol. In the case of IMAP, the configuration support protocol is called IMSP (Internet Message Support Protocol).

DNS – Directory Name Service

The Directory Name Service (DNS) is critical to the operation of the Internet and provides the mapping of simple mnemonic names, called domain names, into their equivalent 32 bit IP addresses, using the DNS protocol. As an example, it is much easier to remember ceres.kingston.ac.uk than 141.241.4.25, and it is the DNS service that provides the mapping between the two. While there are always three periods in an IP address, separating its four constituent bytes, there are a variable number of periods in a domain name.

Internet domains form the basis of the common Internet naming scheme. For example, www.ge.com is a domain name, and ge.com is a domain. Domains are structured in the form of an inverted tree. Each branch or leaf on the tree is labelled with an simple alphanumeric string, and a complete domain name is written by stringing all the labels together, separated by periods. Thus, www.ge.com is a third-level domain name. The root domain is com, the second level label is ge, and the third level is www. The interpretation of domain names ending in ge.com is solely at the discretion of GE, who manage that domain name space.

Top-level domain names (defined in RFC 1591) take one of two forms. First, they can be generic domains and take the form com, edu, org, net, mil, gov and int, all of which are primarily of US origin; secondly, they can use the UN two digit country code and include, uk, fr, de, nl, us, etc.

Internet and X.400 Service Models

As described earlier, the X.400 service model is based around Administrative Management Domains (ADMDs) which now exist in a large number of countries throughout the world. ADMDs services are not only provided by the new PTOs (Private Telecommunications Operators), but also new players known as Valued Added Network (VAN) services providers, made possible through telecommunications liberalization and re-regulation. Many of the ADMDs have established bilateral interconnection agreements to allow subscribers to their respective services to readily communicate with one another. Users pay to send E-mails and receive service guarantees from the ADMD service providers.

In the case of the Internet, a large part is currently based upon academic and research networks which are funded by the individual networks themselves making up the Internet, often from public funding. There is a perception for users of the Internet that its services are free and no-one pays. This is course not correct – someone always pays, but this is not normally seen by the traditional end user of the Internet.

The Internet had operated a non-commercial use policy for many years, but due to pressure from the business community, this was relaxed in the early 1990s and a new framework established for commercial usage of the Internet, including the creation of Internet Service Providers (ISP). Commercial users of the Internet typically pay a monthly subscription fee, which is dependent upon the nature of the network connection provided by the ISP – the higher the speed, the greater the price.

In summary, commercial Internet users subscribe to an ISP that offers connectivity to the Internet, usually one or more mailboxes (mail drop) on their mail server and space on their Web server, all for a monthly fixed charge. Global connectivity is achieved by agreements between ISPs and use the "Commercial Internet Exchanges", sometimes referred to as De-Militarized Zones (DMZ). While service guarantees are not normally given by ISPs, experience seems to suggest that few problems occur with lost messages, and the Internet non-delivery mechanism works well.

Internet E-mail and X.400 Co-existence

Electronic messaging and other information services based upon the Internet community and X.400 are continuing to grow, and it is unlikely in the medium term that either environment will directly displace the other. In addition, there is a clear requirement for users in both communities to communicate with one another, and further efforts are required to improve the mapping between both services. RFC 1327 and associated specifications provides a sound basis for gatewaying E-mail addresses between SMTP (RFC 822) and X.400 allowing for two methods to gateway E-mail addresses. Simply expressed, irrespective of the end user environment, this would ensure that given an X.400 address it would be possible to map to a SMTP (RFC 822) address, and *vice versa*. Users prefer to work with a single mailbox in which to receive all their E-mail, whether this be local or external – the implementation of RFC 1327 allows a user to be known by either their SMTP (RFC 822) or X.400 address and yet receive their E-mail messages into a single mailbox.

EDI Standards

The three basic structural components of EDI standards such as ANSI ASC X12 and UN/EDIFACT are:

- A syntax and encoding scheme for messages (business transactions), which specifies the structure of the data. The schemes are independent of applications, computers and media constraints and ensures that the data transmitted can be for easily interpreted by humans.
- A data dictionary that defines the standard business data elements, such as sender, product code, address, currency, etc. used to create messages.
- Combinations of data elements to be used for standard messages.

A paper invoice, for instance, normally consists of a header portion containing the name and address of the company sending the invoice, the name and address of the company to make the payment, the invoice date, etc. There is then normally another portion of the document providing details of the goods supplied, which may consist of a series of lines, each containing such details product code, expiry date, unit price, etc. Each of these items has an equivalent in an EDI electronic format with data elements combined into segments, and segments combined into messages.

EDI Message Structure

Using UN/EDIFACT as an example, let's explore the EDI message structure in more detail (Fig. 14.4). First, before any effective dialogue can take place between either human beings or computer systems, a common dictionary of terms is required. These terms are the information conveying elements which form the basis of any language. In EDI these terms are called *data elements,* and form the vocabulary of the EDI application. Each data element will identify an individual field or item of data designed for a specific purpose, e.g. product code, expiry date, unit price, invoice number, postal code, etc. Individual data elements may be combined to form composite data elements, e.g. a weight of 24 kilos is represented by the composite data element 24:KG. The "dictionary" which holds all these data elements together is referred to as the data element directory.

In the same way that this paragraph contains information about a specific topic, there is a requirement in EDI to provide logical groupings of data. These logical groupings are called *segments.* A segment is a functionally-related group of data elements or composite data elements which describe a certain aspect of the overall dialogue, e.g. an address segment, a goods description segment, a payments segment, etc. Some of these segments may be applicable to many types of EDI dialogue, e.g. all documents require the same address segment, and hence they can be grouped together in a segment directory.

```
UNA:+.? '
UNB+UNOB:1+RICHARD+CHESHER+971014:1619+3'
UNH+1+ORDERS:D:96A:UN++1'
BGM+105+RS990541+9'
DTM+137:19971014:102'
NAD+BY+++GEIS International+Prof.E.M.Meijerslaan 1+Amstelveen++1183 AV+NL'
CTA+OC+:R.C.Sargeant'
COM+?+31 20 503 5000:TE'
NAD+SU+++GE Information Services+25-29 High Street++Surrey+KT1 1LN+GB'
CTA+SU+:Mike Chesher'
COM+?+44 181 781 2132:TE'
LIN+1++AB-100005:BP'
IMD+F++:::1/2" steel hinge'
QTY+21:50'
MOA+146:0.75'
LIN+3++AA-500023:BP'
IMD+F++:::3 sided corner fitting'
QTY+21:100'
MOA+146:1.50'
UNS+S'
UNT+19+1'
UNZ+1+3'
```

Fig. 14.4 EDIFACT message example.

A *message* is a specific type of EDI dialogue which is formed to support a particular business transaction, e.g. invoice, order, delivery notice, etc. They are formed from a group of segments which have been selected for this specific purpose. Messages are required to adhere to message design guideline and the syntax rules.

EDIFACT messages (made up of user data segments) are enveloped by a hierarchy of header and trailer segments, called *service segments* and shown in Fig. 14.5. In addition to the above, a service segment UNS can be used to divide a message into sections, if so required.

Functional groups refer to groups of messages of the same type, e.g. all purchase orders going to one company.

The *EDI interchange* forms the entirety of EDI based communications between trading partners and can be thought of as the envelope which contains all the messages (within functional groups if so used). The interchange envelope will contain information about the interchange as a whole, while within it will be a logical nested structure of functional groups and EDI messages.

The *syntax rules* effectively specify the grammar for the EDI dialogue. It is these rules which will define how the components (data elements, segments, EDI messages, functional groups and EDI interchange) are formed together to produce a logical and coherent communication that can ultimately be correctly interpreted for the receiving application.

Message design guidelines allow working groups engaged in designing new EDI messages or modifying existing messages to do so in a consistent manner, which will allow other users to understand them.

Operation of EDI

Within an existing trading community, EDI usually starts when the dominant

Service String Advice	UNA	Conditional
Interchange Header	UNB	Mandatory
Functional group Header	*UNG*	*Conditional*
Message Header	UNH	Mandatory
User Data Segments	-------	As Required
Message Trailer	UNT	Mandatory
Functional Group Trailer	*UNE*	*Conditional*
Interchange Trailer	UNZ	Mandatory

Fig. 14.5 EDIFACT message structure.

player in the community decides for commercial reasons to proceed with an EDI implementation. This might be a retailer with several hundreds of suppliers, looking to reduce inventory by speeding-up delivery times. An agreement needs to be reached within the community (usually a decision taken by the dominant player) on the EDI standard to be used, the information to be exchanged, the means and frequency of the information is to be sent. The information can be sent through a direct connection (point-to-point), or through an EDI VAN service.

EDI connector software products are required by the trading parties wishing to exchange business documents in this way. The software will perform the necessary application integration tasks (in our earlier example, collect the information created by the invoicing application), translate the information into an EDI Standard, and finally, establish communications with a EDI VAN Service to send and receive the EDI interchanges. Alternatively, the software will need to schedule a direct communications session with the trading partner, if this method is to be used. In addition to translating the individual messages (business transactions) into the agreed EDI standard, the translation process must also create the electronic envelope containing the sender and recipient details which are wrapped around the messages to form the EDI interchange (really just a file containing structured information). Once received, the process operates in reverse and the EDI interchange is converted by the EDI connector software into the required format for the receiving applications (accounts payable).

EDI Standards Summary

The basic structure of an EDI message has been described above using the EDI-FACT standard as an example. Each EDIFACT message aims to address one business function, i.e. each message carries information that would appear on one business document, e.g. an order, an invoice, etc. Trading partners prepare EDI interchanges, in which they may send one or more EDI messages, based upon well defined rules for the message structure. EDI interchanges split the data to be sent into a header, the individual EDI messages (business transactions), and finally, a trailer that contains certain control information. These divisions are generally known as segments, and are classified either as service or user data segments. This means that data of a particular type should always be found in the appropriate segment, for example the name and address of where goods should be sent to

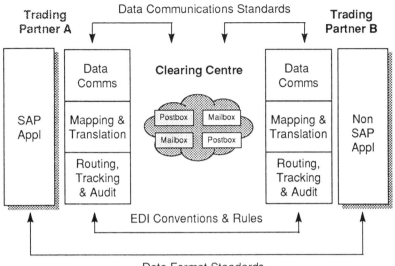

Fig. 14.6 Components of an EDI solution.

on a purchase order would be found in the NAD+ST segment. EDI segments are denoted by a three letter "tag", and more specific meaning can be given by a data element qualifier (ST for ship to; BT for bill to, etc.).

EDI and X.400

The X.400 standard was originally devised for electronic mail and has, shown that it can cater for the needs of this user community. However, the increasing popularity of Internet technologies, have capitalized upon the relatively unfriendly addressing scheme for X.400, lack of integrated Web like capabilities and the ubiquitous connectivity of the Internet. The needs of the EDI community are rather more stringent than those of E-mail users, and there are also differences in the make-up of an EDI message (or Interchange) which impact upon suitability of both the X.400 and Internet technology message relay mechanisms for EDI messages. This section examines the use of X.400 for EDI, while the following section discusses the growing interest and use of EDI over the Internet.

An X.400 system is just a relay system, with no provision for the "value added services" such as standards translations, checking on "trading relationships" or sorting and re-bundling groups of messages.

A more difficult point is raised by the need for positive acknowledgements. A standard EDI message (sent through a conventional EDI system and based, as an example, on the EDIFACT EDI standard) consists of three major parts:

- A Header (referred to as record type UNB), which contains information about the following interchange; this information is more comprehensive than an IPM header and, in particular, allows for "intelligent" acknowledgements to be generated automatically and sent to addressees (which need not be the same as the sender).

- A Body or Interchange, which may contain many different types of document (at least in some implementations of EDI systems) as well as multiple documents of the same type.
- A trailer record (called a UNZ record) which refers back to the header, contains additional control information and acts as a positive marker that the message is now complete, thereby fulfilling part of the requirement for message integrity (Fig. 14.7).

The header, or to be more precise, acting upon the information contained in the header, is what causes the problem. The basic X.400 process will merely indicate that the message has been delivered to the recipient's MTA, whereas the EDI user want to know precisely which messages, as identified by the EDI reference numbers rather than X.400's message serial numbers, have been delivered and accepted by the recipient's application. An additional difficulty is that once the file of EDI messages transported in the body of an X.400 message is accessed, a further application process needs to take place. This will either mailbox the EDI messages, or attempt to pass them directly to the relevant end application (such as the Order Processing application). If format errors are detected at this point, which is completely outside the X.400 environment, the return of resultant error messages has to be handled by a separate application rather than being integrated into the Message Transfer System.

It will come as little surprise to the reader to learn that different groups of EDI/X.400 users or service suppliers have devised a variety of solutions to this problem! The simplest, referred to as the "P0" approach, is to define a new message content type called "Undefined", and deliver it in the usual X.400 envelope without X.400 headers or other information. It is then up to the EDI application to create and send acknowledgements and process the message contents in the

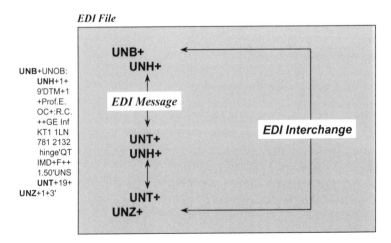

Fig. 14.7 EDIFACT message structure.

EDI	Message Model	Remarks

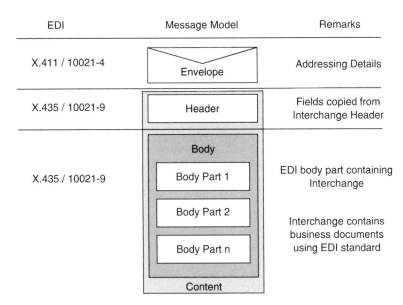

Fig. 14.8 EDI using X.400.

appropriate way. This approach was developed in the United States. The European approach was to treat the entire EDI transaction as the body of an inter-personal message and deliver it with the X.400 header to the recipient user agent.

Clearly, these approaches do not solve the underlying problem of handling EDIFACT addressing and acknowledgement procedures in an "EDI-aware" manner, they just push the problem into an envelope and pass it to the interchange recipient. A more promising approach has made under the aegis of the ITU-T (a technical standards committee of the International Telecommunications Union and formerly known as CCITT) by defining an additional P1 message content type called "protocol for EDI" (P35). This is distinguished by a redesigned header which contains some of the information from the EDIFACT message header (UNB), as well as the information required by the X.400 relay mechanism. It is equally suited for processing messages formatted according to ANSI ASC X12 standard. Therefore, recognizing both the commonalty and differences between E-mail and EDI, in 1992 the ITU-T ratified the X.435/F.435 series of recommendations based upon the original X.400 standard.

P35 brings some new features to X.400 functionality including clear end-to-end acknowledgement rather than relay level acknowledgements, additional security features to cater for the special needs of EDI users, the ability to send positive, negative or forwarded acknowledgements to users other than the original sender and the ability to interface with a wide range of "gateways". Gateways are frequently installed by EDI users to protect their existing investment in hardware and software, and simply act as interfaces between in-house applications and the X.400 delivery mechanism. From the X.400 viewpoint the EDI message is delivered to a user's application; the gateway merely momentarily delays the time when this in fact becomes the case, and allows the user to readily

support a range of session level protocols including support for the X.400 message
delivery standards.

EDI and Internet

Many of the factors discussed in the previous section are equally applicable to the
use of the Internet or Internet technologies for "business-to-business" electronic
commerce. Indeed X.400 "envelopes" in which business transactions are placed,
normally in an EDI format (i.e. structured format according to an EDI standard),
can be transported over TCP/IP Internet networking technology. However, in view
of the lack of support for X.400 based E-mail, as opposed to the ever growing
usage of Internet SMTP E-mail, it seems unlikely that X.400 has any significant
future for transporting EDI messages over the Internet.

The Internet is clearly an ideal medium for opening up "business-to-business"
electronic commerce. The infrastructure is mature and much has been achieved
in recent years by the Internet Engineering Task Force (IETF) through its
Electronic Data Interchange Internet Integration (EDIINT) Work Group to
address the very real and serious concerns of transaction security across the
Internet. This is against a good deal of unwelcome publicity concerning weaknesses in Internet security, from hacking into Citibank's cash management system, inadequacies in Netscape's secure commerce server and browser products,
and systematic hacker attacks on high profile installations.

However, draft IETF standards do exist, that ensure full end to end security of
business transactions may be maintained between co-operating trading partners.
There are a number of competing possibilities, but the favourite IETF standard for

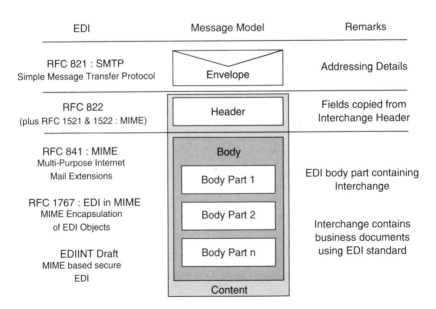

Fig. 14.9 EDI using the Internet.

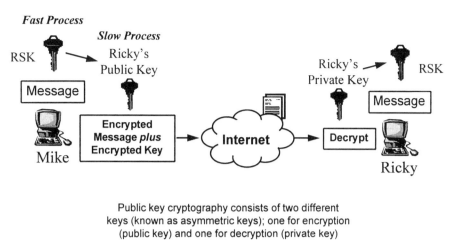

Public key cryptography consists of two different
keys (known as asymmetric keys); one for encryption
(public key) and one for decryption (private key)

Fig. 14.10 Asymmetric keys.

E-mail security is Secure MIME (S/MIME), based upon technology from RSA Data Security, Inc. to transport digitally signed and encrypted information in MIME. S/MIME is based upon Public-Key Cryptography Standards (PKCS), and in particular, one such specification PKCS #7, which defines how to protect a MIME body part, creating a new data structure which itself becomes a new MIME content type, called "application/x-pkcs7-mime". Further details are provided in Chapter 13, but it is sufficient to understand at this stage that through these security standards, "easy-to-use" products are available that employ certificates, encryption, authentication and digital signatures to guarantee data integrity and security of sensitive business transactions (Fig. 14.10).

X.500 Directory and LDAP

X.500 is a directory service based upon international standards (ITU-T X.500 / ISO 9594), and its reference model can be simply thought of as a classical hierarchical structure, where the top represents entries for the countries, under which entries for organizations are made, under which entries for departments are made, etc. The intention is that an X.500 server operated by an organization forms part of a worldwide distributed directory, hence the global database is potentially vast and the information highly distributed. When an X.500 server is deployed to build a single organization directory, it possesses the access control and security features necessary to permit appropriate internal and external access, holding a wide range of object oriented information based around departments, applications, people etc. Commercial implementations of X.500 based directories make it possible to query an individual's E-mail address, as well as ensure that E-mail directories are synchronized.

There are several directory service initiatives aimed at gaining experience in this area, including the Paradise project sponsored by the European Commission, Eurescom, consisting of European PTOs and the North American Directory

Forum (NADF). Each implementation is based upon the X.500 series of recommendations, and seeks to clarify and identify issues of an operational, administrative, commercial and technical nature to assist in the implementation of public directory services. In the case of the Paradise project, largely used by the research and academic communities, over a million entries exist. These entries are maintained by each of the organizations operating an X.500 server on behalf of their users.

X.500 technology provides the potential to create such an infrastructure on a global basis, and despite several successful pilots schemes, it has been slow to take off, due in part to several non-technical issues including a lack of end user priority attached to this requirement. There is strong evidence to suggest that this topic is moving higher up the corporate agenda. The advantages for corporate users of an X.500 directory includes:

- A consistent technology on which to converge all directory services activities and eliminate duplication of effort.
- A solution to the problems of finding E-mail addresses, both within and outside the organization.
- Can be used by both X.400 and Internet based message handling systems for finding addresses, storing routing information and accessing distribution lists.
- A capability that is replacing internal telephone books, as well as external telephone books for white and yellow page services; offering the possibility to look-up phone numbers, postal addresses and display text information together with voice and image annotation.
- A tool to be used by sales and marketing to promote products and services, as well as organizational browsing through the structure.
- The environment in which security key management can be stored, necessary for the effective operation of open EDI.

Access to the X.500 Directory (consisting of directory system agents/servers) is via a directory user agent, based upon a client/server architecture. The Directory Access Protocol (DAP) defined by ISO/ITU-T as part of the X.500 standard, provides the protocol for accessing X.500 directory servers.

However, the Lightweight Directory Access Protocol (LDAP) has become the standard way to access directory services through an intermediate LDAP server, though it does not address how the directory service itself is structured. It was originally defined by the Internet community to allow users to pass text-based queries quickly and easily gain access to directories of people and information, e.g. E-mail addresses, telephone numbers, location etc. As RFC 1777 states the LDAP protocol is "designed to provide access to directories supporting X.500 models, while not incurring the resource requirements of the X.500 Directory Access Protocol. This protocol is specifically targeted at management and browser applications that provide interactive access to directories." The Open Group (merger of X/Open and Open System Foundation) is currently in the process of developing a test suite of software for LDAP server interoperability based upon five separate profiles.

With the growing importance of electronic business communications for many medium/large organizations, open standards based corporate directories are seen as a means to smooth the way towards more spontaneous and effective electronic commerce. As such corporate directories are falling into the IT thick architecture (described in Chapter 3) that many organizations are now constructing. Corporate directories using X.500 are in use, and many larger organizations are planning to introduce them. Electronic mail is the dominant application using corporate directories, which has given an added impetus to the interest in LDAP, that is increasingly being bundled into LAN E-mail implementations. A further stimulus to the growing use of corporate directories will be provided once the Private Telecommunications Operators (PTO) start to offer public X.500 directory services. Corporate directories will be the obvious and natural point at which to connect an organization's directory service to the external public directory services. Organizations will then need to address the difficult question of how much of their corporate directory to make accessible to other members of the business community.

15. *Standards in Electronic Commerce (2)*

Introduction

This chapter unravels the evolution of hardware and software techniques available to bridge the different document formats in use today. Many different tools, of varying functionality, are available and the discussion centres on the strategic implications of the various approaches.

In bygone days, integrated applications were not as great an issue as today – proprietary software solutions were purchased, operating on vendor specific hardware allowing consistency between different applications.

The wide proliferation of personal computers and increasingly sophisticated "off-the-shelf" software devastated the level of integration that was taken for granted by organizations. This lack of interaction was seen as an important issue, especially with the advent of the networked organization. Today, these islands are interacting with surprising success, but the applications are not integrated – there is no co-operation.

In addition, we examine document standards utilized on the Internet and new compression technologies.

The Myth

One of the myths of information technology was that it would reduce the amount of paper that organizations used – it is clear that the paperless society will not exist in the near future. In fact, the opposite seems to have taken place – tools available to make documents look good, encourage several draft copies to be made in order to 'tweak" tiny details. The document is then usually photocopied and sent by standard mail, or faxed resulting in deterioration of the overall quality. If the recipient then requires sections of the document to be reproduced in an electronic format, the text has to be re-typed again – a waste of time and resource.

Rather naïvely, one may question why the emerging digital superhighways are not used to disseminate these documents in electronic format in the first instance. One element of the answer to this is simply the existence of several hardware platforms and different software packages, in use in various organizations, and sometimes departments. Even when applications are standardized throughout the organization, the machine used may not possess the correct fonts for the document to be transcribed correctly, requiring additional effort. Organizations have found that to combat this, staff have maintained several illegal copies of software in order to be able to read electronically distributed documents – for instance, keeping a copy of Freelance Graphics illegally, even though the organization has centralized on Powerpoint. A somewhat unsatisfactory solution.

Analyst estimates suggest that between 5–10% of an organization's gross revenues are spent on putting information onto paper, and then distributing it. Gartner Group[1] further estimate that 95% of all corporate information is located in documents, rather than spreadsheets and databases. The facilitation of document sharing is BIG business.

Manufacturers have not been slow to appreciate the benefits of establishing a standard to allow the interchange of information. The vision is to be a leader in the provision of integrated applications, available across multiple platforms providing a clear path for the emerging technologies of the next century. The initiatives can be categorized into two areas – hardware and software interchange solutions. On the software side, the major players, such as Microsoft and Apple, are trying to establish their own standards.

In addition to these steps forward, the concept of a "compound" document was born – a document that would hold various types of data, perhaps created by multiple applications – in addition, the "link" to this data could be maintained or severed. For instance, in the former case, should the original data in the compound document be changed or altered by the associated application, the changed would dynamically reflected.

Object Linking and Embedding (OLE)

OLE was Microsoft's contribution to the development of integrated applications, with the idea being that all types of information can be treated as "objects" which can be copied and manipulated within any Window packages. A version for the Macintosh was released to provide multi-platform functionality. Objects are not restricted to just text and graphics, but also animation sequences, film clips and voice annotations.

The goal Microsoft was pursuing was richer than just providing a multi-platform exchange medium, but rather a provision of applications that work together, providing for an automated process. OLE provides many functionalities:

- Applications that are OLE supported can export data into objects, regardless of the format they possess. The creation of compound documents is then possible through the manipulation of these objects, regardless of their contents.
- OLE supported applications can possess data that is either linked or embedded. The latter stores information and attributes in isolation of any other application documents that reference that data, and storage is within the resulting compound document. Any changes to the object are local to that document. Linking provides a much richer functionality though, where information is not stored within the compound document. Other documents referencing this information will always reflect the latest alterations.

For instance, take the example of a graph created by a spreadsheet application being incorporated into a word processed document. Using OLE linking, when the data in the spreadsheet is updated, the graph used in the document will automatically mirror the additional changes. This automatic updating and editing is termed as "edit in place". For example, Microsoft Word allows users of Excel, to add spreadsheet data and tables into documents with a click of an icon on Word's toolbar, providing the user with Excels' tools and menus to be accessible within Word.

Selecting objects within OLE supported applications automatically starts up the application that the object was created in. OLE does not support networking extensively, although OLE version 2.0 does allow the user to mount remote disks, allowing for the creation of a virtual domain for the individual user, who is able to access other disk storage areas transparently.

OLE has undoubtedly made significant in-roads within the PC market, and the large number of Windows installations in organizations almost guaranteed this, although its success in the client/server marketplace is not as clear-cut.

OpenDoc

The OpenDoc standard shares the same goal as Microsoft's OLE technology: allowing users to work on different data types within the same document. OpenDoc is stated to be fully compatible with OLE for the Macintosh, and has endorsements from majority of the computer industry's developers.

OpenDoc was conceived as a compound document architecture binding together diverse type of data with documents that could be shared. Efforts were co-ordinated through Component Integration Laboratories, a firm that was supported by Apple, IBM, Wordperfect and some other interested parties.

OpenDoc possesses five main components:

- *System Object Model*: A mechanism free from specific language, for object messaging.
- *Object Storage*: A storage facility, similar to an object-oriented database facility, to store/retrieve compound documents.
- *Open Scripting Architecture*: A cross-platform scripting language, based on AppleScript.
- *Common APIs*: OpenDoc common APIs to provide interaction between applications across different hardware platforms.
- *Interoperability*: OLE interoperability for OpenDoc running under Windows.

OpenDoc was also based on the industry standard CORBA technology, providing full interoperability with CORBA compliant desktop and server systems.

Open Document Architecture (ODA)

ODA is an internationally recognized architecture for compound documents consisting of text, images and graphics defined by large computer manufacturers such as IBM and DEC. ODA defines interchange formats, and the architecture aims to allow blind document interchange. The term refers to documents that can be interchanged between systems, where layout is preserved providing that the two systems adhere to the standard.

ODA is a model for formatting and representing compound documents. Three discernible steps are involved in the process: the editing process, the layout process and the presentation process.

Two interchange formats can be used. The Open Document Interchange Format (ODIF), or an alternative format which utilizes SGML (see later) termed Open Document Language (ODL). ODA based standards are continually being issued, termed Document Application Profiles (DAP), specifying document interchange parameters within certain classes of applications.

ODA had been designed as an architecture for the needs of a broad range of applications, with the interchange formats also usable for the storage of documents, with information contained within the file supporting retrieval operations (such as key words, authors and so on).

Mark-up Languages

Mark-up languages, despite being in existence for many years, are finally playing an increasingly greater role within the domain of Electronic Commerce in the late 1980s and early 1990s. This trend was exacerbated by the need to have a clear and defined process of publishing on the World Wide Web, which was experiencing profound growth. In the following sections, the popular languages are outlined.

SGML

Standard Generalized Mark-up Language (SGML) is an ISO standard (ISO 8879) for defining document structures for the application of mark-up schemes – the specific mark-up tags (discussed later) are not defined but rather a way of describing the mark-up scheme is the underlying philosophy of the standard. SGML developed from generic coding languages that were being developed in the late 1970s and early 1980s, finally resulting in an ISO standard in 1986.

Essentially SGML does not define data content, but provides the flexibility to describe any logical data – books, reports and spreadsheets, for instance. One of the greatest strengths of the standard is the ability to reuse the coded data for a variety of purposes, and to be able to interact with numerous systems. SGML works by modelling a document's contents and identifying structural and content elements of a document. It enables the exchange of documents between different systems, by utilizing a language to define a document's contents in the following main elements:

- *SGML Declaration* – The declaration is a header that determines the environment for the document, specifying information such as character sets used (ASCII, EBCDIC), symbols used, and so on.
- *Document Type Definition (DTD)* – Within a SGML document, rules need to be

established that identify document structures. The DTD interprets and processes these rules, indicated by tags, and also defines relationships between tags. For instance, a heading within a document would not be marked as 18-point bold Helvetica font, but rather as a <lev1> tag, which is defined in that format. The tags then define the structure of the document. Tags may also indicate paragraphs, bullet lists, etc., as illustrated below.

 <Lev1> Glossary
 <p>   The following terms are defined
 <bull1> Commerce:
 <bull1> Data:

Tags can also attributes about each element. For example, specific blocks of text may be marked so as to be accessible to certain qualified personnel, for security or skill levels.

SGML handles text only, and other types of information that is included in documents, such as graphs and illustrations, are referenced and brought in externally. It is thus possible for SGML to be successfully used for documents with a variety of different object types, but it is a difficult and involved process. The further development of SGML is to include other compound document objects, such as graphics and voice.

The goal of SGML is for the compound documents to be used for a large variety of purposes – not only for subsequent paper output. Therefore, the method does not embed formatting information into the document, but rather leaves it to the interpreter to allocate different formats to each tag. Tag1 may require bold point size 14 for paper output, but it might be more readable to use bold, italics and point size 12 if viewed within an on-line service. Hence the data and structure remains the same, but the way they appear may be very different. SGML is being utilized more widely since its formal acceptance, and new generations of products are decreasing the costs associated with its use.

HTML

The huge growth of the World Wide Web had fuelled the need for an effective, standard publishing standard. HyperText Mark-up Language (HTML) addressed this need, and was based on the SGML standard discussed earlier. HTML is a simple language well suited for uncomplicated Web applications, such as hypertext and displaying straight forward documents – this is one of the reasons that HTML has been so widely accepted and utilized.

At its core, HTML documents are simply standard 7-bit ASCII files with the relevant formatting codes that indicate information on layout and hyperlinks – documents written in HTML are usually named with the suffix ".html".

XML

Despite the advantages of HTML's simplicity, this did present some drawbacks, though – with the Web further expanding, there has been a marked push towards more advanced content being published. It was this technology push that spawned Extensible Mark-up Language (XML). XML, developed by the World Wide Web Consortium (W3C), provides the added functionality beyond HTML. The first phase of the development, like HTML, relied on a simplified subset of SGML specially designed for Web based applications, although differed from HTML in the following primary respects:

- New tags could be defined at will; and
- The nesting of document structures was made possible.

The language is not backwardly compatible with existing HTML documents, although parsers have been developed to ease this process. Although the technology is in use today, its use will increase when the applications, currently adequately served by HTML, require added complexity. The trend is certainly visible.

Translation Devices

New software products also promise the same panacea. The release of Adobe's Acrobat (and similar permutations) allowed the distribution of documents of all kinds, across different systems, with fonts accurately transcribed, photographs reproduced accurately and graphics rendered precisely as drawn – Acrobat is a translation device that works very effectively.

Platform Interchange

Interchange between hardware platforms has been becoming a decreasing problem in recent years, with a less proprietary stance being taken by manufacturers. Applications have the functionality to translate from different formats, versions and platforms. Software is available to achieve the same result.

Examples are prevalant in the new releases of software from major software companies, such as Microsoft and Lotus. Their applications incorporate translaters allowing the use of documents prepared on other applications, and other hardware platforms. The solution is not always seamless, and in some cases, the resulting document may still need some minor editing.

Third party manufacturers have also introduced hardware and software solutions to mimic platforms – PC functionality on a UNIX box, or a Macintosh, or vice versa. Apple and IBM have been working on the PC/ Macintosh hybrid based on RISC technology, termed the PowerPC.

Collaborative Environments

Networking capabilities have advanced in quantum leaps within the last few years, with emphasis being on larger amounts of data travelling along network fibres and response times being continually reduced. This focus on one aspect of networking has resulted in less emphasis on the interpersonal, collaborative and integrative aspects of networking – this latter goal has been somewhat more elusive. Manufacturers are waking up to the fact that the next challenge is not so much more advances measured in Mbits and MIPS, but on the more collaborative aspects of network technology.

For instance, consider the average user on a network service, producing a document that needs to be shared with several users. Options for distribution could be to make several copies and mail them via the standard postal service, or if urgent use a courier service. Alternatively, the file could be attached to an E-mail message and sent electronically to those concerned. The user still needs to leave the application being used, launch an E-mail application, look up an address and then attach the message and send it. Hardly an efficient process, and one that can not really be referred to as integrated or collaborative.

Players in the field have developed advanced environments to plug this gap in our work environment, promising huge improvements in efficiency and working productivity.

Open Collaborative Environment (OCE)

Apple's contribution to this new way of working centres on its collaborative environment, OCE, sometimes referred to as AOCE. OCE is a collection of Application Program Interfaces (API) and modules that are embedded in its operating system software, which enable cross-application communication and interaction. In addition, other functionalities required for collaborative working are provided for, such as directory services, E-mail, authentication and digital signatures.

The approach heralds a new scope in working rather than a significant breakthrough in technology, and central to the approach is the idea of a cross-platform environment, supported by mail-enabled applications.

The OCE architecture consists of three main building blocks, as illustrated in Fig. 15.1: Messaging, Directory Services and Security Features.[2]

The establishment of Apple's OCE has already begun to be realized with System 7 Pro, and the PowerShare Collaboration Server, both of which utilize OCE functions. The latest development of the Apple OS provides Applescript, a scripting tool which can be used to customize applications and working environments. The heart of the software, though, lies in the OCE system extensions; Powertalk, based on the blocks outlined in Fig. 15.1. The architecture can be utilized without a server in a peer-to-peer network, although the convenience of having reliable 24 hour E-mail delivery is then compromised.

Messaging

E-mail facilities are provided to exchange letters and documents within their applications. Messaging also allows the exchange of documents within a consistent environment using OCE APIs. Third parties can use Service Access Modules (SAM) to translate between OCE and other services, to allow integration into different services (such as those based on X.400). SAMs act as gateways into the OCE world.

OCE eliminates the need for file translation into specific formats before com-

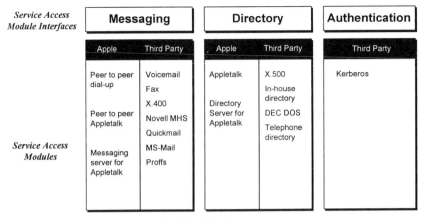

Fig. 15.1 OCE architecture.

munication services can send documents (i.e. ASCII or specific binary formats), allowing for more productive use of the time which would normally be used on this activity.

One In-basket sitting on the desktop holds ALL mail delivered in various formats, rather than several different baskets for different systems (i.e. voice, movies, fax, etc.).

Directory Services

A common information repository stores all users and user group addresses. A standard directory desktop application can be called up within any application.

A new concept has been introduced: the Information Card, a template that holds a variety of information on people such as preferred electronic addresses, physical addresses, pager addresses, ID photos, and so on. The emphasis is on one integrated address book that caters for all your messaging needs.

Security Services

Keeping communications secure and private is facilitated through the provision of encryption and authentication (based on RSA Public Key cryptography technology). Digital signature functionality provides users with a reliable mechanism for transmitting legally binding documents, such as forms-related mail, like purchase orders. This added security helps advance workflow capabilities.

OCE uses a mathematical algorithm to compute a 128-bit number, based on a specific message, which is then encrypted and attached to the original message within a certificate (see Chapter 13 for details on certificates).

OCE has simplified integrated working into a simple "Send" command that may well become as common as the "Print" command that we are all familiar with today. The system handles all the underlying protocols, routing addresses and inter-application issues. Personal directories hold delivery specifics and the user need not get involved with the intricacies.

OCE ties in the variety of communication medias, such as voice-mail, fax, paging and E-mail into one integrated environment. The infrastructure also promotes the development of groupware applications, and group working.

Compression Techniques

With the increasing use of high capacity dependent applications, such as multimedia, there is an increasing dependence and need for effective and fast data compression techniques. For instance, six seconds of CD quality audio, or a single frame of video would require in the order of 1 Megabyte of storage capacity.

There has been extensive research carried out in the field of compression and many innovative approaches have emerged and become defacto standards in their own fields. Research bodies continue to collaborate with interested parties in defining standard techniques for emerging applications.

Many techniques exist to compress data, which can be usefully categorized into two domains – *Lossy* and *Lossless*. The mainstream techniques are outlined in Fig. 15.2.

Lossless Compression

With lossless approaches, the original is recovered perfectly, with no changes made (sometimes referred to as noiseless or entropy methods, as there is no noise added to the compressed signal). What goes in is exactly what comes out. Lossless approaches use arithmetic decomposition (statistical methods) to reduce redundancy and can achieve compression rates of 2:1 for text and up to 15:1 for black and white images.

Huffman decoding reduces the amount of data used for common symbols and run-length encoding replaces strings of the same symbol to achieve compression ratios. For instance take the phrase:[3]

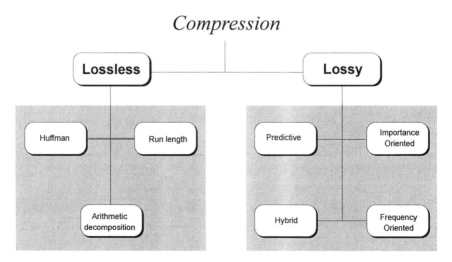

Fig. 15.2 Popular compression technologies.

"The rain in Spain falls mainly on the plain"

The strings of letters "the", "ain" and "in" need only be stored once, and then referred to in subsequent words. Hence the compressed encoded version of the sentence would read:

"The rain <3,3>Sp<9,4>falls m<11,3>ly on <34,4>pl<15,3>"

The brackets denote where to refer to when decoding the sentence, hence <15,3> means repeating the three character string that is 15 characters to the left. In this specific case the compression was 9%, but many data files contain a much higher level of repetition. PKZIP, the popular PC compression utility, uses lossless techniques and shrinks files of text by up to 70%, or more.

Lossy Compression

Lossy compression (or noisy approaches) can achieve very high compression rates, but there is a small loss in quality, the extent of which depending on the compression ratio utilized. This approach decodes an original image into one that is visually very similar to the original, but some information is discarded for good. The challenge is to establish what is not easily discernible and hence a good approximation to the original can be produced. Some common approaches in this area include:

- *Prediction:* Subsequent data values are "predicted" using historical values. The difference between predicted and actual are usually very small, and the technique is use widely in video, or similar, applications where each frame is similar to the previous.
- *Frequency Oriented:* Filters are utilized to segregate different data frequencies, consequently coding with greater fidelity those frequencies that are more noticed by the human eye.
- *Importance Oriented:* Similar to frequency oriented, but as opposed to focusing on frequencies, there is emphasis on the reduction of other factors that are not perceived by the human eye. For example, colour differentials are blurred and more coding bits are used in critical areas such as edges of images.
- *Hybrid:* As the name of the approach suggests, different compression techniques are used in tandem to achieve and overall result – a widely used example being the JPEG standard which is based on the work of a French mathematician, who in 1822 found that spatial patterns can be represented numerically. This mathematical characteristic is utilized in the technology to achieve high levels of compression.

New Advances in Compression Techniques

The field of compression has attracted much commercial attention in the past few years, with application diets being fuelled by the multi-media revolution that demands vast amounts of data – each new application requires a large increase in processing power and storage capacity. Standards are emerging at an incredible rate, in response to consumer demand, but many techniques are almost redundant just as soon as they are established. Nevertheless, much work has been conducted on a new generation of compression techniques, some of which work extremely well within their niche domains, having uses for specific applications (for instance, voice or video), whereas other new technologies are utilized for a wider range of applications.

A case in point is the utilization of fractal mathematic relationships within compression. Fractals are best epitomized by the popular "Mandlebrot Set": a set of swirling patterns that are produced through the use of fractal mathematics. A fractal image has features that are more or less the same, regardless of the level of magnification, and this trait is exploited to produce a high level of compression of data that exhibits this characteristic. A good example is the generation of images, such as mountains – from a distance their appearance is much the same as when they are magnified. The problem with fractal coding is the immense amount of processing power it requires. It can take up to several days of workstation processing to compress two hours of video.

Fractal compression results are impacted by the processing power used to produce the compressed images, unlike established techniques such as MPEG. Whereas traditional techniques produce the same level of quality regardless of the processing platform, the fractal compression image yields better results if more computational power is available.

Other new advances include processing "wavelets", which compress images as a whole rather than block by block (as with most current compression techniques), and the use of objects, which when defined once can be re-used time and time again yielding high compression rates. These, and other related "new" compression technologies are far from mature, but indicate the direction that the research is being directed at.

Multi-media Standards

Initial proponents of multi-media hardware and software have advocated recent standards for images, audio and video with continuous research and innovation improving methods of coding information for new applications.

At the software and network level, much of the work is only recently coming into a robust form. Efforts have been co-ordinated by many interested parties, such as the Multimedia and Hypermedia Information Coding Expert Group (MHEG).

MPEG (Moving Picture Experts Group) has built on the expertise developed with JPEG, and MPEG, developed in 1992, has been upgraded and improved, denoted by the name MPEG-2. An approach, popular in teleconferencing, has been the standard known as Px64. Both MPEG and Px64 are lossy techniques, in that redundant data is removed from individual frames – for instance, when a car is shown moving, the road does not change that much, and hence much of the data used to update the image of the road can be removed.

Approaches have been varied, and there has been much work in integrating the multimedia needs of applications to map onto, whilst extending, ODA and SGML standards. This approach gave birth to HyTime.

Name	Official Name	Standards Group	Designation
JPEG	Digital compression and coding of continuous tone still images	Joint Photographic Experts Group	JTC1/SC2/WG10
H.261	Video code/decoder for audio visual services	Specialist Group on Coding for visual Telephony	CCITT SG XV
MPEG	Coding of moving pictures and associated audio	Moving Picture Experts Group	JTC1/SC2/WG11
HyTime	Hypermedia/ Time Based Structuring Language	Standard Music Representation Work Group	ANSI X3V1.8M
MHEG	Coded represented of multimedia and hypermedia information	Multimedia and Hypermedia Information Coding Expert Group	JTC1/SC2/WG12

Fig. 15.3 Multimedia standards.

Standards in Multimedia Coding

At a lower level, the specific coding requirements for multi-media applications has received much attention and many techniques have been endorsed by standards bodies. Some popular techniques are outlined in Fig. 15.3.[4]

Notes

1. M. Ruport, "Toward Document Sharing", *Software Magazine*, 6 March 1993.
2. D. Baum, "Apple Open Collaboration Environment", *Infoworld*, 31 May 1993, pp. 53–56.
3. "Th bg sqz", *The Economist*, 15 January 1994, pp. 87–88.
4. E. Fox, "Advances in Interactive Digital Multimedia Systems", *IEEE Computer*, Volume 24 Number 10, October 1991, pp. 9–21.

16. *Mobile Computing*

Nomads of the Future

The possibility of becoming a corporate nomadic wanderer, geographically far removed from the organization's web of networks and computers, yet still able to link into this fixed topology via a small portable unit offers many advantages and promises new ways of working and balancing one's working life – mobile computing heralds a different way of working which has profound implications for the psychology of workers and the future organizational structures of our companies. We are beginning to see the evolution of a society where networks of workers, possessing a wide portfolio of skills, are supported by emerging technologies which help facilitate a new way of working. These mobile devices can also provide the gateway into a new world of information, and entertainment, linking into the growing on-line services markets. The vision is especially appealing to vendors attempting to reach those that have not accepted the personal computer paradigm.

Newer technologies are allowing new mobile units to become more human-friendly. As many of the new units being offered are aiming to have broad market appeal in a few years, they will need to be. Human habits can be generally described as analogue, so it not without surprise that adapting to the digital changes that the personal computer has introduced to our daily lives, not only during working hours, but increasingly during our social hours has been a challenge for vendors and users alike. Are we humanizing new technology, or digitizing the consumer? It is a combination of both – the trend is clear with the latter. One only has to examine the popular press, with large amounts of coverage on the concept of the emerging "Superhighways", and promises of productivity tools, that have caught the imagination of the population.

The convergence of the traditionally different spheres of technology – computers, communications and global networks – are hinting at promising something elusive and exciting – the prospect of reaching the two thirds of the population that have not embraced PC technology, in its variety of forms. These consumers have accepted the fax machine, purchased Nintendo or Sega machines for their children, and are perhaps awaiting for the functionally rich, mobile devices to make their lives more productive – whether in a professional or social capacity.

A key aspect of the looming new paradigm is the synthesis of existing and new hardware technologies, creating new challenges for organizations hoping to benefit, and derive advantage. These themes are explored further in this chapter.

The Next Generation of Hardware

Earlier, when examining the desktop environment, we looked at the phenomenal changes that have taken place in the personal computer arena, with respect to the hardware and software advances achieved in the past couple of decades. The birth of a portable computer soon moved on to the first notebook, and then sub-notebook – the emphasis was on faster performance in a smaller box. The consumer was eager to use this tool whilst on the move. Newer, smaller units were enthusiastically received, and sales far exceeded initial expectations. Furthermore, consumers expressed their appetite for this product by paying a premium, and were willing to sacrifice performance in order to obtain this added portability – the trend continues today.

Notebooks have become widespread, and are widely used by workers connecting to corporate networks while on the move travelling around the globe, or squeezing an extra few hours out of the working day while at, or travelling from/to, home. Users have had to accept the poor quality of mobile communication technology available to them – publicly connected computing via the PSTN is slow and of poor quality, yet widely accepted due to the lack of cheap alternatives. Even with the use of cellular technology, the bandwidth is still limited and the coverage is not widespread enough for a reliable pan regional service. This situation continues to improve, as demand for mobile computing increases. Much has been achieved in a relatively short time – one only has to think about how long the telephone system has been in place, and how long it took before achieving broad coverage.

This scenario of the portable personal computer and worker epitomizes the popular concept of mobile computing today. The Information Age is providing new toys for us to play with. Early versions are being tested in the marketplace and are getting progressively closer to delivering, what we hope are, the productivity tools we always dreamed about having. The concept of mobile computing is changing but not without challenges.

Perhaps one of the greatest challenges mobile computing faces, concerns a simple aspect of the portable box – the battery. Energy conservation is of paramount importance in existing, and the new generation of products, with manufacturers facing a paradox: add more powerful energy sources and the units become bigger and heavier; add less and recharging frequency increases. Recharging is a nuisance, and all too often the unit will run out of power just when you need it most. Simple solutions such as carrying an extra battery pack only exacerbates the portability conundrum. Despite the huge leaps in technology advances we have witnessed in other aspects of the computer's anatomy, the lifetime of a battery unit is only estimated to increase by 20% over the next 10 years![1] This has led to an emphasis on energy efficient CPUs and also power saving, energy efficient software.

Electronic Personal Assistants

Classification of the new emerging hand-held computers, seems almost as difficult a challenge as that faced by Darwin, when he was classifying his beetles many years ago. Since sophisticated portable products, such as advanced calculators, storage devices and schedulers, appeared in the early 1980s, we have seen a proliferation of products produced by manufacturers obsessed with miniaturization. The early products, such as Psions', had limited functionality, complicated connectivity and the added restrictions of a small keyboard. Technology has inevitably advanced, and it is now possible to move away from the archetypal keyboard format to a more intuitive form of interaction – hand-written input augmented by icons and voice. We begin the process of further humanising the technology available to us, so that the tools we use everyday more closely reflect the way we naturally think and work.

The new products are small, functionally rich, offer immense communication capabilities and are known collectively as Personal Assistants. The shift towards this type of product, and mobile computing, is being fuelled further by the advent of the flexible worker, whose only future link with the office will be an invisible electronic umbilical cord. This symbiotic relationship between computing devices and communication technologies is exemplified by the emerging market of Personal Digital Assistants (PDA) and Personal Communication Assistants (PCA). The best known early example of the former perhaps being Apple's Newton MessagePad, and the latter by AT&T's EO Personal Communicator.

PCAs and PDAs are often regarded as the same, or very similar products, but today there exists an important core difference in the two products. A PDA can effectively be thought of as the cross between a personal organizer and the mobile phone – the product is the early fertilization of the digital technologies of silicon and wireless telecommunications converging. The Personal communicator (PCA) is a similar product with a different emphasis. Whereas the PDA is essentially organizer oriented, the PCA is completely communications focused, supporting cellular technology modems, and two way fax as standard. An important factor is the price difference, with the PCAs being more expensive units. As the two products mature, there will inevitably be less technological differences between the two, with each adopting characteristics of the other.

CASE STUDY - THE APPLE NEWTON MESSAGEPAD

Apple's Newton MessagePad, was one of the first functionally rich and versatile products launched on the market in the early 1990s. Since then, Apple have launched successive units, incorporating new features that reflect some of the short-comings that users had complained about, such as extra memory and enhanced writing recognition.

The Newton does not use a standard keyboard layout, in favour of a stylus, although a "soft keyboard" graphically represented on the LCD screen is available for those wanting to use this form of input. Handwritten data entry is translated into formatted text, and with use the unit begins to "learn" an individual's personal writing style. There are many functions available to the user, including the standard storage of phone numbers, diary, sketches, notebook memos, and so on. With additional expansion cards, functionality is expanded to offer a variety of different application programs, games, communication facilities, etc.

The Newton will also make "intelligent" assumptions, i.e. writing "Mike, lunch at 1:00, Tuesday" will result in entering a diary entry for that date and associate the name with the one most used, if there is more than one Mike. After confirmation, it will have "learnt", if corrected, and will remember its mistake. It can also fax the entry to a fax machine(s) should you have a wireless/standard modem fitted.

Apple has marketed their product well, and the Newton enjoys perhaps the largest PDA third party software and hardware support, making the product flexible and allowing for a more tailored solution for the user. This is one of Newton's major strengths and corporates have embraced the product (up to 40% of sales have been corporate purchases).

Using the Newton for an enterprise-wide solution necessitates a capability to connect to wireless networks, corporate LANs and desktop machines. These requirements are catered for using either Apple's own solution products or third part vendor offerings (usually via a PCMCIA card solution). Add-ons allow cellular and radio access to other networks (NewtonMail, ARDIS) as well as Internet paging. One in/out box captures faxes and E-mail.

For connection to the desktop, Apple provides kits for both Macintosh and Windows/DOS platforms – interestingly, over half the kits sold have been for Windows connectivity, reflecting a wide user base outside of the Apple Macintosh community. The Newton can also communicate via infra-red beaming, allowing communication between other Newtons and desktops. Perhaps the advent of the Personal Area LAN (PAL) is upon us.

The Newton, like all the new products that continue to emerge in this fast evolving aspect of the market, boast newer technologies with even more fitting in an ever smaller box – the trend continues.

The current PDAs on offer in the marketplace support varying functionalities, depending upon price and size. Perhaps the best known is Apple's Newton product (see the case study above), which was launched with much publicity and media coverage. This product has grown and been adapted, reflecting early criticisms and continues to increase its user base. Amstrad, an UK based company, launched a product at the other end of the scale in 1994 – the primitive PDA without the intelligence capabilities of the Newton but at a much cheaper price. At £299 (sterling), the hope was to appeal to a broad individual consumer market. Others manufacturers are following at their heels, hoping to carve out a share of a market reported to be worth several billion dollars by the end of the century. Sales of PDA units are estimated to grow sharply: BIS researchers predict up to four million PDA units in corporate hands by 1998 (see Fig. 16.1).[2]

The estimates are not surprising. Yankee Group[3] estimates 25 million US workers already work outside their offices, with another 13 million in roles that necessitate being on the road at least 20% of their time as well as a potential 45 million business users in vehicles – the potential market is a large one that continues to grow. As the units are becoming more flexible, users are beginning to evaluate their potential use for simple applications such as text information retrieval, scheduling updates and E-mail. Currently, a large user base of notebooks are lugged around simply for these uses – the PDA offers a much more compact solution.

Despite the high growth potential, there are some inhibiting factors though: the technology is not totally effective at handling cursive (joined-up) handwriting,

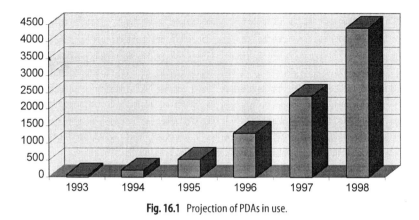

Fig. 16.1 Projection of PDAs in use.

and the cost of the units, although dropping, are still relatively expensive to reach broad market appeal – the more "intelligent" units with connectivity extras cost more. There has also been some complaints about synchronization between desktop applications, although this continues to improve with additional utilities (Windows '95 supports a synchronization tool). There is still dispute over the "standard" operating system to be used, with two major camps – those who support the Windows technology Microsoft have developed for pen-based machines (including the Mobile Computing Initiative), and others like Apple, Sharp, AT&T and Matsushita.

PCMCIA – The Smart Card

The consistent drive to gain increased power in ever smaller units continues at an astounding rate. In response to this, the Personal Computer Memory Card International Association (PCMCIA) was founded in 1989, with a goal of defining a standard integrated circuit card for personal computers. These "smart" pocket sized cards, typically no larger than a credit card, provide complex and sophisticated circuit boards and memory to upgrade functionality. Critical elements included low power consumption, ruggedness and interchangeability between vendor products. The organizations has links with several other standards bodies including the ISO (International Standards Organization), and membership exceeds 350.

PCMCIA cards, named after the organization that sets the standards, are becoming increasingly popular and prevalent, and as take up increases costs are falling. Not only are the cards popular with users of notebooks, but the technology is being used with PDAs allowing the interchangeable model PCMCIA were hoping for at the inception of the card technology.

A wide variety of options are available on PCMCIA cards, ranging from additional memory, peripheral devices such as modems and LAN connectors, to mass storage devices and expansion cards. Currently, three types have been defined by PCMCIA standards, with all types measuring 85.6mm × 54mm, but with different thicknesses. Most notebook configurations favour one Type II, in conjunction with one Type III slot to allow for maximum flexibility. Details of all three config-urations are outlined below:

- *Type I cards* – Being 3.3 mm in thickness, Type I cards primarily house various types of memory options.
- *Type II cards* – These cards are designed to handle memory and input/output (I/O) functions, such as modems, faxes, LANs and host communications. They measure 5 mm in thickness.
- *Type III cards* – The thickest of the three (10.5 mm), Type III cards provide the greatest capacity. The additional capacity allows for miniature hard disks (cur-rently up to 100 Mbytes or more), or various new chip technologies.

To enhance ease of use and flexibility, the cards can be inserted and removed without removing power, or necessitating any re-programming of the computer. The underlying software, termed *Socket and Card Services* is the key to this flexi-bility. *Socket services* monitor the PCMCIA slots continually and detect any inser-tion/removal of cards. *Card services,* operating at an higher level, allocates system resources, automatically if a card is detected, which are released when a card is removed. As new cards are made available, and inserted, Card Services automati-cally reconfigures appropriate domains of the operating system to handle techni-cal interrupts, as well as memory allocation.

This all adds up to a very easy system and flexible solution for the user, who simply needs to insert the relevant card, allowing immediate access to the relevant services. Insertion and removal of the card, even when the computer is powered up, provides easy capability for the use of several cards without the need for any technical knowledge.

Growth Of PCMCIA Cards

When considering the huge growth in the laptop, notebook and pen computing markets, increased flexibility and the ability to upgrade becomes not only more attractive, but a wise investment choice. PCMCIA cards are one important key to the growth in these markets – manufacturers have been very active in producing new innovative cards. Hundreds of vendors already offer PCMCIA card solutions, with new cards boasting increased power (32 bit interfaces) with central process-ing units (CPUs) residing directly on the card.

Market research estimates cite market sales for the cards to grow significantly. The day of easy upgradeability is upon us, where future machines may only be shells with several PCMCIA slots available for customization. Upgrading to a more powerful machine may only be a case of purchasing a new PCMCIA-based microprocessor card.

Cutting the Umbilical Cord

Today we have a whole community of satellites of varying sizes orbiting our planet. Quietly and efficiently, among their many tasks, they facilitate communication around the globe, and are just one of many ways of allowing corporate nomads, away from their home bases, to continue to work, communicate, learn and keep in touch with their personal domains. They are no longer attached to these domains by physical umbilical cords, whether a network or telephone cable, but rather virtual connections utilising the technologies that have been developed over the past years, and are now being deployed on a broader scale. The coming of the wireless network is upon us.

These nomads will use portable computers, whether the new generation of powerful notebooks or smaller Personal Assistants, to connect to information networks using wireless connections. This combination of mobility and portability creates not only a variety of new markets, some of which we already seeing, but also a new way of interacting and working with colleagues and friends. We will see new applications, with by far the most talked about being information services and mail-enabled applications, typically relying on a core E-mail engine. Wireless networks are proving to be a large scale project for those providing them, and for corporations utilising them or building their own. The sphere of communication technologies supporting wireless technology has become known as Personal Communication Services (PCS), and due to the evolving nature of the industry, the term has fast become to be associated with anything and everything. The Cellular Telecommunications Industry Association defines PCS as:

"...a wide range of wireless mobile technologies, chiefly cellular, paging, cordless voice, personal communication networks, mobile data, wireless PBX, specialized mobile radio and satellite based systems"

For large operations looking at PCSs, the myriad of new potential information systems challenges faced by managers are diverse, and often all the answers are not yet available. Nevertheless, the mobile wireless network connectivity model of the future needs to be robust and transparent to the user. We are working towards this vision, and can examine today's technologies that are being used for wireless networks – these can be categorized into the following list, discussed later, which is not exhaustive but covers the major trends:

- Paging Networks.
- Wireless LAN.
- Wireless MAN/WAN.
- Cellular Technology.
- Satellite Technology.

These technologies more or less all face some core challenges, such as coping with a user connected whilst travelling over different coverage areas – this exchange of coverage, termed "handoff", needs to be handled in a manner that does not interrupt data flow. The sheer magnitude of the scale will also require new approaches – imagine a communications network that has to support thousands of wandering users, with machines of varying capabilities all around the globe.

Mobile computing necessitates diverse accessibility to the network – the user could be connecting from anywhere in the world. This poses some very difficult questions regarding security issues, such as access fraud, intentional jamming, eavesdropping, and so on. The potential for abuse increases exponentially as mobile computing becomes a regular service for a corporate network, if security aspects are not considered. Security can be achieved by effectively utilizing technologies such as encryption and challenge and response, where the network will issue a challenge (i.e. prompt for a password from a smart card issued to the user), and the user has to respond within a set period of time. Often there is a belief that wireless computing communication cannot be kept private, due to its broadcast nature. This is not the case, and with effective processes in place wireless networks can be as secure as their terrestrial counterparts.

As usage increases across different sectors, and lessons are learnt, these and other challenges are being addressed.

Paging Networks

These are networks that have high levels of coverage, but low bandwidth restrictions. The major restriction is the fact that these are one way wireless communications (usually receive only). Examples include SkyTel, MobileComm and EMBARC.

Wireless Local Area Network (LAN)

Wireless LAN technology has been available for some time, but is limited in flexibility and range. Typically, usage is restricted to mobile computers that interact with a fixed LAN via an interface card supporting an antenna, which allows the unit to communicate as a node on the network. Due to restricted range, this solution is not widespread, although it does allow relatively high bandwidth communication, between 1 and 2 Mbps.

Wireless MAN/WAN (Metropolitan/Wide Area Network)

There is a high proliferation of private service providers utilizing mobile radio networks (Packet Data Radio), providing low bandwidth data services (up to 19.2 Kbps) offering nationwide coverage. These include providers such as ARDIS (IBM/Motorola with about 1300 radio stations), RAM Mobile Data (Ericcson with about 850 stations) and other Specialized Mobile Radio (SMR) networks, offering a variety of services from wireless E-mail to applications running on hosts. The providers are also offering services utilising Cellular Digital Packet Data (CDPD), although bandwidth is still up to 19.2 Kbps.

Cellular Technology

Cellular technology has impacted our lives in a profound way via the use of cellular phones. The technology handles voice and data services, in an analogue or digital format. We are still restricted to relatively limited bandwidth (typically 9600 bps) and coverage, although expanding, is centred around metropolitan areas.

Satellite Technology

Although satellite services are not widespread today, the networks being built promise high bandwidth and extensive coverage (up to thousands of miles as opposed to up to 50 miles with Packet Data Radio), allowing for true WAN wireless networks. Systems proposed rely on a network of Low Earth Orbit (LEO) satellites, and include Motorola's Iridium Project with 66 LEO satellites and Qualcomm's Globalstar with 48 LEO satellites, as well as others. Services are to include messaging and fax transmissions, though initial offering will be based around paging and voice.

Who is Using Wireless Networks, and Why?

Why the big fuss over wireless connectivity? The key aspect is access to information, in its variety of formats, including E-mail, fax, voice, image or video. The past few years have been characterized by the increasing need for information and has led to a new class of worker, termed "the knowledge worker". Information, and the timely delivery of it, is key to these workers and with increasing requirements to be away from a fixed work location, mobile access becomes of paramount importance.

Knowledge workers, and the information that they use are beginning to define today's organizations. Look back to an earlier era during the industrial revolution, and one could clearly value a company by its assets – typically, these were the large industrial machines that were helping fuel growth around the world. Today, when examining the value of a company, we see its assets typically being information and workers – up to ten or twenty times the value of physical and tangible assets. This information may include research, "know-how", experience, and knowledge. One only has to look at companies as diverse as Microsoft, to companies such as the Wall Street investment firms. Today's environment has levied a large competitive premium on access to information, and the ability to communicate it to those that need to know.

Earlier we examined the archetypal mobile worker; the white collar professional using a portable computer whilst away from the office – whether this was whilst travelling on business or working at home. The users of mobile services are in reality somewhat more diverse, and in fact the greatest use of this technology in the past few years has been in other areas. A more realistic list would include:

- *Mobile Office Workers* – white collar professionals using services such as E-mail, file transfer and various desktop/LAN applications.
- *Field Services* – these include white collar workers such as sales/insurance representatives and blue collar workers in data collection, repair, customer service and distribution.
- *Fixed Location* – applications such as Point-of-Sale and electronic display and control.
- *Personal Communication* – private consumers using information services, messaging, etc.

Certainly, by far the greatest market size of these segments will be represented by the professional mobile workers segment, who collectively will perhaps constitute almost a half of the potential market by the end of the century. In the early 1990s, the picture has been a little different, with the majority of users being field service workers, who have derived tangible benefits from the technology. Some of the inhibiting factors for the other segments have included cost, size of specialist modems (such as radio or cellular), complexity and unpredictable coverage and usage costs. For mobile workers, the major impediment has been the lack of wireless solutions operating on the corporate client/server LAN level. This is changing, and we can examine two popular methods of remote LAN access in use today; remote control and remote client, discussed later.

Mobile workers, or telecommuters as they may be sometimes referred to as, will clearly represent a large market, and the concept has been one that is favoured by employees and employers, as both benefit. Although the concepts of a mobile worker overlap with a telecommuter, the two possess some fundamental differences – the mobile worker is based full-time at an office and requires access whilst away from their home location. A telecommuter may spend a period of their working week based outside of their office (from one to several days of the week, every week). Both share the same challenge though – that of *ad hoc* access to corporate network resources from diverse geographical locations and in the context of this chapter we view both in the same vein.

Telecommuting has promised much over the years, and there have been some very successful cases. These have typically involved workers spending extended periods away from the organization's central site, allowing the organization to learn, and finally benefit. The concept is an appealing one, especially as the touted benefits include tangible financial savings, as well as the more desirable intangible benefits. Mobile computing addresses issues such as balancing family values, flexible schedules and commuting time frames, as well as allowing organizations to achieve considerable savings in expensive office space when employees are located elsewhere. This latter concept has become to be known as the SOHO (Small Office Home Office) model, and differs from the principal requirements of the mobile worker, who would dial-in where-ever they happen to be located; this does, of course, include the home, and more often then not, mobile workers establish a semi-permanent set-up at home, including peripherals such as a printer.

The philosophy behind working away from the office has suffered some impediments, as the proponents of telecommuting know all too well. Although some were technological or cost benefit related, these reasons are less of an hindrance today. By far the largest reason remains cultural, and organizations have been wrestling with the new way of working that is inferred. The Orwellian nature of some management has restricted the concept of telecommuting as workers cannot be "seen" to be working – in fact, the ideology behind telecommuting can be viewed in the opposite sense: the technology allows more working hours in the day, suiting ambitious employees burning the midnight oil.

This new way of working has some significant implications in terms of a organizational cultural shift, and an adjustment of working patterns. The key aspect is perhaps a question of trust – without it advantages of working away from the office are diminished, as overtly or covertly, those against the philosophy try their best to oppose it. Organizations are experimenting with small user bases, and are realizing tangible results, especially with their sales professionals. This shift is being accelerated by more mobile users requiring *ad hoc* access to corporate LAN resources, and consequently having the means to spend more time away from the office.

Remote Access

Today, despite the increasing proliferation of wireless networks based on newer technologies, by far the greatest number of mobile users connecting to disparate networks, corporate or public information service providers, utilize the existing infrastructure of the PSTN. Corporations are utilizing available software solutions to provide remote access services to mobile users of their network, and using sophisticated security solutions in an attempt to ensure confidentiality.

Users demanding remote access to corporate LAN resources are also growing in number – armed with the required hardware, typically a notebook with modem, they are discovering the productivity advantages and convenience that remote access can provide. As a greater number of notebook configurations, in conjunction with a desktop docking solution, are introduced into organizations, so the challenge to provide what is becoming a necessary function on a LAN increases. The notebooks can provide local access to application software residing on the machine's hard disk unit, but users still demand access to LAN-based corporate databases, schedules and E-mail facilities. Users are also fuelling the supply for remote access products, as technological functionality overrides price, encouraging vendors to bring to market newer more powerful solutions to this growing requirement. Currently, typical access speeds range from the more prevalent 14.4 Kbps to some 33.6 Kbps implementations, with the two most popular approaches to providing remote access to the LAN being remote control and remote client.

Remote Control

Remote access in the early 1980s was characterized by the PC technology of the day. This typically translated into a 286/386 processor based machine, or one with similar processing characteristics, coupled with a modem operating up to 9600 bps, but usually at 2400 bps. This led to remote access solutions being built around the limitations of this technology; namely slow modem speeds and a need to limit processing on the dial-in machine.

Remote Control is a remote access technique that allows the dial-in machine to essentially assume control over a dedicated LAN-based PC. This can either be a one-to-one relationship, where there is a PC for every dial-in user, or a virtual PC in a multi-user operating system running on a server. Usually, the latter is implemented via a rack of PCs, with processing clustered and shared amongst dial-in machines. A typical configuration is illustrated in Fig. 16.2. With a one-to-one relationship, dial-in PCs A and B would communicate with different dial-in slave PCs. In a multi-user configuration, the processing would be shared between all the slave PCs.

When using a remote control solution, the dial-in PC is effectively a dumb terminal – all processing is performed at the LAN level on the slave PC, with screen updates and keyboard/mouse interaction sent over the dial-up connection. As the central suite of software is used, additional software licenses are not required for the dial-in machine. As a result, the dial-in PC capabilities are not important and a relatively low performance machine will suffice, although this does have an

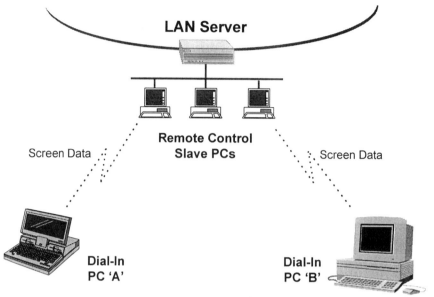

Fig. 16.2 Remote control access.

impact when using applications which support high levels of graphics – such as Windows-based software.

Although sometimes perceived as dated technology, remote control access has several benefits, and can be an excellent solution depending upon the particular needs of an organization. For instance:

- For text based services, the solution is fast.
- When interrogating databases, as the slave PC's capabilities are used, performance is excellent as only screen updates are transmitted through the connection. As the dial-in PC's processing capabilities are not an issue, older machines can be used for remote access.
- Depending on software licensing deals, there is no requirement for additional licenses on the dial-in machine, which can represent a significant saving.

The increasing use of Windows-based applications has put a strain on this type of access model, and although popular remote control products have been improved to work with Windows, access is still slow. Furthermore, there are confusions when using this model as simple tasks such as file transfer can be convoluted. For instance, take the example of copying a file from a network drive to a local drive – the result will be files copied to the slave PC's local drive rather than the dial-in machine. Hence, users need to be aware of the distinction between the slave and their dial-in PC.

Remote Client (RC)

The Remote Client solution makes the most of inexpensive new technologies, such as PCs (usually notebooks) with faster processing speeds, used in conjunction with high speed modems. As opposed to connecting to a slave PC on the LAN, and

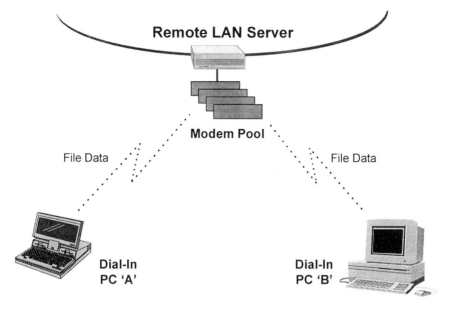

Fig. 16.3 Remote client.

having all processing performed by that machine, RC software allows the dial-in machine to be essentially viewed as a client on the LAN, by the software emulating a network interface card. The software operating on the Remote LAN Server (see Fig. 16.3) then receives data as if being sent to an interface card and sends the data over the modem link as opposed to the LAN. As illustrated in Fig. 16.3, the dial-in PC would connect directly to the LAN, usually through a pool of modems, hence benefiting from the same software environment as users local to the LAN, including higher-layer functionality.

Unlike remote control, a remote client does make full use of the dial-in PC's processing capability, and uses application software running on the dial-in machine. Consequently, this solution is relatively more expensive in terms of hardware and software, especially if an unlimited software license is not in place. The higher functionality afforded by this approach does result in degraded response time, as the modem link is not as fast as the network speed. Despite this, the remote client approach is becoming the first choice for organizations implementing a remote access solution, especially as this model works best with Graphical User Interfaces (GUI) such as Microsoft Windows, Apple System OS, Unix Windows – the most popular operating systems in use today.

The Future of Wireless Networks

As we see the dawn of the next century, mobile workers will enjoy the luxury of not having to worry about how their communications to diversely located information is being handled. One access point will allow them to communicate, receive and peruse through information repositories at their will. The segregation of existing communication systems and technologies are merging into a intricate wireless solution, providing the ubiquitous service that mobile workers will demand. When examining the trends of wider geographical coverage and higher bandwidths required to support throughput hungry multi-media applications, it is not surprising to see PCS being increasingly supported by cellular and Low Earth Orbit (LEO) satellite technologies. LEO satellites are a little different to satellites we most familiar with, known as geosynchronous satellites. These are much further away from the Earth's surface, approximately 22,000 miles, and orbit the Earth once day as opposed to several times a day for LEOs which orbit just a few hundred miles above the Earth.

Since 1990, when the first few large scale LEO projects were filed, satellite-based PCS solutions have grown, and commercial services have been available since the mid 1990s. A good example of the satellite approach is being headed by a spin-off initiative by Motorola, known as the Iridium project. The initiative was named after the element Iridium, as the original project called for 77 LEO satellites orbiting the Earth; the element has 77 electrons rotating around its nucleus. The name was kept after the project was scaled down to 66 satellites as Dysprosium, the element with 66 electrons, was not deemed as "catchy" enough. Iridium will be a worldwide cellular telephone network offering both voice and data services available in rural areas, underdeveloped countries and other remote locations.

Clearly, the availability of widescale wireless connectivity, at a cheap price is an appealing prospect not only to commercial interests, but also to the wide population of everyday users of the new mobile technologies being developed and coming to market. This availability will herald a new type of commerce – imagine exchanging business cards electronically via infrared communication between personal assistants. More far reaching is the prospect of handling more information, and hence perhaps less personal attention – digital communication will allow incoming calls to be identified and perhaps your personal electronic agent can handle the call. The key question will one of time; we only have look at what E-mail is doing to the art of letter writing.

The increasing use of cellular technologies will have a profound impact of what we call "my office" or "home". No longer will people be tied to one location by virtue of a telephone number – that person could be anywhere. As with most new technology, it has a tendency to creep up on us, and before we know it, it becomes widespread within our organizations. The potential changes are numerous, and those that will benefit the most will be the ones that understand the implications of the new technology and how organizations will change and adapt around it – much of it will be cultural.

Notes

1.   S. Sheng, A. Chandrasekaran and R. W. Broderson, "A portable multimedia terminal for personal communications", *IEEE Communications Magazine*,   December 1992, pp. 64–75.
2. "Portable and Personal", *Managing Office Technology*, November 1993, p. 49.
3. J. Daly, "Move Over Dick Tracy", *Forbes*, p. 48.

Reference List

EDI & Electronic Commerce

Cronin MJ (1994), *Doing Business on the Internet*, Van Nostrand Reinhold
Kalakota R & Whinston AB (1997), *Electronic Commerce – A Manager's Guide*, Addison-Wesley
Sokol PK (1995), *From EDI to Electronic Commerce*, McGraw-Hill

Telecommunications & Networks

FitzGerald & Dennis A (1996), *Business Data Communications and Networking*, John Wiley & Sons
Goldman JE (1995), *Applied Data Communications – A Business-Orientated Approach*, John Wiley & Sons
Stallings W (1990), *A Business Guide to Local Area Networks*, Howard W Sams & Company

Standards & Standardization

Cargill CF (1989), *Information Technology Standardization – Theory, Process and Organizations*, Digital Press
Gray PA (1991), *Open Systems – A Business Strategy for the 1990s*, McGraw-Hill

IS/IT & Competitive Advantage

Benjamin RI, Rockart JF, Scot Morton MS & Wyman J (Spring 1984), Information Technology a Strategic Opportunity, *Sloan Management Review*
Cash J & Konsynski B (1985), IS Redraws Competitive Boundaries, *Harvard Business Review*
Hamal G & Prahalad CK (1994), Competing for the Future, *Harvard Business Review*, July–Aug 1994 pp 122–128
Hammer M & Mangurian G (1987), The Changing Value of Communications Technology, *Sloan Management Review*
Johnston H & Vitale M (1988), Creating Competitive Advantage with Inter-organizational Information Systems, *MIS Quarterly*
Kanter RM (1994), Collaborative Advantage, *Harvard Business Review*, July–Aug 1994 pp 96–108
Keen PGW (1986), *Competing in Time*, Ballinger Publishing Co
McFarlan FW (1984), Information Technology changes the way you compete, *Harvard Business Review*, May–June 1984 pp 98–103
Parsons GL (1983), Information Technology: A New Competitive Weapon, *Sloan Management Review*
Porter ME (1985), *Competitive Advantage – Creating & Sustaining Superior Performance*, The Free Press

Porter ME & Millar VE (1995), How information gives you competitive advantage, *Harvard Business Review*, July–Aug 1995 pp 149–160

Rackoff N, Wiseman C & Ullrich W (1985), Information Systems for Competitive Advantage: Implementation of a Planning Process, *MIS Quarterly*

Saloner G (1989), *The Changing Patterns of Interfirm Competition and Collaboration*, MIT – Sloan School of Management

Stalk G (1989), Time – The Next Source of Competitive Advantage, *The McKinsey Quarterly*

Tapscott D & Caston A (1993), *Paradigm Shift – The New Promise of Information Technology*, McGraw-Hill

Business Process Re-design

Doherty N & Horsted J (1996), Re-engineering People – The Forgotten Survivors, *Business Change and Re-engineeering* Volume 3 Number 1 1996 pp 39–46

Drucker PF (1988), The coming of the new organisation, *Harvard Business Review*, Jan-Feb 1988 pp 45–53

Hammer M, Champy J (1993), *Reengineering the Corporation*, Harper Collins

Johansson HJ, McHugh P, Pendlebury AJ & Wheeler WA (1993), *Business Process Reengineeering*, John Wiley & Sons

Towers S, Business Process Re-engineering – Lessons for Success, *Management Services*, August 1993, pp 10–12

Information Systems Management & Planning

Beath CM (1991), Supporting the Information Technology Champion, *MIS Quarterly*

Blumenthal SC (1969), *Management Information Systems: A Framework for Planning and Development*, Prentice-Hall

Cash JI, McFarlan FW & McNerney JL (1988), *Corporate Information Systems Management*, Dow Jones-Irwin

Currie W (1995), *Management Strategy for IT – An International Perspective*, Pitman Publishing

Davis GB (1974), *Management Information Systems: Conceptual Foundations, Structure and Development*, McGraw-Hill

Duffy NM & Assad MG (1980), *Information Management: An Executive Approach*, Oxford University Press

Earl MJ (1989), *Management Strategies for Information Technologies*, Prentice Hall

Edwards C, Ward J & Bytheway A (1991), *The Essence of Information Systems*, Prentice Hall

Ennals R & Molyneux P Eds (1993), *Managing with Information Technology*, Springer-Verlag

Henderson J & Venkatraman N (1989), *Strategic Alignment: A Process Model for Integrating Information Technology and Business Strategies*, MIT – Sloan School of Management

Laudon KC & Turner J Eds (1989), *Information Technology & Management Strategy*, Prentice Hall

Robson W (1997), *Strategic Management & Information Systems*, Pitman Publishing

Scott Morton MS (1991), The *Corporation of the 1990s – Information Technology and Organizational Transformation*, Oxford University Press

Sullivan CH & Smar JR (1987), Planning for Information Networks, *Sloan Management Review*

Tricker R (1982), *Effective Information Management*, Beaumont Executive Press

Venkatraman N & Leghorn R (1989), *IT Induced Business Reconfiguration: The New Strategic Management Challenge*, MIT – Sloan School of Management

Ward J & Griffiths P (1996), *Strategic Planning for Information Systems*, John Wiley & Sons

Wiseman C (1985), *Strategy and Computers*, Dow Jones-Irwin

Standards

Baum, D (1993), Apple Open Collaboration Environment, *Infoworld,* 31 May, pp 53–56
Bryan, M (1988), *SGML: an author's Guide to the Standard Generalized Markup Language,* Addison Wesley
Fox, E (1991), Advances in Interactive Digital Multimedia Systems, *IEEE Computer,* Volume 24 Number 10, pp 9–21
Ruport, M (1993), Toward Document Sharing, *Software Magazine,* 6 March
The Economist (1994), Th bg sqz, 15 January, pp 87–88
van Herwijnen, E (1994), *Practical SGML (second edition),* Kluwer

Security

Chapman, D and Zwicky E (1995), *Internet Security Firewalls,* O'Reilly
Cheswick, W and Bellovin S (1994), *Firewalls and Internet Security: Repelling the Wiley hacker,* Adisson-Wesley
Diffie, W and Hellman, ME (1976), New Directions in Cryptography, *IEEE Transactions on Information Theory,* Volume IT-22, pp 644–654
Elkins M (1996), MIME Security With Pretty Good Privacy (PGP), RFC 2015, September
Ford, W and Baum, M (1997), *Secure Electronic Commerce: building the infrastructure for digital signatures and encryption,* Prentice Hall
Sneider, B (1995), *E-mail Security,* John Wiley & Sons
Sneider, B (1996), *Applied Cryptography (second edition),* John Wiley & Sons
Spafford E (1989), The Internet Worm: Crisis and Aftermath, *Communications of the ACM,* Volume 32 Number 6, June, pp 678–688
Morris, R and Thompson, K (1979), Password Security: A Case History, *Communications of the ACM,* Volume 22 Number 11
Warman, A (1993), *Computer Security Within Organisations*
Wheatman V and Bsik D (1997), *X.509 Certification Authorities for Enterprise Security and Electronic Commerce,* Gartner Group – Strategic Anlalysis Report, August 6
Wu, S (1992), MHS Security – A concise survey, *Computer Networks and ISDN Systems* Volume 25, pp 490–495

Desktop Computing and Groupware

Daly, J (1996), Move Over Dick Tracy, *Forbes,* p 48
Cohen, SA (1995), Forrester Research, *Re-engineering Workflow,* Volume 11, Number 5
Coleman, D (1994), Justifying Groupware, *Network World,* January 10, p 27
Jones, P V (1993), A GUI Puts a Friendly Face on Computing, *Business Quarterly,* Spring, pp 110–113
Ovum (1996), *Markets for Operating Systems,* August
Forrester Research Inc. (1994), *Server O/S shootout,* Volume 11 Number 12, October
Levin, S (1995), Gartner Group – Are Suite Dreams Made of This?, Research Note: March 8
Sheng, S, Chandrasekaran, A & Broderson, RW (1992), A portable multimedia terminal for personal communications, *IEEE Communications Magazine,* December, pp 64–75
Yankee Group (1993), *Videoconferencing: The Future of Group and Desktop Systems*
Gartner Group (1997), Matter: Summer/Fall 1996 – The Future of Collaboration, *Strategic Analysis Report,* April 4

Part D

Acronyms and Glossary

ActiveX	Microsoft's response to Java, used to extend the functionality of applications running within a browser
AFNOR	Association Francaise de Normalisation is the national standards body in France – other examples include BSI (UK), ANSI (US) and DIN (Germany)
Agents	Software routines which personalize Web access
AIAG	The US Automobile Industry Action Group is an active EDI forum and has developed a sub-set of the ANSI ASC X12 standard for use in the US motor industry
ANA	UK Article Numbering Association affiliated to the European Article Numbering Association (EAN)
Anonymous FTP	Internet sites that allow anyone to connect to them and transfer files using FTP
ANSI	American National Standards Institute represents the US in the International Standards Organisation (ISO)
API	Application Programming Interface
Applet	A small computer program written in Java that runs inside a Java compatible Web browser
Application Messaging (AM)	A process that uses a mapper/translator to transpose data from one internal application into the required format for input into another internal application
ARPA	Internet suite of protocols was developed by the Advanced Research Projects Agency (formerly DAPDA – Defence)
ASCII	American Standard Code for Information Interchange that assigns numeric values to characters
ASN.1	Abstract Syntax Notation One is an OSI language for describing abstract syntax (description of data types)
Asynchronous	A basic method of data communications that uses start and stop bits to separate individual characters
Asynchronous Transfer Mode	ATM is a means of transmitting data, voice and video over high speed networks – ATM is a connection oriented protocol using a fixed-length packet or cell
ATM	Automated Teller Machines allow banking customers the ability to obtain cash and account information on a 24 hour basis

Backbone	The portion of the network that manages the main traffic volume
Basic Rate ISDN	An Integrated Services Digital Network (ISDN) service that offers two bearer channels (64K bits/sec) and a control channel (16K bits/sec)
Baud	Measurement of data communications speed, that does not always correspond to bits per second
Binary	Raw data represented by a string of zeros and ones
Biometric Security	Security approaches that use human characteristics to distinguish between individuals
Bit	Bit is a basic unit of information representing 0 or 1 in the binary system (BInary digiT)
Bits per second (bps)	Number of binary digits transmitted each second
BPR	Business Process Engineering – term coined by Michael Hammer to signify the radical redesign of business processes
Bridge	Hardware device to connect similar local area networks
Browser	Software running on a PC to navigate the World Wide Web – Netscape Communicator and Microsoft Internet Explorer are market leaders
Bulletin Board System	A centralized database application that contains information to be 'pulled' off as required by end users
Byte	Usually a group 8 bits (BinarY digiT Eight)
CA	A Certificate Authority is a trusted third party that attests to an individual's electronic identity (public key)
Campus Network	A series of interconnect local area networks (LANs)
Card Services	Software that allocates system resources as PCMCIA cards are inserted/removed
CCITT	Comité Consultatif International Télégraphique et Téléphonique forms part of the International Telecommunications Union (ITU) – CCITT has been renamed ITU-T
CERT	The Computer Emergency Response Team monitors the Internet for illegal or fraudulent activities
Certificate	Means of exchanging an individuals public key (see X.509)
CGI	The Common Gateway Interface is used when capturing or displaying information from a Web HTML form – it also integrates databases with Web functions
Ciphertext	Text that has been disguised through encryption technologies
Client	Usually an application that makes use of services from a server
Client/server architecture	A computing architecture, where client applications request and receive, information and services from server applications

Clipper chip	A low cost encryption device that the US Administration proposes to make available to the public
Compound Document	A document that holds various types of data, with dynamic links to the data sources
Conference Call	Facility that allows individuals at different locations to participate in a meeting by phoning into a conference bridge
CORBA	Common Object Request Broker Architecture is designed to ease the manner in which applications interact with one another
CRL	Certificate Revocation Lists highlight certificates that should not be trusted, or those withdrawn or cancelled
Cryptography	Art or science which renders plaintext unintelligible or converts encrypted messages into intelligible text – used to protect messages and transactions to ensure they can not be read without the right 'key'
CSCW	Computer Supported Collaborative Working
Cyberspace	A term created by William Gibson in his novel 'Neuromancer' used to describe the collective world of networked computers
Daemon	Background program that runs unattended
Database	Collection of related objects with data attributes, such that information can be extracted
DES	The Data Encryption Standard is a popular encryption algorithm adopted by the National Bureau of Standards in 1977 and is used extensively in the Financial Sector
Directory Services	A listing of users and resources located on a network and designed to help locate them
Domain Name	In the Domain Name System (DNS), an easy way to remember an Internet host address, as opposed to its numerical IP address
DOS	Disk Operating System termed MS-DOS was developed and marketed by Microsoft for use on personal computers and licensed to IBM as PC-DOS
e-commerce	Electronic Commerce on a business-to-consumer basis
E-commerce	Electronic Commerce on a business-to-business basis
ECR	Efficient Consumer Response eliminates inefficiency in the supply chain using a combination of technologies and business process redesign
EDI Internet Gateway	Software that allows EDI messages to be securely exchanged on a point-to-point basis with trading partners over the Internet
EDI VAN Service	A Value Added Network service provider that facilitates the exchange of EDI messages between trading partners

EDIFACT (UN/EDIFACT)	United Nations/Electronic Data Interchange for Administration Commerce and Transport is an EDI standard
EEMA	European Electronic Messaging Association
EFT	Electronic Funds Transfer used in the financial services sector
Electronic Business Communications	Describes the use of computing and telecommunications technologies for the exchange of information within and between organisations
Electronic Commerce	Any interaction between an organisation and its trading community undertaken in an electronic manner – really a sub-set of Electronic Business Communications, but tending to replace it
Electronic Data Interchange (EDI)	Electronic Data Interchange (EDI) is the electronic transfer of structured data using agreed message standards between computer applications
Electronic Mail (E-mail)	Electronic Mail (E-mail) is person to person electronic messaging also known as inter-personal messaging (IPM)
Encryption	Process of encoding information to make it secure
ERP System	Enterprise Resource Planning Systems are fully integrated packaged software applications supplied by SAP, BAAN, Oracle, PeopleSoft, etc.
Ethernet	Popular LAN network media access protocol, evolved into IEEE 802.3 and ISO 8802.3 standards
EWOS	European Workshop for Open Systems
Facsimile (FAX)	A system for the transmission of images (text/graphics)
Facsimile Modem	Modem adapter that fits into a PC providing the ability to send and receive Group 3 FAX (analogue)
FDDI	Fibre Distributed Data Interface, a high speed media access protocol used in LAN backbones
Firewall	Security device that protects a network from unwanted access by unauthorized users
Frame	A block of data suitable for communication as a single unit, also known as a packet or cell
FTP	File Transfer Protocol (part of the TCP/IP architecture) that enables a user to log onto another computer and exchange files
Gateway	A device that interfaces two different environments, such as SMTP to X.400
GOSIP	Government OSI Profile and required by US and UK governments when purchasing IT products/services
GSM	Global System for Mobiles is designed to replace all Europe's analogue cellular mobile systems by a digital system
GUI	Graphical User Interface with 'point and click' characteristics using a mouse

HDLC	High-Level Data Link Control is the ISO standard for the data link layer protocol – ITU-T adapted HDLC for its link access protocol (LAP) used with X.25 networks
Home Page	The initial starting page on the World-Wide Web
HTML	HyperText Markup Language comprises a set of formatting commands used to build Web pages
HTTP	HyperText Transfer Protocol provides the session level protocol to access a Web site
Hypertext	A method of presenting information so that it can be displayed in a non-sequential way
IAB	The Internet Architecture Board is the co-ordinating committee for the management of the Internet
ICT	Information and Communication Technology
IETF	The Internet Engineering Task Force specifies protocols and other related standards
Imaging	The process of capturing, storing, cataloguing, displaying, and printing graphical information, as well as scanning paper documents for archival storage
IMAP	Internet Message Access Protocol is used to move E-mails from a mail server/mail drop a PC
Interchange	A file of EDI messages transmitted between two trading partners in a single transmission
Interconnectivity	First of two stages in a successful networking environment, providing the secure path to move digits around
Internet	Short for Internetwork; two or more networks connected together by bridges, routers or gateways; and the name of the World's largest computer network
Internet Commerce	Same as electronic commerce, but implies the use of Internet technologies to govern the interaction between trading partners
Internet Service Provider (ISP)	An Internet Service Provider offers Internet access usually for a fixed monthly charge based upon the access speed
Interoperability	Usually considered to be outside the networking environment and implies co-operation between communicating applications
Interworking	Second stage in a successful network environment that adds meaning to the digits being moved around
Intranet	Internal (within the same company) messaging and information management environment based upon open Internet technologies
IP	Internet Protocol is part of the TCP/IP architecture providing a connection-less service at the network layer
IP Address	Internet Protocol address relates to a unique network destination that usually has a mnemonic equivalent

IPX	Internet Packet Exchange is part of the Novell protocol stack
IRTF	The Internet Research Task Force researches new technologies to be referred to the IETF
ISDN	Integrated Services Digital Network capable of transporting voice, data and moving image (video)
ISO	International Standardisation Organisation responsible for a wide range of standards, including computing
ISO/OSI Model	Open System Interconnection model consisting of seven layers
IT	Information Technology is an all embracing term to describe the whole of the computing landscape
ITU	Internal Telecommunications Union is a UN umbrella organisation for world-wide telecommunications
ITU-T	International Telecommunication Union – Telecommunication, a standards making body for telecommunications operators (previously CCITT)
Java	A network-aware, multi-platform programming language created by Sun Microsystems that creates programs called applets to add functionality to Web browsers
Java Beans	Java's component architecture that can be parts of Java programs or self-contained applications
JPEG	The Joint Picture Experts Group standard is a lossy compression technique based upon the work of a French mathematician
Just-in-Time	Term used to describe the close coupling of goods arriving at a factory and their use in the manufacturing process – Quick Response is a similar philosophy in retail
LAN	A Local Area Network is a series of connected computers/ peripherals in a discrete geographical location
Layer	A layer in a network architecture is a discrete group of services, functions and protocols, that is one of several
LDAP	The Lightweight Directory Access Protocol has become a standard way to access directory services
Leased line	Permanent physical connections between two or more computers that can form the basis of a network – sourced from a private/public telecommunications operator
Legacy System	Computer applications that have been in use for a long time
Lossless Compression	Data compression method where there is no loss of original data when the file is decompressed
Lossy Compression	Data compression method that discards certain unwanted data , such that original data is lost during decompression – used for shrinking audio and image files
Lotus Notes	Popular groupware product from Lotus
Lotus Smartsuite	Popular software suite (word processing, spreadsheets, presentations, etc.) from Lotus

MAC	The Message Authentication Code is a check value appended to a message to ensure integrity – widely used in the financial services sector
Mailbox	An electronic storage area in which information sent to a particular recipient is stored until retrieved by them
Mail-enabled Application	Applications that use E-mail as a transportation function
MAPI	Messaging Application Programming Interface from Microsoft that defines how applications and E-mail systems relate to one another
Mapper/Translator	Computer application that maps data between an internal (application) data format and an EDI standard
Media Access Protocol	The rules that workstations use to avoid collisions when sending information over a local area network (LAN)
Messaging Handling System	The ITU-T X.400 standard protocol for global store and forward messaging
Microsoft Office	Very popular software suite from Microsoft comes as Small Office and Professional editions
Microsoft Windows	Graphical operating environment that runs under DOS and brings many of the features found in the Apple Macintosh environment
Microwave	Line of sight communications that use high frequency waves (1 to 33 gigahertz)
MIME	Multi-purpose Internet Mail Extensions enhancing basic Internet Mail (see SMTP); allow multiple attachments to be transported in similar manner to X.400 body parts
MNP	Microcom Networking Protocol is a set of data compression and error detection protocols
Modem	A MODulator/DEModulator is used to transmit data over the public switched telephone network by converting digital signals to analogue signals and vice versa
MPEG	Motion Picture Experts Group
Multi-media	Refers to the simultaneous usage of different media, such as text, sound, graphics and video
Multiplexing	A function that allows two or more communications sessions to share a common physical connection
NADF	The North American Directory Forum focuses upon the issues of public X.500 directory services
NC	A Network Computer relates to a basic PC based machine
Netscape Communications	Company known for its popular World-Wide Web browser and Internet commerce applications
Netware	A series of popular local area network operating systems from Novell
Network	Series of computers and associated devices connected by a communications channel enabling the sharing of file storage and other resources

NII	National Information Infrastructure is a Bill Clinton term to describe the US programme for an information superhighway
NIST	National Institute of Standards and Technology – US government agency involved in setting commerce related standards
NOS	Network Operating System used by local area networks
OBI Standard	The Open Buying on the Internet standard that aims to make purchasing over the Internet easier
ODA	Open Document Architecture is an internationally recognized standard for compound documents
ODBC	Open Database Connectivity is an application program interface from Microsoft
ODETTE	European Automotive Association active in developing EDI and communications standards for its members
OLE	Object Linking and Embedding is a Microsoft protocol for application-to-application exchange and communications, using data objects
Open Group	Formed by the merger of X/Open and OSF organisations
Open Standards	Standards developed by recognized international bodies that are freely available in the public domain
Open Systems	Those systems and components which provide true vendor independence for users, achieved by conformance to open standards
OpenDoc	Compound document specification from a group of suppliers including Apple, IBM and Novell – similar in concept to OLE from Microsoft
OSF	Open Systems Foundation formed in 1988 to maintain the open nature of Unix development
OSITOP	European user organisation
Outsourcing	To subcontract out all or part of an organisation's information technology department
Packet	A block of data sent over a network
Packet Switched Network	A term usually used to describe networks using the ITU-T X.25 standard
PARADISE	European pilot for X.500 directories
PCMCIA	Personal Computer Memory Card International Association formed in 1989 that developed standards for connecting devices to portable computers
PDA	Personal Digital Assistant that usual fits on the palm of a hand and provides organizer/E-mail functions
PEM	Privacy Enhanced Mail is a popular security technology widely used on the Internet

Pentium	64 bit microprocessor introduced by Intel in 1993
PGP	Pretty Good Privacy is a security technology developed by Phil Zimmerman and distributed freely on the World-Wide Web
PKCS	Public-Key Cryptography Standards were created by a consortium of major computer vendors
PKZIP	Popular PC based compression utility that uses lossless techniques
Platform	An operating system environment such as Unix, sometimes also used to refer to hardware such as RS6000
Platform Independence	The ability of programs to run on nearly any kind of computer
POP3	Post Office Protocol (version 3) is the designed to retrieve E-mails from a mail drop and has less features than IMAP
PPP	Point to Point Protocol is sometimes called dial-up TCP/IP and transmits IP packets over a telephone connection
Proprietary Software & Standards	Software and standards developed and owned by an organisation that are not in the public domain
Protocol	A set of rules/conventions that need to be respected if communications are to be achieved between two parties
PSPDN or PDN	The Packet Switched Public Data Network is a global infrastructure operated by Private Telecommunications Operators based upon the X.25 standard
PSTN	The Public Switched Telephone Network is a global infra structure operated by licensed Telephone Operators based upon international standards
PTO	Private Telecommunications Operators emerged from the re-regulation of telecommunication services in Europe to introduce greater competition into service provision
PTT	The Postal, Telephone and Telegraph organisations were the original government agencies (affiliated to the ITU) established in each country providing monopoly services
Public Key Encryption	An encryption scheme that uses two keys – the public key encrypts the data and the corresponding private key decrypts the data
RFC	A Request for Comment describes either a proposed or accepted Internet standard sponsored by the IETF
RISC	Reduced Instruction Set Computing processors usually only recognize a limited number of assembler level language instructions
Router	An intelligent communications device for connecting dis similar networks
RSA	Popular algorithm named after the developers (Rivest, Samir and Adleman) that uses prime numbers and keys

S/MIME	Secure Multipurpose Internet Mail Extension used to send E-mail attachments securely over the Internet
SDLC	Synchronous Data Link Control is a predecessor to HDLC, developed by IBM and used for the data link layer in SNA networks
Search Engine	Application that uses intelligent agents to index information available on the Web – users can use search engines to locate information and then hyperlink to the selected home page
Service Provider	Term used to describe companies that provide network based services to user organisation
SET	Secure Electronic Transaction is a standard particularly orientated towards credit card usage in an electronic commerce environment
SGML	Standard Generalized Markup Language (ISO 8879)for defining digital document structure – HTML is a sub-set of SGML
SHA	Secure Hash Algorithm
SITPRO	UK Simplification of International Trading Procedures is a government agency
SME	Term used to describe Small and Medium Enterprises
SMTP	Simple Mail Transfer Protocol is used to send messages over the Internet to a mail server/mail drop
SNA	IBM's proprietary System Network Architecture
Socket Services	Software that monitors PCMCIA slots to detect insertion/removal
SPECint	System Performance Evaluation Cooperative integer – relates to a standard benchmark used to measure CPU performance
SQL	Structured Query Language is an ANSI and ISO relational database query language standard
SSL	The Secure Sockets Layer is a protocol developed by Netscape Communications providing security services for Web based applications
SWIFT Network	Society for World-Wide Interbank Financial Telecommunication is a global network utilized by the financial services industry
Synchronous Communications	Communications that use a clock/synchronisation signals to control traffic flow
TCP	Transmission Control Protocol is part of the TCP/IP architecture providing end-to-end reliable transport of data
TCP/IP	The Transmission Control Protocol/Internet Protocol provides interconnection/transport services across TCP/IP Networks

Telecommunications	The transmission of electronic signals over a distance that can be used for voice, data or image
Telecommuting	Working from home using a portable computer connected to the office via a modem and the Public Switched Telephone Network
Telnet	Terminal emulation protocol and part of the TCP/IP suite providing host connection for remote terminals
Thick Architecture	The result of reducing choice of IT conventions, rules and standards in use throughout an organisation
Token Ring	Popular LAN network media access protocol, developed jointly with IBM as IEEE 802.5 standard (ISO 8802.5)
TQM	Total Quality Management aims to optimize the internal working practices of an organisation and eliminate unnecessary cost
Trading Partner	Companies with whom an organisation does business
Unix	A 32 bit multi-user, multi-tasking, portable operating system and very popular together with Windows NT in a client/server environment
URL	Uniform Resource Locator usually written url, identifies a specific location on the Web, which could cause an HTML form to be displayed or result in the running of a script – an example of a url is http://www.geis.com
V.32	An ITU-T recommendation that defines how modems are to encode, modulate and transmit data at 9600 bps (V.n refer to analogue standards for connection to the PSTN)
VANS	Value Added Network Services are service providers that provide additional services, e.g. E-mail, EDI, Applications, etc. rather than just networking
Videoconference	Use of voice and video linked by communications to allow individuals at different locations to participate in a meeting – groupware products provide desktop video and chalkboards to help people work together
Voicemail	Computerized store and forward system for voice messages
VSAT	Very Small Aperture Terminals provide a physical connection service via satellite links
W3C	World Wide Web Consortium
WAN	A Wide Area Network is a series of connected computers/ peripherals (or LANs) in dispersed geographically separate locations
Web Page	Information (text, images and sound) stored on a Web server for subsequent display using a Web browser
Webcasting	Allows Web broadcasting of events as they happen with video and sound
Windows 95	Replacement for DOS/Windows 3.1 from Microsoft that is a 32 bit multitasking operating system

Windows NT	A 32 bit New Technology multitasking portable operating system from Microsoft running on a wide range of platforms
World-Wide Web	A killer application that has done much to accelerate the growth of the Internet – hypertext links connect information stored in separate pages on servers, that can be explored using a Web browser
Worm	Program that replicates itself in order to infect connected computers
X Window	Windowing environment developed in the US by MIT for Unix workstations
X.25	ITU-T recommendation that provides support for the physical, data link and network layers of the OSI model (X.n refer to digital standards for PSPDNs)
X.400	ITU-T recommendation for inter-personal messaging (IPM) that may run over a number of network protocols
X.435	ITU-T recommendation that enhances X.400 to cater for the rather special requirements of EDI
X.500	ITU-T recommendation for private and public electronic directory services
X.509	ITU-T recommendation defining digital certificates
X/Open Company	Founded in 1984 by a group of vendors and very active in open systems matters
X12 (ANSI ASC X12)	X12 is an EDI standard developed by the US American National Standards Institute Accredited Sub-committee
XML	The eXtensible Markup Language is a more powerful markup language than HTML for Web publishing and has potential to simplify Web EDI

Index